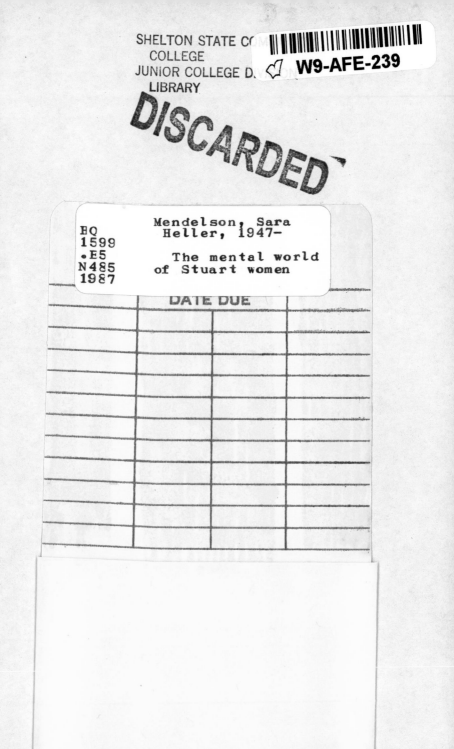

The Mental World
of Stuart Women

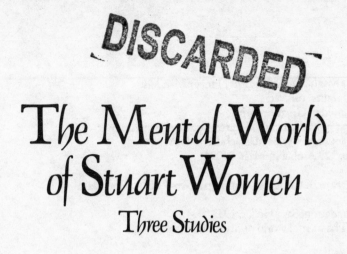

The Mental World of Stuart Women
Three Studies

Sara Heller Mendelson

The University of Massachusetts Press
Amherst 1987

Copyright © 1987 by Sara Heller Mendelson
All rights reserved
Printed in Great Britain
First published in the United States of America by
The University of Massachusetts Press
Box 429 Amherst, Mass. 01004

Library of Congress Cataloging-in-Publication Data

Mendelson, Sara Heller, 1947-
　The mental world of Stuart women.

　Bibliography: p.
　Includes index.
　Contents: Margaret Cavendish, Duchess of
Newcastle—Mary Rich, Countess of Warwick—
Aphra Behn.
　1. Newcastle, Margaret Cavendish, Duchess of,
1624?-1674.　2. Rich, Mary, Countess of Warwick,
1625-1678.　3. Behn, Aphra, 1640-1689.　4. Women—
England—Biography.　5. England—Social life and
customs—17th century.　I. Title.
HQ1599.E5N485　　1987　　　305.4′0942　　　　87-5972
ISBN 0-87023-591-5

To The Memory Of My Father

Contents

Acknowledgements

This book is a modified version of my Oxford D.Phil. thesis (1982), entitled 'Women in Seventeenth-Century England: Three Studies'. In writing it I have incurred many debts. I should like to thank numerous librarians and archivists for their help, particularly those of the Bodleian Library, the University of Nottingham Library, the Folger Shakespeare Library, and Chatsworth. Several friends read earlier drafts and made helpful suggestions, including Linda Brownrigg, Patricia Crawford, Phyllis Mack, Alan Mendelson and Mary Prior. I should also like to thank my thesis examiners, Gerald Aylmer and Blair Worden, for useful and stimulating comments. I owe an incalculable intellectual debt to my thesis supervisor, Keith Thomas, for his unfailing wisdom and patience. Above all I am grateful to my husband Alan; without him, nothing would have been conceivable, let alone possible.

Introduction

When Adam delved and Eve span
Who was then the gentleman?

The couplet chanted by the peasant rebels of 1381 harks back to a fictive past when no distinctions of wealth or status had emerged. Yet the rhyme assumes that gender had already split the first couple into two occupational classes. An economy based on the sexual division of labour seemed so natural to Englishmen that they found it difficult to conceive of any society, however inchoate, in which gender domains did not exist. In early seventeenth-century England, the boundaries defined by gender were as fundamental to the ordering of everyday life as those dictated by class. Its distinctions were marked by dress and deportment and were exhibited in virtually every social situation. At the Sunday church service, where the collective notion of the social order was mapped on to physical space through the arrangement of the congregants, villagers were first separated by gender and then ranked according to the stepwise hierarchy of degree. Even the early Quakers retained a form of segregated seating despite their radical notions about women's equality.[1]

This partitioned seating arrangement suggests a world in which male and female domains were seen as different in kind but essentially parallel. It is an appropriate symbol of everyday village life, in which the husbandman and his wife divided the complementary tasks of household and field according to a rough and ready equality. Although men and women worked in separate spheres, each sex was regarded as sovereign in its own domain, and each half of the partnership was deemed

1

essential to the family economy.[2]

But a simple complementarity of the sexes will not serve to describe Tudor-Stuart society in its official or institutional guise. Wherever society moulded itself into formal structures, hierarchies were created in which the female domain was pronounced inferior or subordinate to the male. This assumption was reflected in seventeenth-century usage: the word 'effeminate' denoted whatever pertained to the female domain but carried a pejorative connotation in other contexts. The doctrine of women's innate inferiority was given 'scientific' status by contemporary medical theories which postulated that men were composed of the more perfect hot and dry humours and women of the defective cold and wet humours. A gender-specific code of prescriptive morality and personal honour carried a similar force.[3] The feminine virtues were the passive qualities of a subject race: chastity, obedience, piety, and silence. Gender also determined the unequal allocation of power and prestige. Women's activities earned less esteem and a smaller pecuniary reward than those of their male counterparts.[4] Finally, the worldview which assigned women a subordinate place was enshrined in institutions, from Parliament down to the humblest family. In the more traditional centres of power, women were apt to disappear from view altogether. According to a legal fiction of the common law, a married woman was deemed a non-person because she was 'covert' or included in the person of her husband. Contemporaries offered a similar rationale for women's exclusion from representative government. 'See here the reason that women have no voyse in Parliament...' wrote the author of *The Lawes Resolutions of Womens Rights* (1632), 'All of them are understood either married or to be married and their desires are subject to their husband...'[5]

The axiom of female subordination was so much a part of the mental apparatus of the time that it unconsciously influenced contemporaries who attempted an analytical description of their own society. William Harrison's *Description of Britain* (1577) distinguished four 'degrees of people', but his classification was concerned only with adult males. Either he assumed that the female domain was represented by the male, just as wives were 'covered' by their husbands, or else he regarded the existence of a gendered social structure as a fact too obvious and too trivial to require comment. Most subsequent writers have looked at seventeenth-century England in much the same way that William Harrison did. As long as the subject matter of history was limited to the narrative of past politics, traditional historians ignored the female domain altogether. Queens and courtesans might be included because of their public role, but the rank and file of the female populace appeared to have no part to play in the historical drama.

More recently, social historians have espoused wider historiographical aims whose objectives include the study of women as well as other groups that lacked formal political power in past societies. But even the most fervent practitioners of *histoire totale* have been handicapped by the archival consequences of women's dependent status in seventeenth-century England. Those who advocate the historical reconstruction of past communities confess that the sources permit them to reconstruct only the male half of the populace.[6] Although women's literary works increased in volume and variety throughout the seventeenth century, they display the expected bias toward the upper end of the class spectrum.[7] To investigate the illiterate majority it is necessary to resort to indirect sources such as court records, which by definition refer to a deviant segment of the community. While the records of the ecclesiastical courts yield a wider sample of 'normal' behaviour, even this kind of evidence entails methodological and epistemological problems.[8] There is no comprehensive source which directly charts the two groups that made up the vast majority of the female population: married women of the lower ranks and unmarried maidservants. Indeed it is often impossible to establish a woman's social and occupational status except by the dubious expedient of tracing her husband and identifying his occupation.[9]

The problem of historical evidence is most acute with respect to female *mentalité* rather than material life. Through the painstaking collection of a wide range of economic sources, Alice Clark pieced together a classic account of women's productive life during the Stuart age.[10] Demographers have added a statistical dimension to our knowledge of women's everyday experience by charting nuptuality and fertility. Although many parts of the picture are still missing, we have some information on the occupations women followed, how much they were paid for their labour, at what age they married, and how many children they bore. But we do not know what women themselves thought and felt about it all.

As the anthropologist Edwin Ardener termed it in a different context, women were a 'muted group' with respect to the 'dominant male culture' of seventeenth-century England.[11] Because of their subordinate status they were less able or less apt to express their own views in ways that an outside observer can interpret. This 'muted' quality of female discourse does not mean that women were inarticulate in the intimate *milieu* of the family and village. On the contrary, women were proverbially known as the talkative sex. Their reputation can be attributed in part to men's low threshold of tolerance for women's speech.[12] But it also arose from their cultural role in village society, for feminine discourse was part of the social 'glue' that helped bind the community together. Gossip was a means of social control, and feminine sociability formed a key element in the exchange of goods and services which promoted the communal virtue of neighbourliness.[13] The ideal of the 'silent woman' was far from the reality of village life.

For the purposes of the historian, however, most women were not merely inarticulate but mute, since they were incapable of leaving a written record of their thoughts. In fact the vast majority could not sign their names, let alone compose their memoirs for posterity.[14] Even the minority who had learned to write were diffident about chronicling their experiences, for the pen—like the sword—was considered a masculine prerogative. It is true that the idea of authorship as an exclusively male attribute was beginning to break down by the middle of the century. The flood of pamphlets by female authors of the Interregnum paralleled a general rise in popular publications, inspired by the heady atmosphere of social ferment in the absence of censorship. But if women were beginning to express their views to the public at large, their eloquence was usually channelled into a few well-defined areas. The majority of female printed works are on religious topics, partly because piety offered women a socially acceptable excuse for breaking into a male preserve.[15] While there is evidence of a great deal of private 'closet writing' by Stuart women, the survival of female manuscripts is heavily biassed towards the upper ranks. Contemporary male manuscripts of the labouring classes are exceedingly rare, but female manuscripts of the same class are virtually non-existent. If we seek to recover women's view of their world, the muted 'counterpart model' postulated by Edwin Ardener, we are limited in practice to the middle and upper ranks who left a record of their thoughts. And in order to place feminine *mentalité* in its social context we must turn to an even smaller group, those women whose families preserved archives.

For some historians this elite minority is of merely antiquarian interest, for it is difficult to imagine how upper-class women could be representative of the rest of their sex. Seventeenth-century England was an extremely inegalitarian society, and at first sight it may appear reasonable to assume that the difference in outlook between women of the highest and lowest ranks was as great as the disparity in their income. Indeed some writers have questioned whether seventeenth-century women formed a group in any meaningful sense of the word. They were not a caste, for the occupational boundaries of gender were blurred in certain sectors of society, particularly at the upper and lower ends of the social spectrum. Queens behaved in accordance with masculine canons, not feminine ones. At the other end of the social scale, the struggle for subsistence dissolved traditional occupational divisions between the sexes. Families of impoverished labourers practised by-employments which were undifferentiated by gender. For those who had neither cottage nor land, the complementary domains of household and field had little relevance.[16] Even biology is not an infallible touchstone for characterizing seventeenth-century women as a uniform group. Upper-class women's practice of handing their children over to wet-nurses to be breastfed was apt to produce two different fertility patterns, one for wealthy women and another for their lower-class counterparts.[17]

Finally, although Stuart women suffered a wide range of disabilities because of their sex, their knowledge of the fact did not mould them into a cohesive group. Class interests are certainly more obvious than a sense of gender solidarity among seventeenth-century women, although this rule does have its exceptions. The pious humanitarian designs of the Countess of Warwick led her to conduct charitable missions among the 'poor widows' and 'weeding women' of her neighbourhood, and her diary reveals a sympathy with their mental outlook as well as with their appalling material conditions.[18] Still, most contemporaries who voiced complaints about the feminine condition showed little enthusiasm for overcoming class barriers. The Duchess of Newcastle did not conceal her contempt for women of the lower orders; her utopian fantasies had reference only to titled women like herself. In real life she expressed more empathy for wild animals than for the poor in her midst. Some of the most outspoken proponents of female equality during this period were also the most socially conservative. Pamphleteers like Mary Astell displayed a social elitism much like that of suffragette leaders of the early twentieth century.[19] Those who seek in the seventeenth century the roots of a universal feminism that embraced the entire sex in the bonds of sisterhood are liable to be disappointed.

Yet the aim in studying women in past societies is not to establish a pedigree for modern feminism but to reconstruct women's mental and material world in all its rich complexity. If we look at Stuart society on its own terms, beginning at the level of women's everyday life, it becomes clear that gender entailed certain common experiences which transcended class differences. To postulate a degree of shared feminine experience is not to minimize the immense gulf created by social and economic inequalities. Women's perception of the world was always two-dimensional. In some contexts their outlook reflected their social class as defined by husbands and fathers, but in other contexts class distinctions were superseded by more fundamental priorities of gender. The ambiguities and contradictions inherent in this dual status led to baffling paradoxes for contemporaries, just as they have created conceptual confusion among present-day historians. Queens represented an especially perplexing problem, and their proper gender role was the subject of much debate during the sixteenth and seventeenth centuries. But political theorists were aware that similar anomalies existed with respect to the entire sex in the contradiction between women's 'natural' condition as freeborn human beings and the dependent role assigned to them by civil society.[20]

Modern historians have been beset by similar conceptual difficulties in attempting to place female *mentalité* within the matrix of class and gender. To what 'culture' did women belong? It is clear that they did not participate in the masculine culture appropriate to their social class. Aristocratic women were excluded from the 'great tradition' of the grammar schools and universities which moulded upper-class male culture, and wives of the middle and lower ranks did not join in the camaraderie of alehouse or guild.[21] As to whether women produced a culture of their own, historians have had little to say, pleading lack of evidence. Yet women's mental and material world is reflected in their own writings and a variety of other sources. For example, the elements of this feminine *milieu* can be glimpsed in the Countess of Warwick's 'Occasional Meditations', a series of moralistic essays composed during the 1660s and 1670s.[22] The Countess was the daughter of one earl and the wife of another, the sister of an eminent scientist and the relation by marriage of several prominent court figures. Yet her meditations are 'homely' in both senses of the word. There is almost no evidence of the educated culture of her male relations and relatively little to indicate her social class. Instead, her imagery is drawn from the female domain of the household and its immediate surroundings of garden, henhouse and dairy. Analogies are inspired by a feminine constellation of domestic concerns: housecleaning, childrearing, cookery, needlework, dress, hospitality, the behaviour of relations and servants and neighbours, the world of nature in its most accessible aspects.

During the seventeenth century, the female domain included some activities which were exclusive to the sex and others which were strongly linked to women although common to both sexes. Aside from its association with the household, female culture in most of its guises represented the non-literate obverse of literate male culture, almost as if women sought to compensate for their lack of literate skills through other modes of expression. The bare minimum common to women of every rank was a knowledge of housewifery, 'from which neither wealth nor greatness can totally absolve them' as the author of *The Ladies Calling* (1673) reminded his readers. Just as aristocratic women were not excused from these duties, lower-class servants were encouraged to learn them: good mistresses were enjoined to teach even their lowest maidservants the fine points of domestic management. The branches of the art were considerably more numerous than they are today. Gervase Markham mentioned the following topics in the title page of *The English Housewife* (1618):

> physic, surgery, the extraction of oyls, banqueting stuff, ordering of great feasts, preserving of all sorts of wines...distillations, perfumes, ordering of wool, hempe, flax, making cloth, dying, the knowledge of dayries, office of malting, oats, brewing, baking...

Some omissions from the list are women's responsibility for everyday cooking, the kitchen garden, and the care of small livestock.

Women's primary productive task was thought to be the bearing and rearing of children. During the seventeenth century, the continual round of pregnancy, childbirth and childrearing still took place in a feminine context. The 'lying-in' was exclusively the affair of women: every female friend and relation was expected to come to the labour, and midwives rather than male physicians were employed by rich and poor alike.[23] Throughout the Tudor-Stuart period these feminine customs and rituals were virtually the same for all ranks, except that the wealthy were more able to indulge in conspicuous consumption for the lying-in and christening parties. Aside from basic housewifery and childcare, needlework and other textile crafts were considered the archetypal female occupations. Needlework formed the main item of the female curriculum, whether of queens or of charity apprentices. It was so much the badge of gender that it was simply called 'work'. The only discernible difference between social ranks was the expense of the materials and the degree of decorative uselessness of the final product.[24]

Other occupations associated with the feminine sphere had a more mixed character: they were practised by women of every rank for little or no remuneration, while at the same time they were pursued on a lucrative professional basis by a small number of men. Medicine, for example, was a highly-paid male profession, but as an amateur feminine art it was dispensed by every good housewife, from pious noblewomen down to illiterate 'wise women'.[25] Medicine also exemplifies the literate/non-literate division between the sexes, for professional medicine was based on the academic complexities of Galenic theory, whereas the housewifely variety usually relied on a hodge-podge of herbal remedies derived from popular lore.

Music, another feminine desideratum, exhibited strong associations with the sex. Virginals, as their name implies, were played chiefly by young girls, and titles of Elizabethan music collections suggest the same female bias. Indeed Gerrard Winstanley merely followed convention when he assigned textiles and music to girls and learning and trades to boys in his utopian commonwealth.[26] Like needlework, music was the prerogative of the entire social spectrum, varying chiefly in the costliness of the instruments and complexity of the music. While the wealthy played highly ornamented airs on expensive instruments, labouring women had their own tradition of 'plain' songs associated with the female textile occupations:

> ...come, the song we had last night.
> Mark it, Cesario, it is old and plain;
> The spinsters and the knitters in the sun
> And the free maids that weave their thread with bones
> Do use to chant it...
>
> (*Twelfth Night*, Act II, sc. iv)

Piety was another feminine 'ornament' regarded as a special talent of the sex. It was customarily listed as one of the female virtues, perhaps because women were pre-eminent in its devotional aspects—faith, prayer, and occasionally prophecy. The devotional routine was adopted as a kind of self-imposed career by large numbers of seventeenth-century women. There are also indications that women were preponderant in many religious groups, notably the sects. Like other feminine concerns already enumerated, piety was practised widely by women of all ranks.[27]

In a society in which both material and intangible benefits were so unequally allocated, it is remarkable that the spectrum of activities in which Stuart women engaged was much the same for those of dissimilar social and economic backgrounds. But while the tasks performed by women comprised a large and specialized contribution to the Stuart economy, an occupational comparison between the sexes has an anachronistic air. In Stuart society the crucial categories for women were not occupational but matrimonial and 'sexual'. It is this premise which has created such difficulties for those who have sought to measure statistically what kinds of work women actually did in the past. Local records rarely include occupational designations for women, because to the seventeenth-century mind the matrimonial label 'spinster' or 'widow' offered as complete a description for females as the occupational term 'yeoman' or 'joiner' did for males. This assumption, which is everywhere implied in contemporary documents, is spelled out in the conduct books. *The Ladies Calling*, for example, declared that 'the principal and distinct scenes in which a woman can be supposed to be an actor, are these three, virginity, marriage and widowhood'.[28]

Thus there was a fundamental asymmetry in the way the two sexes were perceived. Matrimonial status or sexual activity was a relatively minor addendum to a man's occupation, whereas it designated the core of a woman's being. This asymmetry was closely connected with women's dependent status in marriage and their primary role as childbearers and childrearers. Moreover, just as matrimonial or sexual categories defined each stage of a woman's life-cycle, attitudes to female sexuality in a wider sense determined a code of behaviour that applied to all women regardless of age, marital status or social rank. Indeed restraints on women's sexual behaviour served as the paradigm for asymmetrical relations between the two sexes as expressed in the Tudor ideal of 'honour and shame'. This normative code controlled not just women's sexuality but virtually every aspect of their lives. The feminine ideal of 'modesty', the outward expression of female chastity, defined the strictures governing women's limited education, their dress and conversation, their lack of independent choice of a marriage partner, their appropriate sphere of activity, and much else besides. Nor was this behavioural code the sole prerogative of the gentry. The records of the ecclesiastical courts confirm that village society was guided by notions of feminine shame and honour which were much the same as those of the upper classes.[29]

Given the hypothesis that seventeenth-century women did undergo certain common experiences, how shall we investigate their world? Their oral traditions and much of their material culture are lost to the historian except for tantalizing allusions in contemporary sources. And like other subordinate groups, women developed cultural characteristics that can render their actions difficult to interpret. They discovered indirect ways of circumventing official strictures on their independent activities, but generally found it prudent to conceal their stratagems while paying lip-service to conventional ideals. To accept women's declared opinions at face value without investigating their behaviour can sometimes lead to a distorted view of their attitudes and objectives. In any case women's life and thought were so intertwined in practice that their worldview is liable to be divested of meaning when divorced from its social context. For example, it would be possible to piece together a feminine 'counterpart model' of marriage by citing women's statements about wedlock as an institution. Yet such an artificial construct would ignore the fact that the matrimonial bond entailed a multi-dimensional mesh of disparate elements: family politics and kin networks, patriarchal authority, social and financial 'preferment', sexual honour, altered legal status, emotional fulfilment, and the beginning of the cycle of childbearing and childrearing which comprised the archetypal female vocation. Without exploring the relations between these elements in real life we can hardly pretend to understand what marriage meant for seventeenth-century women.

To recover the wider context in which women's *mentalité* was embedded, the following chapters take the form of biography. This is one method among many which might afford an entrée into the complex subject of women's mental world, and no claim is made that the three women whose lives are described in these pages provide us with an exhaustive or even a representative picture of Stuart women. The case studies do, however, offer the opportunity to explore some prototypical feminine themes of the seventeenth century: female life stages, patriarchalism in theory and practice, the control of female sexuality, the limitations inherent in women's conventional role and the reactions provoked by those who sought to challenge them. These biographies are also a reminder that historical narrative is ultimately the concretion of individual life stories.

> You accumulate Particulars, & murder by analysing, that you
> May take the aggregate...
> But general forms have their vitality in particulars, & every
> Particular is a man...[30]

Or, as in the following studies, a woman.

CHAPTER I
Margaret Cavendish, Duchess of Newcastle

i. Margaret Lucas: Family and Education

The Lucas family of Colchester achieved its mid-sixteenth-century ascent to gentility as if to furnish an illustration of Tawney's 'rise of the gentry'. A fortune acquired through the fruits of office was used to buy local monastic lands, the former St. John's Abbey. The family estate was further augmented by lucrative marriages to tradesmen's heiresses.[1] In 1625, Thomas Lucas was reported to be a 'gentleman...of good quality being a man of £4000 [a year] in lands...'. A list of Essex royalists drawn up in 1643 ranked the Lucas rentals second in the county. But the same list accorded the Lucas family only sixth place in social standing.[2] Behind this disparity between income and status lies half a century of growing alienation from social and political connexions within the county. Its beginnings can be traced to Margaret Lucas's father, Thomas Lucas, who brought the family's upward social momentum to a halt. As a young man in 1597 he killed a relative of Lord Cobham in a duel and was forced to remain exiled in France until his Court enemies fell from favour. Simultaneously he introduced a scandal into the family. He had left behind him a London girl, Elizabeth Leighton, who bore him a son out of wedlock. Although Thomas married Elizabeth on his return, their child was disbarred from inheritance. Aside from one uneventful term as High Sheriff of Essex, Thomas Lucas left no record of his activities. In 1625 he died plain Master Lucas, having engendered two legitimate sons and five daughters. Margaret, the youngest child, was only two years old at the time.

Elizabeth Lucas assumed control of family affairs, revealing herself as a more forceful and ambitious figure than her husband. She looms large in the memoirs of her daughter Margaret, who described her as a practitioner of the liberal mode of childrearing.

...we were bred tenderly, for my mother Naturally did strive, to please and delight her children, not to cross or torment them, terrifying them with threats, or lashing them with slavish whips; but instead of threats, reason was used to persuade us, and instead of lashes, the deformities of vice was discovered, and the graces, and vertues were presented into us.[3]

But other sources suggest that Elizabeth Lucas maintained a firm hold upon her children. Her ruthless business capacity was shown by her skill in intriguing for her son John's wardship.[4] Although the entire estate should have passed to John upon his majority, Elizabeth exercised joint supervision for another twenty years. Perhaps her managerial talents had earned her the privilege. Margaret described her mother as 'very skillful in leases, and setting of lands, and court keeping, ordering of stewards, and the like affairs'. The financial aspects of this arrangement were also advantageous to Mrs. Lucas, as her daughter noted:

...although after my Father's death the Estate was divided, between my Mother and her Sonns, paying such a sum of money for Portions to her Daughters, either at the day of their marriage, or when they should come to age; yet by reason she and her children agreed with a mutuall consent, all their affairs were managed so well, as she lived not in a much lower condition than when my father lived.[5]

The Lucas clan had little to do with their Essex neighbours. Elizabeth Lucas's attitude to the lowest ranks is suggested by her attempt to have her poor rates reduced soon after taking over the estate. The citizens of Colchester were not fond of the Lucas family either, for John was continually embroiled in petty disputes with townsmen during the 1630s.[6] And none of the family was affiliated with the local gentry, either socially or matrimonially. Instead, Elizabeth Lucas matched her children with offspring of courtiers and Cavalier businessmen outside the county. Even with regard to these connexions, the Lucas clan remained unfriendly. Margaret observed that her sisters were 'so far from mingling themselves with any other company, that they had no familiar conversation or intimate acquaintance with the families to which each other were linked by marriage...'. At a time when a network of useful acquaintances was a major benefit of matrimony, this preference for isolation was almost aberrant. The family spent part of each year in London, but even in the capital Margaret observed that 'they did seldome make Visits, nor never went abroad with Strangers in their Company...'[7]

The family's disinclination for sociability affected the development of Margaret's character. During her early years there was no occasion to 'fashion herself to all companies, times and places' as one of her dramatic characters put it. In short, she failed to acquire the social desideratum termed 'civility', a crucial ingredient of a gentlewoman's breeding. To add to her isolation, there were no companions close to her own age even among her siblings, who behaved more like grave aunts and uncles than playfellows, as Margaret recalled:

> ...my brothers and sisters, were for the most part serious, and stayed in their actions, not given to sport nor play, nor dance about, whose company I keeping, made me so too.[8]

She saw little of her three brothers, who were educated away from home. Of her four sisters, three had already married by the time Margaret turned twelve. Margaret's most intimate companion at this time was her young waiting-woman, Elizabeth Champlain. The latter, to whom Margaret signed herself 'Your loving friend' in a preface to her first book, was to remain a bosom companion for the rest of her life.

Margaret's education at home did little to repair her lack of the conventional social graces. As she herself was the first to admit, it was even more lax than usual for one of her sex and rank:

> As for tutors, although we had for all sort of Vertues, as singing, dancing, playing on Musick, reading, writing, working [i.e. needlework] and the like, yet we were not kept strictly thereto, they were rather for formalitie than benefit...[9]

Reading and writing were taught by an 'ancient decay'd gentlewoman' whose incompetence Margaret blamed for her own 'ill hand' and extraordinary orthography. Under this indulgent regime, Margaret failed to progress in the basic female requisites.

One of her prefaces lists a whole gamut of 'ladies works' of which she professed complete ignorance, with one significant exception: somehow Margaret had acquired her mother's knowledge of the art of managing a sheep-farming estate.[10] Since this was a part of the masculine domain, we can conclude that Margaret was never thoroughly initiated into the domestic concerns of Stuart femininity.

As an adult Margaret bemoaned her 'negligent' education, although by this she did not mean the female accomplishments she had scanted. In her stories and plays, she dreamt of receiving a *male* education in the liberal arts and sciences. One of her heroines declared:

> I would my Parents had kept me...as birds...when they are taught to sing Artificial Tunes...so would I have had Tutors to have read to me several Authors, as the best Poets, the best Historians, the best Philosophers, Moral and Natural, the best Grammarians, Arithmeticians, Mathematicians, Logicians...[11]

But all this was in retrospect. Margaret seems to have enjoyed a happy childhood because her permissive education allowed her leisure to do exactly as she pleased. 'My Mother did not Force me to Learn to Work with a Needle, though she found me always Unapt thereto...', Margaret recalled. 'As for my studies of books it was little, yet I chose rather to read, than to imploy my time in any other work [needlework] or practise [of a musical instrument]'. Instead, she preferred solitary diversions which displayed her taste for fantasy and eccentricity:

> ...my serious study could not be much, by reason I took great delight in attiring, fine dressing and fashions, especially such fashions as I did invent my self...also I did dislike any should follow my Fashions, for I always took delight in a Singularity.[12]

Even as a child she spent her time in a sort of philosophical contemplation, 'being more taken or delighted with thoughts than in conversation with a society, insomuch as I would walk two or three hours...in a musing, considering, contemplating manner, reasoning with myself of everything my senses did present'. Before she was twelve years old, Margaret had begun to record her contemplations in what she later termed her 'Baby

Books'. Unfortunately she found these youthful essays too anarchic for her taste and 'for want of good method and order' would never divulge their contents.[13]

While Margaret was left to her own devices, her family made itself unpopular in the Colchester neighbourhood as the county became polarized on political and religious issues. The Lucas family had always been High Church in its sympathies. In 1634 John Lucas challenged the Puritan hegemony of the Earl of Warwick and Sir Thomas Barrington by soliciting Archbishop Laud's subscription to repair St. Paul's; in 1637, serving as High Sheriff, he broke the back of ship-money opposition in the county, and was knighted as a reward.[14]

By this time Sir John and his mother had alienated every sector of the Colchester populace, and in 1640 and 1641 they were the targets of a series of mysterious 'riots'. Popular outrage culminated in the anti-royalist riot of 22 August 1642, provoked by information that Sir John had secreted horses and arms intended for the King. In the ensuing mêlée Sir John and his mother were nearly lynched and the manor house was looted.[15] It is not clear whether Margaret was a witness to these events, or, if she was, whether she took in their full significance. Yet we may conjecture that Margaret's lifelong hostility toward the local populace was rooted in her youthful perception of her family's social alienation from its surroundings.

Margaret apparently accompanied her sisters when they joined the King in Oxford, probably in late 1642. She recorded in her memoirs that as soon as the Queen had arrived there,

> I had a great desire to be one of her Maids of Honour, hearing the Queen had not the same number she was used to have, whereupon I wooed and won my Mother to let me go, for my Mother being fond of all her Children, was desirous to please them.... But my Brothers and Sisters seeme'd not very well pleas'd, by reason I had never been from home...for though they knew I would not behave my self to their, or my own dishonour, yet they thought I might to my disadvantage....[16]

Although this passage represents Mrs. Lucas as indulging her daughter's whim, Margaret's fictionalized reminiscences suggest that her mother's motives were more worldly. In the play *Youths Glory, Deaths Banquet*, Mother Love is portrayed as plotting to send her daughter Lady Sanspareille (Margaret) to Court to ensnare a rich husband. Lady Sanspareille rejects the idea, but in real life Margaret shared her mother's ambitions. *The Presence*, a dramatization of Margaret's experiences at Court, made no secret of her urge to conquer the world with her beauty and wit.[17]

Unfortunately, Margaret was not fitted for social success at the *précieuse* Court of Henrietta Maria. Aside from her lack of French and the female ornaments, Margaret was unaccustomed to sociable discourse. And the mores at Court were baffling to a girl brought up in rural solitude. Margaret found the young women astonishingly bold and their male counterparts even more intimidating. In *The Presence* Margaret offered an acerbic portrait of the Court gallants:

> be bold, rude, and vain, talk much without sense, swear much without cause, brag much without reason, accoutre your self fantastically, behave your self carelessly, and imploy time idly; and be sure you raile of all Women generally, but praise every particular one...[18]

Isolated and bewildered, Margaret was unable to distinguish where the line was drawn between honourable and dishonourable female behaviour. And Mrs. Lucas had made sure that her daughters were over-careful on this point, no doubt in compensation for her own youthful indiscretion. Margaret had been told that 'the world was apt to lay aspersions even on the innocent',

> for which I durst neither look up with my eyes, nor speak, nor be any way sociable, insomuch as I was thought a Natural Fool...[19]

This fear of an unwitting slip resulted in paralysing bashfulness, an affliction which was to trouble her for the rest of her life. In the alien milieu of the Court, Margaret was perennially tongue-tied. 'I am told you stand amongst Company like a stone Statue, without life, sence, or motion...', her mother reproached Lady Bashful (Margaret) in the latter's dramatic reconstruction.[20] Mortified by her failure, Margaret wanted to return home immediately. But Mrs. Lucas argued that 'it would be a disgrace for me to return out of the Court so soon after I was placed'. Margaret's mother was also willing to invest heavily in the enterprise: her daughter was so well supplied with funds that she was 'in a condition to lend rather than to borrow'.

Margaret accompanied the Queen to Paris, where she was tongue-tied in two languages, for even after five years in the country she was unable to speak French. In April 1645, Margaret was still enduring her miserable existence at Court when the 51-year-old Marquis of Newcastle arrived in Paris. As an inveterate womanizer, the marquis was inclined to play the gallant to the young women at Court. Having heard of Margaret from her brother Sir Charles Lucas, Newcastle made a point of being kind to her. By autumn his courtesy was transformed into courtship.

ii. Courtship and Marriage

Since the marquis was to be the predominant influence upon Margaret for the rest of her life, a sketch of his career is in order. William Cavendish, Marquis and later Duke of Newcastle was an aristocratic dilettante. Born in 1593, he was made heir in lieu of his elder brother Charles, probably because of the latter's physical deformity.[21] William's education included a stint at Cambridge and a continental tour in the train of Sir Henry Wotton. His early manhood was spent in collecting titles and inheritances and in marrying a rich widow.[22] Newcastle's first wife bore him ten children, of whom two sons and three daughters survived to adulthood. Meanwhile the 1630s saw him dissipating the fortune he had accumulated during the 1620s. As Lucy Hutchinson commented:

> ...no man was a greater prince than he was in all that Northerne quarter; till a foolish ambition of glorious slavery carried him to Court, where he ran himselfe much into debt, to purchase neglects of the King and Queene and scornes of the proud Courtiers.

Newcastle spent five years intriguing to be appointed governor to Prince Charles. He was granted the post in 1638, but was forced to resign in 1641 when Parliament learned of the royalist Army Plot. In 1642 his influence in the north enabled him to raise an army of his own, whose service to the King earned Newcastle a marquisate.[23]

The marquis's military successes were mixed. Although everyone conceded his courage in the heat of battle, rumours at Court described him as sybaritic and negligent. More damaging were the intimations that Newcastle was too vain to subordinate himself to any other commander, to the detriment of royalist strategy.[24] Yet his fears were justified by events: when the marquis joined forces with Rupert at Marston Moor, the result was a disaster. Newcastle's reasons for bolting to the continent the day after the battle were acutely analysed by Clarendon:

> ...the strange manner of the prince's...undeliberated throwing himself, and all the King's hopes, into that sudden and unnecessary engagement, by which all the force the marquis had raised and with so many difficulties preserved was in a moment cast away and destroyed, so transported him with passion and despair, that he could not compose himself to think of beginning the work again, and involving himself in the same undelightful condition of life, from which he might now be free.

In addition to the disgrace which clung to Newcastle, his flight had left him in severe financial straits. Yet characteristically, as soon as he had secured credit the marquis purchased a 'coach and nine horses of an Holsatian breed', turning his hang-dog retreat into a triumphal progress through Flanders to the English Court at St. Germain.[25]

Despite the marquis's misfortunes, he was still an eligible matrimonial prospect. The Court was surprised, and his friends dismayed, when he fixed his attentions on 22-year-old Margaret Lucas, one of the most insignificant of Court personages. Yet she was the type of young woman most likely to appeal to the marquis. One asset was her figure; twenty years later Mrs. Evelyn grudgingly allowed her 'a good shape, which she may truly boast of'. However eccentric Margaret's fashions may have been, they were invariably designed to set off this quality. All her portraits show her in an extraordinary décolletage which seems to have been her habitual style of dress, one which was daring enough to shock Pepys in 1667.[26] It did not fail to attract the marquis, who described her as 'all well shap'te' in his first poem to her; subsequent verses dwelt on her 'skinne...softer then softest silke' and her 'plumpe fleshe'.[27] Yet this palpable appeal was accompanied by so modest a demeanour that the contrast heightened her allure. The marquis's poetry celebrated Margaret's ability to provoke lust yet remain insensible to it; 'like the Sunne, that powre shee now hath gott/ To inflame others, yett herselfe not hott...'. To Newcastle this modest demeanour was preferable to the impudence of the Court ladies. Margaret's naiveté and her uncritical admiration of the marquis were also flattering to a man still recovering from wounds to his self-esteem. As Margaret observed:

> ...my Lord the Marquis of Newcastle did approve of those bashfull fears which many condemned, and would choose such a Wife as he might bring to his own humours, and not such a one as was wedded to self conceit...[28]

Newcastle was infatuated, but it is doubtful that he was initially interested in matrimony. His reputation for amorous conquests was well established. Even his daughters had composed several songs describing their father's prowess at casual seductions:

> ...his true gallantry, sweetnes of fame
> which doth our Sex garrison ever soe take
> soe desirous to yeild, their conditions not make....[29]

But Margaret had been forewarned of this danger. Her first note to the marquis confronted him with the counsel of friends who had told her 'they heer of your profesions of afeetion to me, which they bed me tak hed of, for you had ashured your selfe to many and was constant to non'. Adroitly manoeuvring Newcastle into honourable intentions, Margaret told her friends that 'my lord Newcastll was too wis and to honest to ingag himself to many...'. Soon the marquis was scribbling verses exalting the ideal of two platonic souls virtuously intermingling. He heaped scorn on the courtier who 'takes lust for love, runnes over Woman kinde', and boasted about the 'long lent' he endured while waiting for his 'blest ascension' with Margaret in wedlock. Yet the marquis had not abandoned his hope of sexual conquest. Almost until the day of the wedding, Margaret still reminded Newcastle that 'ther is a custumare law that must be sineed before I may lawfully call you husban...'. She was not about to repeat her mother's mistake. A 'headless maid' is the worst monster in nature, one of her characters quipped.[30]

Even if the marquis had been converted to the idea of remarriage, his friends were convinced that Margaret was a poor choice. It is not clear on what grounds they based their opposition, since their objections have been relayed in garbled form through Margaret's own writings.[31] Most likely Newcastle's advisors thought he could have made a better bargain both in social and pecuniary terms. The Lucas family was of minor gentry stock, and Margaret's portion was only £2000. Newcastle's cronies insinuated that Margaret was a designing young woman determined to throw herself in his path. His children from his first marriage formed the same opinion.[32]

There was some basis for their suspicions. Not that there was any doubt about the sincerity of Margaret's feelings for the marquis. With his impressive military rank, his facetious conversation, his bent for poetry, he combined Margaret's three 'dead loves' of her childhood: '*Caesar*, for his Valour...*Ovid*, for his Wit, and *Shakespear*, for his Comical and Tragical Humour'. Thirty years her senior, he became the father she had never known. And he alone had discovered the worth that lay behind her shy exterior. Margaret's dejected solitude at Court had inflamed her desire to be admired. The marquis's attentions released a grateful flood of affection that had been dammed up for two years. Eventually she came to love him with an intensity which exceeded that reserved for the dearest members of her family. The speech she composed for a dying widow might have been her own:

> My Love to my Husband was not only a Matrimonial Love...but a Natural Love, as the Love of Brethren, Parents, and Children, also a Sympathetical Love, as the Love of Friends,...a Loyal Love, as the Love of a Subject...[33]

But however strong her attachment to Newcastle, Margaret's role was not as innocent as her memoirs would lead us to believe. In her autobiography Margaret appears passive, even hostile to matrimony: 'I did dread marriage and shunn'd Mens companies as much as I could...'. She accepted Newcastle's proposals because he was the onely Person I ever was in love with:... it was not Amorous Love, I never was infected therewith, it is a Disease, or a Passion...I onely know by relation...neither could Title, Wealth, Power or Person entice me to love; but my Love was honest and honourable, being placed upon Merit...[34]

All Margaret's disclaimers are significant. Her professed indifference to title, wealth and power should not be taken seriously, as these were part of Newcastle's allure. In her play *The Presence*, her exultation at having secured a magnificent prize is evident. And in her subsequent career Margaret displayed the exaggerated respect of an *arriviste* for a title.[35]

The most interesting clue to Margaret's character is her disavowal of 'amorous' or romantic love. In her hostility to this ideal she presents a striking contrast to her female peers, who were addicted to a diet of romances which often provided the terms of reference for real life. Margaret declared her contempt for romances and for the moral economy which they described:

As for those Tales I name Romancicall, I would not have my Readers think I write them, either to please, or to make foolish whining Lovers, for it is a humor of all humors, I have an aversion to...[36]

There was a profound difference between Margaret's fictional fantasies and the romances she affected to despise. Stuart romances portrayed the sensation of being in love as an end in itself. In Margaret's tales the focus is not on love *per se* but on a woman's 'will to power', expressed as the chronicle of her extraordinary ambitions, or as her psychological conquest of a male protagonist. Love assumes a secondary role as one vehicle by which the struggle may be played out. Sometimes Margaret's heroines used the customary arsenal of their sex, especially beauty, 'the Light of our Sex, which is Eclips'd in Middle age, and Benighted in Old age, wherein our Sex sits in Melancholy Darkness...'. Beauty was prized because it brought attention from men and power over them which could not be obtained in any other way:

...if Nature had not befriended us with Beauty, and other good Graces, to help us to insinuate ourselves into men's Affections, we should have been more inslaved than any other of Natur's Creatures she hath made; but Nature be thank'd, she hath been so bountiful to us, as we oftener inslave men, than men inslave us; they seem to govern the world, but we really govern the world, in that we govern men...

And in her own daydreams, she associated fantasies of absolute power with visions of irresistible or even lethal feminine beauty:

> I did imagine my self such a Beauty, as Nature never made the like.... And then that a great powerful Monarch...fell desperately in love with me, seeing but my Picture.... As I went out of the City where I dwelt, all the streets were strewed with dead Lovers, which had lived only on hopes...I should have govern'd all the world before I had left off Contemplating...[37]

Such aspirations were still conventionally feminine, if somewhat exaggerated, but a number of Margaret's heroines attained their ends by more active contrivances. And even those who were rejected by their lovers still sought revenge as a consolation. The most energetic expedient, adopted by nearly all Margaret's heroines, was to commit suicide. In their hands it became an aggressive instrument of retaliation, for the faithless lover invariably killed himself on discovering his mistress' dead body.

Despite the improbable fantasies that comprised Margaret's plots, their underlying theme of a power struggle between the sexes offers insight into the principles that guided her conduct in real life. Indeed the chief difference between art and life was that in fiction Margaret could concoct incredible circumstances to satisfy her ambitions, whereas in the real world these urges were limited by convention. One constraint shrewdly noted by Margaret was that the exercise of feminine authority in a male world must be concealed:

> ...what man is he, that is not govern'd by a woman more or less?... And not only Wives and Mistresses have prevalent power with Men, but Mothers, Daughters, Sisters, Aunts, Cousins, nay, Maidservants...yet men will not believe this, and 'tis the better for us, for by that we govern as it were by an insensible power, so as men perceive not how they are Led, Guided, and Rul'd by the Feminine Sex.[38]

The progress of the marquis's courtship of Margaret displays all the elements of one of her fictional power struggles artfully adapted to the limiting conditions of reality. Like an angler hooking a fish, Margaret alternately drew Newcastle in with ingenuous professions of love and admiration, then offered to 'delever up' her 'intrest' in him whenever he displayed the slightest resistance. Each of her offers to withdraw elicited more fervent protestations of commitment from the marquis. Meanwhile Margaret transformed each apparent disadvantage into a strategic advantage. Her unpopularity at Court was represented to Newcastle as a by-product of her severe virtue. Since Newcastle himself had experienced the courtiers' malice, it was easy to persuade him of this interpretation. So well did Margaret play on his *amour-propre* that he refused to believe anything to her discredit, even when reported by his friends. Fear of Court gossip also served Margaret as a pretext for being tantalizingly coy: 'For know, me Lord, Saintjarmanes is a place of much sencour [censor]...'. Sulking was also useful whenever matters were not progressing smoothly. Judging from Newcastle's poems, Margaret's sullen moods elicited the desired effect: 'When your least sadder looke on me, it still/ Doth make me thinke which waye my selfe to kill...'. Finally, Margaret betrayed a shrewd grasp of the need to expedite matters before Newcastle's friends could help him to recover his rationality. 'If you are so passhonit as you say...it may be feared it cannot last long, for no extrem is parmenttary [permanent]...'. Once the marquis was securely hooked she drew up the line with a jerk: 'My Lord, sence our affeetions is poublished it will not be for our honours to delay our marreg'.[39] In fact Margaret took charge of the wedding arrangements, choosing John Cosin to perform the ceremony, and promising Lady Browne substantial largesse for the use of Sir Richard Browne's Paris chapel. The wedding took place there in early December, 1645, after only a few months of courtship.[40]

In his poems to Margaret the marquis affected scorn for the material side of matrimony, composing droll fantasies of their life together as travelling beggars.[41] Nevertheless Margaret's portion of £2000 would have been a substantial help. Once the wedding was a *fait accompli*, however, Elizabeth Lucas informed the couple that the money was not forthcoming:

The state of the Kingdom is such yet that...her brother cannot give
unto her with that wch is hers, nether can I show my love and
affection towardes my Daughter as I would, in respect of the great
burdens we groane under.

Actually Mrs. Lucas's own lands were never sequestered, and
Margaret's brother John flaunted excess cash while paying a £500
bribe to John Ashburnham (and a larger amount to the King) to
be made Baron Lucas of Shenfield. But Margaret could do
nothing, and her portion was not relinquished until two years
later.[42]
Financial insecurity was to plague the couple for the next
decade, until Newcastle's relatives had compounded for their
estates and began sending him a fixed annuity. Meanwhile the
marquis fell into a cyclical pattern of credit and crisis. He
borrowed large sums from friends and set up a magnificent
establishment whose splendour enabled him to obtain credit with
local tradesmen. He lived on credit until some depressing turn in
royalist affairs brought his creditors to the door. Newcastle then
borrowed another lump sum and started the process again.
Meanwhile he never abated his luxurious style of life—indeed it
was one ingredient of his success in creating the illusion of
solvency in the eyes of his creditors. But Margaret lived in
continual fear that the marquis would be carted off to prison for
debt.[43]
There were other causes for anxiety. Margaret failed to
become pregnant, and by 1648 the couple were seeking medical
advice. Newcastle's concern was unambiguous. As Margaret
wrote,

he was so desirous of male issue that I have heard him say he cared
not...although they came to be persons of the meanest fortunes...[44]

Margaret was more ambivalent. In later years she was to assert
that wives wished for offspring chiefly for social reasons: '...many
times Married Women desire Children, as Maids do Husbands,
more for Honour than for Comfort or Happiness, thinking it a
Disgrace to live Old Maids, and so likewise to be Barren...'. But
there were no rational grounds for these feelings:

...though it be the part of every Good Wife to desire Children to

Keep alive the Memory of their Husbands Name...yet a Woman
hath no such Reason to desire Children for her Own Sake, for first
her Name is lost...also her Family, for neither Name nor Estate goes
to her Family...Also she Hazards her Life by Bringing them into the
World, and hath the greatest share of Trouble in Bringing them up.[45]

Margaret also displayed annoyance at what she felt was the
affected and self-indulgent behaviour of pregnant women, who
took 'more pleasure when they are with Child, than when they
are not...not onely in Eating more...but taking a Pride in their
great Bellies...'. Pregnancy was also the excuse, Margaret
claimed, for 'Feigning Laziness', 'Unnecessary Complaints', and
the wasteful expense of fancy childbed linen and other
accoutrements of the 'lying-in'.

Again to redouble the Charge, there must be Gossiping, not only
with Costly Banquets at the Christening and Churching, but they
have Gossiping all the time of their Lying-in...[46]

Yet Margaret's acerbic portraits of her pregnant acquaintances
betray envy and perhaps even guilt that she had not fulfilled her
childbearing role. In 1648 she was as concerned as the marquis
about her infertility and was dosing herself with all sorts of
remedies. Aside from a strong tendency to hypochondria,
Margaret apparently suffered from amenorrhoea, and her
interpretation of the current humoral theories induced her to be
'Purged & Let Bloud very much'. She also tried 'Doctor Farrers
Receipt for the Sterrillite in women', a herbal compound to be
taken internally, injected 'into ye Matrix [womb]' and to 'anoynt
allso ye Navill'. Dr. Mayerne referred to the 'Melancholyk
Hypocondriak' humour that afflicted the marquis and his wife,
suggesting that perhaps they were too depressed to engender
children:

Touching Conception, I know not if in the estate she's in you ought
Earnestly to desire it, It is hard to get Children...when One is
Melancholy...it will be but tyme Lost if you enter that race
frowningly...[47]

Political events were a major cause of the couple's melancholy.
In 1645, Newcastle had thought it only a matter of weeks before

he would return to England at the head of a victorious army. But an Irish invasion planned for 1645 came to nothing; the next engagement in which Newcastle was involved was to follow Prince Charles to Holland in July 1648. The Prince had already left when Newcastle arrived, and he sat idle in Rotterdam for six months trying to gather an army of his own. The subsequent royalist débâcle took its course without his aid.[48]

After the King's execution, followed by a Parliamentary order which barred Newcastle from England as a traitor,[49] the couple faced a more permanent exile. They settled in Antwerp, where Newcastle rented a luxurious villa and purchased expensive horses in order to practise the art of the *manage*, or horsemanship. Margaret returned to her childhood occupation of recording her 'contemplations'. Its original impetus was escapist. Margaret's ill-health and childlessness, the deaths of four members of her family within the space of a year,[50] the blasting of royalist hopes and of her own vicarious political ambitions had left her in a state of nervous torment. As she recalled,

> my own thoughts...were like travellers seldom at home...busying themselves on that as nothing concern'd them, or could any wayes advantage them...putting my minde in disorder....

But as she discovered, the imagination enabled men to 'Conquer their Unruly Passions...and order their Minds according to their Fortunes'.[51] At any rate it was a harmless way to pass the time. There were already several 'closet poets' within the Cavendish family. Aside from Newcastle himself, who printed two plays in 1649, his daughters Elizabeth and Jane had written poems and a comedy a few years earlier.[52] It is not clear whether Margaret considered publishing her work at this stage. If the next royalist venture had succeeded, she might have remained a closet poetess like other female members of the Cavendish family.

In 1650 the marquis was still part of the King's inner circle. In April he was sworn into the Privy Council and took part in negotiations with the Scots. Yet there were signs of his waning influence. In June, Hyde wrote to Nicholas that Newcastle was 'a very lamentable man and as fit to be a gen[era]ll as a B[isho]pp'. The Scots shared Hyde's opinion; the following February Newcastle described himself as 'one of the cast Privy Councellors his Majesty left here behind'. The marquis spent the next few months negotiating with the Elector of Brandenburg for the loan of 10,000 troops, but the bargain was not consummated until 7 September, four days after the battle of Worcester. When Newcastle heard that the Scots had been defeated and that no one knew what had become of the King, he fell into 'so violent a passion' that Margaret believed it would endanger his life.[53]

At this low ebb of royalist fortunes, Newcastle's creditors became importunate. There was one resource left: Newcastle persuaded his brother Sir Charles Cavendish to travel to England to compound for his lands. Margaret accompanied Sir Charles in order to petition for a share of Newcastle's estate as the dependant of a delinquent.

The two left for England in early November, 1651. Margaret's own petition was rejected on 10 December on the grounds that she had married Newcastle after his delinquency. She remained in England nearly a year and a half, presumably awaiting the completion of Sir Charles' composition. Away from Newcastle, she became even more anxious and depressed. Sir Charles attempted to divert her by describing his own interest, the latest theories in science and mathematics. Both Cavendish brothers had been 'virtuosos' in science since the 1630s, but Sir Charles was the true scholar of the family. Although his chief love was mathematics, he entertained a wide acquaintance and an even wider correspondence with the foremost scientific figures of the period.[54] His fascination with atomism and scientific topics of the early 1650s can be discerned clearly in Margaret's works, albeit grotesquely transformed. Sir Charles' revelations had filled her mind with exciting new ideas, and she threw herself into her writing. Within nine months she had finished a book of scientific speculations in verse entitled *Poems and Fancies*. The idea of printing it apparently originated with Margaret herself. In 'The Poetresses Hasty Resolution' she described the process as an irrational impulse. Having written her book so quickly, she thought of writing more verses to build a 'Pyramid of Fame'. When 'Reason' advised her to burn her work, she rushed it off to the press before she had a chance to change her mind.[55] An overpowering urge had set aside not only social convention but her own judgement.

Margaret's obsession with fame had already come to the

surface in her work begun in Antwerp. *The Worlds Olio* began by observing that 'The desire of Fame proceedes from a doubt of an after being'. Margaret's preoccupation with death, heightened by what her doctor had perceptively diagnosed as 'Melancholyk Hypocondriak' tendencies, led to cravings for some form of immortality. A conventional woman might have found solace in religion, but piety was not to Margaret's taste. And even if there were to be a heavenly resurrection, it did not offer Margaret sufficient compensation for the loss of this world. She conjectured that man's soul might delight in earthly fame after it had left the body, or grieve if it had been forgotten.[56] Others sought immortality in their offspring, but by 1651 Margaret must have suspected that she would never bear children. There are strong hints that her books served as a substitute: 'Condemne me not for making such a coyle/About my Book, alas it is my Childe'. She tried to convince herself that the surrogate was superior to the original:

> Fame...the older it groweth, the more it florishes, and is the more particularly a mans own, then the Child of his loines...many times the child of his loines deceives the parent, and instead of keeping his father's fame, brings him an infamy.[57]

Margaret's motivation differed from that expressed by some of the first Englishwomen to appear in print. Women's fear of death in childbirth inspired a specific genre, the maternal advice-book intended for children whom the mother might not live to educate. Elizabeth Joceline's *The Mothers Legacie to her unborne Childe* (1624) exemplifies the altruistic intention of such works.[58] Since they were regarded as an extension of women's childrearing role and were generally printed posthumously, they did not encroach into the 'male' realm of publication. Female religious writers of the Interregnum were on shakier ground for choosing a 'male' topic. But they likewise renounced masculine ambition, representing themselves as passive instruments of the divine purpose, not as competitive theological authorities.[59]

The upsurge of feminine writing and preaching in Interregnum London attracted Margaret's notice and may have given her the courage to print her first book.

> ...this Age hath produced many effeminate Writers, as well as

Preachers, and many effeminate Rulers, as well as Actors. And if it be an Age when the effeminate spirits rule, as most visible they doe in every Kingdome, let us take the advantage, and make the best of our time, for feare their reigne should not last long; whether it be in the Amazonian Government...or in witty Poetry, or any thing that may bring honour to our Sex.[60]

But Margaret's intention was unlike that of her female contemporaries. There was never any question of hiding behind an excuse of maternal or religious altruism. She admitted that her aspirations had originated in 'Pure Self-love'.

The ambition to build a 'Pyramid of Fame' through her writings was an extraordinary one, as Margaret herself noted. 'Women have seldome, or never, (or at least in these latter Ages) written a Booke of Poetry'. She tried to account for the fact by suggesting that heretofore her sex had been daunted by the scarcity of female authors: 'Women writing seldome, makes it seem strange, and what is unusuall, seems Fantasticall...and what seemes odd, Ridiculous'.[61] But her prefatory epistles reveal that she was acutely conscious of the social conventions which had discouraged women from pursuing a literary career.

The disapprobation accorded to female authors arose less from their novelty than from a restricted definition of women's role, which embraced a time-consuming round of feminine tasks. A wife who discharged her domestic responsibilities should have had no leisure for another métier. Mary Evelyn expressed the prevailing view when she asserted that

Women were not born to read authors, and censure the learned...to give rules of morality, and sacrifice to the Muses...all time borrowed from family duties is misspent; the care of children's education, observing a husband's commands, assisting the sick, relieving the poor, and being serviceable to our friends, are of sufficient weight to employ the most improved capacities amongst us...[62]

This limited view of women's calling made no exceptions for rank or wealth, and Margaret acceded to it despite her stubborn eccentricity. Her earliest works were sprinkled with epistles which countered the imaginary accusation that she had abandoned her proper role of housewife to become an idle scribbler. While she was willing to admit the charge, Margaret felt obliged to justify her aberrant behaviour by proving that she was incapable of performing those tasks considered appropriate to her sex.

Initially, Margaret blamed the exigencies of exile for compelling her to seek alternative employment: '...my Lords Estate being taken away, [I] had nothing for Huswifery, or thrifty Industry to imploy my selfe in...'. But this was hardly a credible excuse, and elsewhere she confessed that it was not the want of materials but her lack of proficiency in the feminine arts which had hindered her.

> True it is, Spinning with the Fingers is more proper to our Sexe, then Studying or writing Poetry, which is the Spinning with the braine: but I having no skill in the Art of the first...made me delight in the latter...[63]

Margaret pointed out that she possessed more leisure than most women, because she had no children. She also considered herself excused from domestic responsibilities because of her husband's unusual complaisance. Despite their financial exigencies during the Interregnum, he provided Margaret with several waiting-maids and a governess, who discharged all the tasks associated with running the household. He never asked her to perform household chores or give up writing, except to spare some time for exercise. The marquis even encouraged his wife in her literary career, helping to overcome her diffidence by praising her works. As she wrote in a dedication to her *Orations*:

> I cannot chuse but declare to the World how happy I and my works are in your Approvement, which makes me confident and resolute to put them to the Press...

As Margaret was aware, most men were not likely to be so tolerant of their wives' ambitions.

> ...Husbands will never suffer [their wives] to climbe, but keep them fast lock'd in their arms, or tye them to houshold imployments, or through a foolish obstinacy bar up their Liberty...[64]

iii. A Feminine Critique of Marriage

Since her personal and professional life benefited from her marriage, Margaret's numerous critiques of matrimony raise certain questions. Why did the majority of her fictional heroines condemn wedlock in the strongest possible terms, resolving never to marry? And why, on the other hand, did these same heroines always break their resolution and marry anyway? First, Margaret's pampered position encouraged her to adopt a critical view of marriage as an institution. The shackles which bound her were so loose as to afford a glimpse of what it might be like to be entirely extricated from the encumbrances of domesticity. Margaret was aware, too, that her ambitions were more elevated than those of most women, a fact she often lamented:

> . . .it is very strange, since every Creature naturally desires and strives for preheminency, as to be superiour, and not inferiour. . .and are unwilling to obey. . .even the Beasts of the Field, the Birds of the Air, and the Fishes in the Sea. . .only Women, who seem to have the meanest souls of all the Creatures Nature hath made; for women are so far from indeavouring to get power, as they voluntarily give away what they have.[65]

But despite a diversity of circumstances, Margaret perceived certain features in the structure of marriage which led her to condemn it. No matter what a woman's condition might be, Margaret asserted, she was more likely to be happy if she remained single. In Margaret's own life, the satisfactions outweighed the disadvantages. But for the ideal woman Margaret wished she might have been, marriage offered too many distractions from the contemplative life.

> . . .marriage is an incumbered life, although the Husband and the Wife were fitly matcht for years, Births, Fortunes, Dispositions, Humours, Capacities, Wits, Conversations, Constancies, Vertues, and affections. . .at the best it is but the womb of trouble, which cannot be avoided. . .[66]

The choice of simile is fitting for it is a reminder that women were unable to avoid bearing children unless they were naturally barren. Margaret's elaboration of the metaphor implied that a woman must choose between bearing real children, or a 'Child of Fame':

> I am resolved for my part [her heroine declared] to live a single life, associating my self with my own Thoughts, marrying my self to my own Contemplations, which I hope to conceive and bring forth a Child of Fame, that may live to posterity, and to keep alive my Memory....[67]

For the ordinary woman, the likelihood of finding permanent happiness in marriage was small. The most obvious reason for this, in Margaret's view, was a woman's complete subordination to the will of her husband. One of her heroines asked rhetorically,

> ...who that is free, if they be wise, will make themselves slaves, subjecting themselves to anothers humour, unless they were fools, or mad, and knew not how to choose the best and happiest life.

The combination of social and biological roles that marriage imposed upon the ordinary woman could only result in a life of continual pain and grief.

> ...all the time of their lives is insnared with troubles, what in breeding and bearing children, what in taking and turning away servants, directing and ordering their Family, counting their expences, and disbursing their revenues, besides the vexations with their servants...and if they have Children, what troubles and griefs do ensue? Troubled with their forwardnesse and untowardnesse, the care for their well being, the fear for their ill doing, their grief for their sicknesse, and their unsufferable sorrow for their death... But if these troubles be joyned with an ill husband, it heightens their torments...[68]

If women's lot in marriage was so hard, then why did women persist in marrying? Of course, Margaret recognized the role of social pressure in persuading young women to seek husbands:

> ...it is an Honour for Maids to get good Husbands, because it is a kind of Reproach to live unmarried; for Marriage is Honourable, and gives a Respect to Women...[69]

A significant clue is provided by the fate of the handful of women in Margaret's plays and stories who manage to avoid matrimony. Of three such examples, one died young, another became a 'she-anchoret' who spoke to visitors through a grating, and a third gave public lectures in natural and moral philosophy.[70] The last of these alternatives was not conceivable in mid-seventeenth-century England except in the recesses of Margaret's mind. The other two are hardly appealing. Even her fertile imagination was incapable of endowing her heroines with employments that were attractive to a woman of rank and feasible in the society in which Margaret lived.

iv. Writing as a Vocation

The original impetus for Margaret's writing was a conventional one: a desire to pass the time during her exile. Margaret's real break with convention was to print her work, for the inhibitions against publishing were far more formidable than those against writing. Although theological tracts by female authors had begun to emerge as part of the religious controversies of the Interregnum, printed works by Englishwomen were still rare when Margaret's first book appeared in 1653.[71] Because of their reluctance to publish, it is difficult to estimate how much writing was done by women, especially since those who did write were secretive about it. The Countess of Bridgewater wrote

> divine meditations upon every particular chapter in the bible, written in her own hand, and never (till since her death) seen by any eye but her own...to the admiration both of her eminent piety in composing, and of her modesty in concealing....

Elizabeth Walker set down her memoirs while the rest of the family was asleep; when her husband caught her in the act, she made him promise never to look at her writings during her lifetime. And when Katharine Philips's poems were published without her knowledge, 'this ungenteel and ungenerous treatment, proved so oppressive to her great modesty, that it gave her a severe fit of illness'.[72]

To understand why women did not print their writings, we

must take a closer look at the Stuart ideal of female 'modesty'. In its narrow sense modesty was responsible for controlling female sexuality. But in broader terms it was a measure of the polarity of male and female roles. Hence the same attributes which were virtues in men became vices when adopted by women. The aspiration for fame, a key quality in the Renaissance ideal of masculinity, was a blot on a woman's character. Only such exceptional figures as female monarchs might legitimately cultivate 'masculine' traits.[73]

Margaret knew that she courted aspersions of immodesty for her incursion into the male realm of publication. She predicted that 'Men will cast a smile of scorne upon my Book because they think thereby, Women incroach too much upon their Prerogatives...'. Accordingly, she tried to redefine the ideal of female modesty so that it was reduced to simple chastity. Certainly readers could point to nothing unchaste in what she had written. Furthermore, she argued, the very practice of writing promoted chastity in women, for it was an antidote to the most dangerous enemy of feminine virtue—idleness.

...those of nearest Relation, as Wives, Sisters, & Daughters, may imploy their time...in honest, Innocent, and harmelesse Fancies, which if they do, Men shall have no cause to feare, that when they go abroad in their absence, they shall receive an Injury by their loose Carriages. Neither will Women be desirous to Gossip abroad, when their Thoughts are well imployed at home.[74]

In her endeavours to seek fame through her writing, Margaret encountered further difficulties that stemmed from the limitations imposed upon her sex. Heretofore women who published books had confined themselves to a narrow range of feminine subjects. Margaret remarked contemptuously,

when any of our Sex doth Write, they Write some Devotions, or Romances, or Receits of Medicines, for Cookery or confectioners, or Complemental Letters, or a Copy or two of Verses...which express our Brief Wit in our Short Works....[75]

But it was understandable that women should limit their discourse to household affairs, pious meditations, and romantic fantasies. These were the only topics on which women could claim competent knowledge, for they lacked worldly experience and bookish learning. Margaret, whose defects of education have already been described, entertained a lively sense of her deficiencies. This never prevented her from writing on any subject she fancied, but it did exert a negative influence on her work. Although she showed discernment when judging the works of others,[76] she accepted a low standard in her own endeavours in conformity with her assumed lack of ability. As she wrote in an epistle to *Natures Pictures*, 'I desire my readers to judge this book of mine according to the harmless Recreations of my idle time, and not as a laborious, learned, studious, or a methodical work...'. Given the fickle quality of popular taste, Margaret calculated that her works had as good a chance as any of achieving renown.

> The Reason why I print most of what I write, is, because I observe, that not only the weak Writings of men get Applause in the World, but the infinite weak Translators of other Works; thus there are many simple Books take the World by the Ears;...[77]

It followed that she had little to gain by revising her works. Debating whether to correct *The Worlds Olio*, Margaret observed that readers '...would have found fault with it if I had done it as I could, and they would but dispraise it as it is'. On the other hand, she did not wish her readers to assume that she was unaware of the defects that marred her works. Hence she prefaced each volume with an inventory of its imperfections. By this means she hoped to forestall criticism and create the impression that she could have written far superior works had she wished to do so. But this stratagem did not have its intended effect:

> those Faults or Imperfections I accuse my self of in my Praefatory Epistles, they fling back with a double strength against my poor harmless Works, which shewes their malice and my truth.[78]

It was partly an awareness of her educational disabilities that had led Margaret to choose a subject which did not require special qualifications: 'natural philosophy' or science. Mid-seventeenth-century science had not yet become the exclusive domain of professional 'scientists' but included practitioners of widely varying qualifications: true professionals like Robert Boyle, 'virtuosos' like Sir Charles Cavendish, and dilettantes like Margaret's brother John. Moreover, the concept of science as an experimental discipline was not fully established until later in the seventeenth century. Those of 'virtuoso' calibre described scientific endeavour as the conjecture of probabilities rather than the accumulation of experimental results. As Hobbes wrote to Newcastle in 1636:

> In thinges that are not demonstrable, of wch kind is the greatest part of Naturall Philosophy, as dependinge upon the motion of bodies so subtile as they are invisible...the most that can be atteyned unto is to have such opinions, as no certayne experience can confute, and from wch can be deduced by Lawfull argumentation, no absurdity....[79]

It was this aspect of 'natural philosophy' that Margaret enthusiastically seized upon. Natural speculation was accessible to anyone, even a woman unlearned in Latin or Aristotle:

> nature...is so free to teach, for every straw, or grain of dust, is a natural tutor...there is a natural education to all, which comes without pains taking, not tormenting the body with hard labour, nor the minde with perturb'd study, but comes easy and free through the senses...

She saw no reason why her conjectures should be less probable than those of anyone else. Moreover if she erred it was 'no great matter',

> For I had nothing to do when I wrot it, and I suppose those have nothing, or little else to do, that read it.[80]

This was why she had written her atomic theories in verse, thinking that 'Errours might better pass there, then in Prose, since Poets write most fiction, and Fiction is not given for truth, but Pastime'. Accordingly, her notion of 'natural philosophy' was almost a sub-branch of poetry, running the gamut from atomic theory to unbridled fantasies about the fairies and other worlds.

In her magpie-like way Margaret had picked up some scientific and mathematical ideas from her husband and her brother-in-law Sir Charles: atomism, the squaring of the circle, the notion of expressing human passions in mathematical form. Hyde, who had been presented with a copy of *Poems and Fancies*, wrote to Newcastle,

> I have now diligently studied my Ladyes booke…and cannot enough admire the worke…and could not have believed (if a lesse credible Authour had avowed it) that so many tearmes of Arte, and such expressyones proper to all sciences & to all kindes of learninge, could have flowed from a person unskilled in any but our Mother tounge…[81]

Others were more sceptical, alleging that Margaret had 'pluckt Feathers out of the Universities' or had stolen her ideas from Hobbes and Descartes. The physician Walter Charleton informed Margaret that

> among those, who have perused your Writings, I meet with a sort of Infidels, who refuse to believe, that you have alwayes preserved your self so free from the Contagion of Books, and Book-men.[82]

He provided a list of 'Terms of the Schools' whose appearance in Margaret's work had excited suspicion. Some thought that she was not the author of her books. Margaret professed herself glad that anyone would 'thinke my booke so well writ, as that I had not the wit to do it…'. But she was incensed at the imputations of plagiarism and countered them with renewed professions of her originality. She assured her readers that she had read few books and had never conversed with any 'professed scholar'. All her knowledge had been gathered from the discourse of her husband and brother-in-law who were not 'professed scholars'.[83] Of course, this meant that Margaret had merely acquired her learning second hand. Another aspect of Margaret's lack of originality was her tendency to express her ideas in trite literary forms that had already become old-fashioned by the mid-seventeenth century. 'Encyclopedic' verse, allegories of fancies, fairy poems, dialogues of birds or animals were all derivative forms that had begun to wane in popularity by the time Margaret adapted them to her own use.[84]

Some aspects of Margaret's thought bear a curious relation to the structure of the society in which she lived. Her view of nature was an inversion of the religious, hierarchical and male-dominated world of Stuart England, with King and God the Father at its apex. Margaret's universe was materialistic (although infused with spiritual forces), more or less egalitarian, and animated by feminine principles, for Nature herself was a woman. Within this perspective human pretensions were deflated: man's upright shape rather than any innate superiority made him apt for speech, action and reasoning. Animals were likely to be as knowledgeable as man, although man arrogantly assumed the contrary for lack of the kind of evidence he was able to interpret. Moreover, in moral terms man compared unfavourably with beasts. In her poetic fantasy, Margaret extended her inversion of the social order. Several passages identified beasts as the 'male' component of the natural world; they were heavy and stupid, careful and solid. Birds, in Margaret's imagination, represented women. Full of spirit, ingenious and subtle, birds were the poets of nature; beasts, its politicians.[85]

The events of the 1650s served to confirm Margaret in her writing career. On the one hand, the couple's financial situation had improved markedly. Newcastle, who had been dunning the King for £10,000 which he had lent to Charles I in 1639, received a first instalment of £6,500 in 1653. The marriages of Newcastle's children provided additional funds.[86] The couple received a steady income from the estate of Sir Charles Cavendish, who had died in 1654. Both the marquis and his wife indulged in publishing lavish editions of their works: Newcastle's first edition of his book on horsemanship cost £1,300 to print, and Margaret produced five books between 1653 and 1656. Walter Charleton mentioned the 'great summs of money' she bestowed in printing her works.[87]

While Newcastle's finances improved, his political influence deteriorated. He perceived this as early as 1654 and asked Secretary Nicholas to ensure that the King would grant him the northern offices which he had held under Charles I.[88] By 1655 Newcastle was complaining that he was left out of royalist counsels altogether. In 1658 Newcastle attempted his old method of hospitality. He provided a grand ball for the royal family, at which Charles wryly remarked that 'he perceived my Lord's credit could procure better meat than his own'. A week after this entertainment, the quarrel with Hyde's faction came to a head when the King's cabal failed to inform Newcastle of Ormonde's secret mission to England. Newcastle learned of it anyway and was 'industrious to deny the King's estate, being piqued that he did not know of its settlement...' as an informant told Nicholas late in February. The same informant wondered why anyone would trust Newcastle with the secret, 'for it might as well be proclaimed at the cross'. Newcastle was rebuked by Hyde and the King, the latter 'having real kindness for him, rather pitying his weakness than forgetting his inadvertency'. The chief blame was attached to Margaret for her presumptuous interference. It was reported that she 'swears that the affair cannot and shall not be effected without her husband'.[89] Margaret knew she was 'Accused for some Words...spoken concerning G.K. and L.O. which Words were Prejudicial to their Great Affairs, and Dangerous Designs, as Doubting their Successes, and Slighting their Proceedings...' as she confessed in a lengthy defence of herself in one of her 'sociable letters'. But her mortification at the incident of February 1658 exacerbated her resentment at Newcastle's exclusion from royalist counsels. The fact that other women were trusted agents in royalist cabals made the rebuff to Margaret more galling.[90]

The only way to revenge herself was to pour her energy into her works. It was no accident that Margaret's literary activities waxed as Newcastle's political influence waned. Poets and philosophers were the happiest men, Margaret declared, since

> they are so delighted with Transcendency, as they will not Descend to consider, or regard the Actions and Designs of Men...they are of Nature's privy Counsel, wherefore they scorn to be in Temporal or Human Counsels of Men.[91]

Elsewhere she admitted that her frustrated dreams of worldly power had been transferred to the literary realm:

> I confess my Ambition is restless, and not ordinary; because it would have extraordinary fame: And since all heroick Actions, publick Imployments, powerfull Governments, and eloquent pleadings are denied our Sex in this age, or at least would be condemned for want of custome, is the cause I write so much...[92]

In 1659 the general disorders in England revived Newcastle's hopes of a restored monarchy and royal preferment. When

Charles arrived at the Hague, the marquis rushed there to ask for the place of Master of the Horse. But the post had already been given to General Monck. The gesture was supremely ironic. Newcastle saw himself as the finest horseman in the world and a nobleman of the first rank who had endured eighteen years' exile for his loyal services to the Crown as northern general. Now his place had been usurped by a so-called 'Northern hero' of mean extraction who had fought against the King, and whose accidental loyalty to Charles had lasted less than two months.

In his flight to the Hague and England, the marquis had left Margaret in Antwerp as 'pawn' for his debts. When she finished their affairs and arrived in London, there were unpleasant surprises in store. She found Newcastle in lodgings which were 'not fit for a person of his rank and quality.... Neither did I find my Lord's condition such as I expected'. In other words, no Court office had been offered.[93] Some time in 1660 Newcastle had written a long 'Advice' to the King on internal and external affairs.[94] But this, like Newcastle himself, was ignored, and it ended up among Clarendon's papers. Margaret was so incensed at the reversal of her expectations that she demanded their immediate removal to Derbyshire. But Newcastle stayed in London to see a bill passed for the restoration of his estates. On his departure the marquis begged leave from the King to retire to the country with a revealing disclaimer:

> I am not ignorant, that many believe I am discontented; and 'tis probable they'll say, I retire through discontent: but I take God to witness, that I am no kind or ways displeased...I am so joyed at your Majesty's happy restoration, that I cannot be sad or troubled for any concern to my own particular...[95]

As late as the following May, when the marquis and his wife were installed at Welbeck, their chaplain Clement Ellis still harped on the couple's alleged lack of discontent: 'I know you think it greater happiness to enjoy my Lord Marquis...at Welbeck, than all the offices and honours which your exemplary loyalty has merited'.[96]

Like the marquis's reactionary 'Advice' to Charles II, his mode of life at his restored northern estates was an attempt to turn back the clock to the England of his youth. Much energy was devoted to rebuilding his ruined castles, restocking his parks, and increasing his rentals. In the latter enterprise Margaret's personal touch can be discerned. Her protégé Francis Toppe, a merchant who had married her waiting-maid Elizabeth Champlain, became overseer of Newcastle's financial affairs. In collaboration with Newcastle and Margaret, Toppe pursued a policy of enclosure and rackrenting which resulted in handsome pecuniary dividends. It also provoked a stream of protests from Newcastle's tenantry.[97] Eventually the financial cabal between Margaret and Toppe was to inspire rebellion in Newcastle's own children and estate stewards, who had been accustomed to a more indulgent regime. Meanwhile it produced a series of increasing jointures for Margaret. The first, dated 21 October 1662, assigned her £1,125 per annum as well as a life interest in Bolsover castle.[98]

Newcastle returned to his literary and artistic interests of the 1620s. During his youth he had patronized Ben Jonson; at the Restoration he bestowed his patronage on Jonson's imitators, like Thomas Shadwell, and other contemporary playwrights and poets. In this endeavour the marquis' two roles as 'Maecenas' and amateur playwright were apt to merge in an unfortunate way. Of the five plays he presented to the world as his own work, two were written almost wholly by Shadwell, one by Shirley, and another by Dryden.[99] Although Margaret had too fertile an imagination to need such wholesale theft, her own worst tendencies were exacerbated by Newcastle's aristocratic contempt for the labour of revision. Like her husband, she distributed largesse to second-rate poets in return for flattery. She also paid an anonymous drudge to 'correct' the stylistic errors of her earliest works for second editions.

By the mid-1660s Margaret had experimented with nearly every medium that had been fashionable in the past half century: 'fancies', tales, imaginary voyages, plays, even 'orations' on the model of grammar-school disputations. But her chief energies were poured into an effort to 'systematize' her scientific notions. As she explained her method, she deduced effects by analogy: she inferred the internal motions of animals or other phenomena by their external motions, or by their forms, figures or shapes.[100] She had long since abandoned the simple materialistic atomism of her earliest works for a system of hierarchical spiritual and material forces. These she named 'rational matter', 'sensitive matter', and 'inanimate matter'; all three together made up the 'infinite matter of nature', but each higher form was a purified quintessence of the others. The idea has affinities with Baconian and Cartesian currents of thought, but Margaret's expression of her theories is so obscure and contradictory that it would be a fruitless enterprise to try to trace their ultimate origins or their precise analogies among other seventeenth-century thinkers. In any case Margaret had become convinced that her own ideas were both true and unique. Indeed she was confident they would have been readily accepted as such if it were not for men's training in the ancient authors, which had predisposed them to condemn new opinions out of hand.[101] By the mid-1660s the diffidence of her early prefaces had disappeared, to be replaced by a progressive certitude which is revealed by her titles: *Poems and Fancies* and *Philosophicall Fancies* (both 1653), *Philosophical and Physical Opinions* (1655), *Observations upon Experimental Philosophy* (1666), and *Grounds of Natural Philosophy* (1668).

Margaret's attitude toward the male realm of scholarship had also begun to change. In her youthful works she affected contempt for learning. It was a mistake to assume that scholars were necessarily great wits, Margaret assured her readers, for their wit was merely borrowed from the books they had read. A character in one of her plays asked rhetorically, 'What do you call Wisdome? to speak Hebrew, Greek and Latine, and not understand them?... Or to cite dead Authors?... Or to make Sophisterian Disputes?' This prejudice against pedantry was heightened by Newcastle's aristocratic revulsion for the exacting discipline of scholarship. 'It were worse to be a pedantick woman, than a pedantick man', Margaret declared, 'yet so ill it is in a man, that it doth as it were degrade him from being Magnanimous and Heroick'. She had also heard that learning 'spoiles the natural wit', much like 'troublesome guests that fill up all the rooms of the house'.[102]

But Margaret's own activities had drawn her into the orbit of learned men. Her habit of donating her works to libraries and private scholars had elicited a great deal of obsequious flattery. The practice had also resulted in a few genuine philosophical friendships with scholars and virtuosos: Christiaan Huygens, who solicited her opinion on the mechanism behind 'Rupert's drops'; Walter Charleton, the physician from whom she learned medical terminology; and Joseph Glanvill, with whom she engaged in a protracted correspondence about physical and spiritual phenomena.[103] Eventually Margaret realized that her isolation hampered her efforts to disseminate her opinions. Having inferred that the obscurity of her terminology had hindered the acceptance of her theories, she began a massive reading programme so as to be able to employ conventional terms for her descriptions.[104]

Realizing that other thinkers defended their views against contrary opinions, Margaret attempted to do likewise. In her *Philosophical Letters* she attacked the theories of such prominent philosophers as Hobbes, Descartes, Van Helmont and Henry More. This venture merely disclosed to her the extent of her own isolation. The targets of her challenge apparently thought it ignominious to engage in public disputation with a woman. In a letter to Lady Conway, Henry More suggested that *she* reply to Margaret's criticisms, for he would not put on petticoats to do so.[105]

The most frustrating limitation imposed by her sex arose from Margaret's inability to teach her opinions. She had become convinced that it was the lack of opportunity to expound her theories that had prevented their being understood and adopted.

> ...there is not any Famous Philosopher, that ever I heard of, which did not Teach and Explane his Own Opinions...Wherefore I fear the Right Understanding of my Philosophical Opinions are likely to be Lost, for want of a Right Explanation...for it is not Proper for my Sex to be a Publick Oratour, to Declare or Explane my Opinions in Schools,... Neither is it fit I should be a Private School-Mistress...[106]

Although the universities were closed to Margaret, she had her books distributed to the college and university libraries. The receipt of her books was acknowledged by adulatory letters, especially from Cambridge, where hopes of largesse had been aroused by the Cavendish family connexions there.

Margaret herself addressed equally flattering dedications and epistolary prefaces to university scholars. In one passage she wrote,

> ...if any of your Noble Profession should Humble themselves so

Low as to Read my Works,...Consider my Sex and Breeding, and they will fully Excuse those Faults which must Unavoidably be found.... But although I have no Learning, yet give me leave to Admire it, and to wish I were one of your Society....[107]

Despite her frequent barbs against scholars, Margaret had a deep admiration for their attainments. Both hostility and approbation stemmed from the same source, a feeling of envy for accomplishments that lay forever beyond her reach, and resentment at the supercilious treatment she received:

...wise learned men think it a discredit to discourse learnedly to ignorant women, and many learned men speak most commonly to women, as women do to children...[108]

Giving what she believed was a realistic view of her abilities in a preface to *Philosophical Letters*, Margaret insisted that she was incapable of learning, since she had not been able to acquire a single foreign language. In the fantasy world of her plays, an entirely different picture emerged. Several of her heroines followed a 'virtuoso' course of studies. One young woman was tutored by an uncle in philosophy, history and poetry, and carried to lectures in physics, chemistry, music and judicature. Another, who received a similarly gruelling training, grew up to give public lectures in natural philosophy.[109]

Fantasies such as these could have no reference to the universities. Margaret's dealings with Oxford and Cambridge were of a purely epistolary nature. But a professional scientific body had recently been founded which did not explicitly assert a '*Salique* Lawe in Philosophy' (as Walter Charleton phrased it): the Royal Society. Indeed Margaret's own daydreams of giving public lectures in natural philosophy may have been inspired by her friends' descriptions of the Royal Society's weekly presentations.

v. *London* Persona *and Northern Exile*

When the Duke of Newcastle and his wife paid a lengthy visit to London in the spring of 1667, Margaret expressed a desire to

attend one of the meetings of the Royal Society. An invitation
was tendered to her on 23 May, but not because of her scientific
credentials. The motion to invite her was passed only after 'much
debate pro and con', as Pepys noted; 'it seems many being against
it, and we do believe the town will be full of ballets of it'.[110] Both
Margaret's sex and her reputation for eccentricity were
outweighed by her aristocratic connexions within the group. In
1665 Newcastle had achieved his ambition of a dukedom, and
several of his friends were influential members of the Royal
Society, among them Lord Berkeley and the Earl of Carlisle.
These two lords were deputed to escort Margaret to the meeting
of 30 May, at which she was to be shown a series of scientific
demonstrations by Robert Boyle and Robert Hooke.

Margaret and the Royal Society prepared to make an awesome
impression on each other. Margaret expressed herself as she had
done since childhood, through the medium of dress. On this
occasion she chose a peculiar blend of male and female. The
feminine element was represented by her petticoat, whose train
was so long that six maids were required to carry it. Other
aspects of her costume were detailed in a ballad which Evelyn
composed to describe the occasion:

> ...her head-geare was so pritty
> I ne'ere saw anything so witty
>   Tho I was halfe a feard
> God blesse us when I first did see her
> She look'd so like a cavaliere
>   But that she had no beard.

It was not the first time Margaret had experimented with male
dress. In 1665 Sir Charles Lyttelton described her as 'dressed in a
vest, and instead of courtesies, made legs and bows to the ground
with her hand and head'.[111]

Margaret was introduced to the company by her friend Walter
Charleton, whose prefatory speech stressed that Margaret and
the Society bestowed equal honour on each other. Yet Margaret
played a passive role in the proceedings. The Society had prepared
a dramatic selection of experiments. Air was weighed, roasted
mutton was dissolved in sulfuric acid, and the power of a magnet
weighing sixty pounds was demonstrated. Boyle illustrated his

theory of colours, and Hooke displayed his skill with the microscope.[112] Under this barrage of astonishing phenomena Margaret was tongue-tied. Pepys noted that she had nothing to say, except that she was 'all admiration'. No doubt her bashfulness was exacerbated by the all-male assembly. Years before, she had described a dream in which she was invited to dine with the immortal poets,

> which when I Saw, I was extremely out of Countenance, as being all Men...insomuch as I knew not how to Behave my self...[113]

Aside from the discomfiture induced by the evening's entertainment, Margaret's observations of genuine science as practised by professionals of the 1660s had a more lasting impact. The year before, in the preface to *Observations Upon Experimental Philosophy*, Margaret had asserted that Hooke's microscopic investigations set forth in his *Micrographia* (1665) were the product of delusions. But the testimony of her own eyes proved that her methodology of 'rational conjecture' was mistaken. Her misgivings must have been reinforced by her correspondence with Joseph Glanvill during the succeeding months of 1667. Despite Glanvill's insistence on the supernatural powers of witches, he was nevertheless a firm believer in the Baconian experimental credo of the Royal Society. After discussing some difficulties connected with the Platonic theory of the soul, Glanvill set aside such matters as idle speculations:

> ...the manner of the most obvious sensible things is to us unknown; And by this we can only prove, that we have yet no certain Theory of Nature...all that we can hope for, as yet, is but the History of things as they are, but to say how they are, to raise general *Axioms*, and to make *Hypotheses*, must, I think, be the happy priviledge of succeeding Ages; when they shall have gained a larger account of the *Phoenomena*, which yet are too scant and defective to raise Theories upon...we have yet no such thing as Natural Philosophy; Natural History is all we can pretend to; and that too, as yet, is but in its Rudiments...[114]

Margaret made her last effort at a comprehensive synthesis of her theories in *Grounds of Natural Philosophy* (1668), a much revised version of *Philosophical and Physical Opinions* (1655). But after her visit to the Royal Society Margaret's succeeding scientific publications were second or third editions, not original works: she printed no new revelations on natural philosophy.

The protracted London visit of 1667 coincided with the publication of Margaret's most significant non-scientific work, *The Life of the thrice Noble, High and Puissant Prince William Cavendishe, Duke, Marquess, and Earl of Newcastle...* (1667). The biography of the duke was the most laborious enterprise she ever attempted. She had begun working on it as early as 1662 with the help of Newcastle's secretary, John Rolleston, who supplied military details.[115] Newcastle himself had laid down two constraints. First, he vetoed Margaret's idea of writing the *Life* in a 'high rhetorical style', a plain style being more suitable for plain unvarnished truth. Secondly, Margaret was forbidden to make reflections on Newcastle's enemies. Since Margaret was eager to settle old scores this condition proved irksome, although she did her best to circumvent it through periphrasis and dark hints. But the injunction to employ a 'plain style' aided her in her aim to create a glorious myth of Newcastle as the perfect Cavalier. The work was not simply an *apologia pro vita sua*. As in the stylized Lely portraits of the time, art improved on life. Newcastle's biography was to exemplify nothing but nobility and wisdom, the 'Caesar...Ovid...Shakespeare' of Margaret's childhood fantasies.

Margaret concentrated chiefly on Newcastle's role as 'Caesar'. She herself had been inspired by Plutarch's account of Caesar to remark:

> I cannot but wish that Nature and Fate had made me such a one as he was; and sometimes I have that Courage, as to think I should not be afraid of his Destiny, so I might have as great a Fame.[116]

No doubt she felt a vicarious satisfaction in extolling Newcastle's military career, which she managed to transform into a successful enterprise by ignoring his defeats and strategic mistakes.[117] Some facts were more difficult to ignore. Margaret explained Newcastle's desertion of England after the battle of Marston Moor both in the text and the preface to her work.

By 'Caesar' Margaret meant stateman and ruler as well as military strategist. To prove Newcastle's acumen, she cited

instances of his alleged ability to forsee the outcome of events.[118]
Yet she never confronted the real test of Newcastle's
wisdom—the ability to devise a successful strategy for effecting
the King's restoration. It was this issue which had increasingly
divided Newcastle's counsels from those of Hyde and the
King.[119] Newcastle's solution relied on brute force, a policy
which emerges as an *idée fixe* in his correspondence in the
Clarendon State Papers, as well as his 1660 'Advice' to Charles
and the maxims which Margaret quoted in her biography. Hence
he spent his exile trying to recruit foreign troops, but never asked
himself how Englishmen might remain in quiet submission under
a Scottish, Irish or continental standing army. Of course Hyde
was proved right in the end, as Newcastle himself admitted after
the Restoration. But if Margaret realized that this constituted a
reflection on her husband's wisdom she never mentioned the fact.

More explicit contradictions emerge from Margaret's portrayal
of Newcastle as the suffering martyr for his king. Throughout
her biography she repeated her husband's professions of suicidal
attachment to Charles. In her dedication to the King, she
asserted:

> I have heard him often say, he loves your royal person so dearly, that
> he would most willingly, upon all occasions, sacrifice his life and
> posterity for your Majesty...

Yet Newcastle's own advice to Charles has a Hobbesian flavour,
and Clarendon was nearer to the truth than Margaret when he
remarked that Newcastle 'loved monarchy, as it was the
foundation and support of his own greatness....'.[120] Margaret was
far more Hobbesian than her husband, and her lack of sentiment
in the *Life* was an excellent foil for Newcastle's professions of
altruistic devotion to royalty. As she observed, 'It is better to be
at the latter end of a feast than at the beginning of a fray'. She had
also noticed that 'those that meddle least in wars...are not only
most safe and free from danger, but most secure from
losses...the wisest way is to be a spectator, rather than an
actor...'.[121]

Finally, Margaret's reckoning of Newcastle's financial
sufferings was as distorted as her depiction of his military
prowess. By exaggerating his rentals, omitting his pre-war

indebtedness, and leaving out embarrassing details such as his efforts to dun the King, she arrived at the inflated total of £941,303 for Newcastle's losses during the Interregnum.[122] Yet even if the figure had been correct, the image of Newcastle's 'sufferings' makes an incongruous contrast to Margaret's glowing description of the couple's luxurious style of life during exile: their villa with its staff of servants, Newcastle's expensive horses, Margaret's publications, and their banquets for the King and European nobility.

The myth of the duke's sufferings which Margaret had created with such art was meant to serve a particular purpose. It was to prove to the world that Newcastle had been Charles' wisest, noblest and most loyal subject. Hence his exclusion from Court office at the Restoration had been proportionately unjust. This is why the *Life* was dedicated to Charles himself as a rebuke for his ingratitude, and why the biography ended with Margaret's invidious sentiments:

> I have observed, that it is more easy to talk than to act; to forget than to remember; to punish than to reward; and more common to prefer flattery before truth, interest before justice, and present services before past.

*

The reasons for the duke and duchess' prolonged London stay in the spring of 1667 are not clear. The last such visit had been a short trip in 1665 when Newcastle received his dukedom. The title had proved powerless to advance the couple's social ambitions. Not only did Charles ignore Newcastle, but the Duke of York failed to attend a grand 'Entertainment' planned for him at Welbeck. Was the 1667 visit designed to coincide with the publication of Margaret's biography of Newcastle for one last assault on Court favour? In publishing the *Life* at this time Margaret may well have had this notion in the back of her mind, although the main purpose of the biography of Newcastle was to settle scores with her contemporaries and create a myth for 'future ages'. Yet Margaret's behaviour in London revealed that her desire for social pre-eminence was stronger than ever. With her fantastic apparel and idiosyncratic mannerisms, she created a sensation wherever she appeared. On Mayday Pepys went to the park with the rest of London:

> That which we and almost all went for was to see my Lady Newcastle; which we could not, she being fallowed and crowded upon by coaches all the way she went, that nobody could come near her; only, I could see she was in a large black coach, adorned with silver instead of gold, and so with the curtains and everything black and white, and herself in her cap...

He spent the entire day in an unsuccessful effort to get a closer view of the duchess. With her magnificent eccentricity she had managed to turn herself into a one-woman circus, earning the nickname 'Queen of Sheba'.[123]

There were several motives for Margaret's unusual behaviour. Since childhood she had always 'delighted in a singularity'. Now that she was a duchess she could indulge this propensity. She hungered for fame from the vulgar if she could not earn the accolades of the judicious: 'For all I desire, is Fame, and Fame is nothing but a great noise, and noise lives most in a Multitude'. Margaret had also persuaded herself that she must create an image in conformity with the notoriety inspired by her works:

> ...so Foolish are Most, especially Women, as when they see a Famous, Learned Man, or Witty Poet...they will streight say, Lord! Is this the Learned Man that is so Famous...how Simply he Looks...all such Famous Men, if they would not have their Works the Less Esteemed...must put on a Constrain'd Garb, and Speak some Gibbrigge...and then they shall be Admired, both for their Conversation and Contemplation...[124]

But perhaps the fundamental reason for Margaret's eccentric exterior was a compensatory one. Never in her life had she enjoyed easy sociability with her acquaintances. Hence she built up an armour of affectation to hide her bashfulness. Her social problems were fewest with men, because the convention of male gallantry guaranteed the flattery she craved. Of course Margaret saw through the pretence of men's civilities to women. Men were not allowed to interrupt women, Margaret noted,

> Neither must Men Contradict Women, although they should Talk

Nonsense...but must seem to Applaud and Approve, with gentle
Nods and Bows, all they say; also they must View their Faces with
Admiring Eyes, although they were Ill-favour'd...[125]

But while Margaret understood the artificiality of male gallantry,
she was unwilling to dispense with its gratifications. Moreover,
she felt she had matters of importance to discuss with men, and
they reciprocated her overtures by relishing her as a curiosity.
Glanvill opened his correspondence with Margaret by baldly
confessing, 'I am, Madam, an Admirer of Rarities, and your
Grace is really so great an one, that I cannot but indeavour some
Testimony of a proportion'd respect and wonder...'. Evelyn
similarly was 'much pleasd, with the extraordinary fancifull habit,
garb and discourse of the *Dutchesse*' when he visited Newcastle at
their London mansion. Yet a few weeks later he composed a
ballad mocking her eccentricities.[126]

Even if Margaret's male contemporaries had been entirely
sincere in their admiration, she herself was convinced that it was
unsafe to form close friendships with men with the exception of
near relations. Free and private association with men was too
dangerous to women's reputation:

> the society of men and women is much more inconvenient, then men
> with men, and women with women, for women with women can do
> little inconvenience...but of the society of men and women comes
> many great inconveniencies, as defamations of womens honours, and
> begets great jealousies...tempts the vertues, and defames the
> chast...[127]

Of course Margaret was free to choose female friends, but her
social difficulties with her own sex were greater than those with
men. Although Margaret occasionally voiced the opinion that
men were more vain and foolish than women, her negative
comments about men were vastly outnumbered by scathing
criticisms of her own sex. She frequently remarked on women's
envious and spiteful dispositions, the stupidity of their conversations, their inability to form stable friendships, their vain
diversions and their petty minds.[128] The condemnation of her
own sex was in part a consequence of Margaret's attempt to rise
above it, not only because she had adopted a higher standard by
which to judge the attainments of other women, but because her

own singularity aroused more resentment among women than among men. Whereas men enjoyed her as a novelty, women viewed her as a threat to their self-esteem and an affront to their code of conduct. Margaret found it difficult to converse with other women, for she assumed that they would have nothing of interest to say. Even those women whom she might have regarded as her intellectual equals did not become her friends, for they were offended by her pretensions and exasperated by her defiance of convention. In any case, women who shared Margaret's interests were exceedingly rare. One female contemporary who was capable of conversing with Margaret on equal terms was Mary Evelyn. Mrs. Evelyn's account of Margaret in a letter to Mr. Bohun reveals the characteristics of Margaret's behaviour which conventional women found intolerable.

> Her mien surpasses the imagination of poets...her gracious bows, seasonable nods, courteous stretching out of her hands, twinkling of her eyes...show what may be expected from her discourse, which is as airy, empty, whimsical, and rambling as her books, aiming at science, difficulties, high notions, terminating commonly in nonsense, oaths, and obscenity.... I found Doctor Charlton with her, complimenting her wit and learning...which she took to be so much her due that she swore if the schools did not banish Aristotle and read Margaret, Duchess of Newcastle, they...deserved to be utterly abolished. My part was not yet to speak, but admire; especially hearing her go on magnifying her own generous actions, stately buildings, noble fortune, her lord's prodigious losses in the war, his power, valour, wit, learning, and industry...Never did I see a woman so full of herself, so amazingly vain and ambitious.[129]

Margaret would not have been surprised to learn of this diatribe against her, for she believed that envy and competition were typical characteristics of upper-class women. Women of mean fortune, in contrast, 'cast not Envious, Spiteful Eyes at each other, but meet Friendly and Lovingly'. While this distinction may have contained an element of truth, it merely underlined Margaret's isolation from the rest of her sex. Unlike women of rank, from whom she was estranged for personal reasons, women of the lower orders had little reality for Margaret. Either she lent them idealized traits when she wished to contrast their homely virtues to upper-class vice; or, more often, she saw them as vicious, mercenary and barely human. They were fit only as stock figures for low comedy.[130]

It is ironic that Margaret failed to relate to her female contemporaries. For when she rose above the empirical observation of her sex's deficiencies in order to explore its theoretical potentialities, she was transformed into an eloquent 'feminist'. Although her first written work assumed the Galenic orthodoxy that women were innately inferior to men,[131] in successive writings she leaned towards the hypothesis that education and environment might be responsible for the differences of intellect between the sexes. Her preface to *Philosophical and Physical Opinions* asked that her work be received without mockery 'for the good incouragement of our sex, lest in time we should grow as irrational as idiots',

> ...as if we had not rational souls as well as men, and we out of a custom of dejectednesse think so too...being employed only in low and pettie imployments, which takes away not only our abilities towards arts, but higher capacities...we are kept like birds in cages to hop up and down in our houses, not suffered to fly abroad to see the several changes of fortune...we are shut out of all power and Authority by reason we are never imployed either in Civil nor marshall affaires...the best of our actions are trodden down with scorn, by the overweaning conceit men have of themselves and through a despisement of us.

This constituted a 'conspiracy theory' of male domination. In her *Orations* Margaret took up the same theme of women's 'dejected condition', asking herself what her sex could do about its plight.[132] The alternatives were presented in the form of a disputation between women, in what was probably the first feminist debate in English history, although it all took place in Margaret's mind. The debate began with the radical proposal that women should 'unite in prudent counsels' to break out of slavery. The second speaker pointed out the impracticality of this suggestion, since men possessed all the power:

> we may complain and bewail our condition, yet that will not free us; we may murmur and rail against men, yet they regard not what we say...our power is so inconsiderable, as men Laugh at our weakness.

The discussion shifted to women's desire to improve themselves. There was much disagreement concerning the ideal for which they should strive. Should women try to imitate men by increasing their knowledge and experience in male activities, frequenting schools, colleges, courts, and even taverns, gaming-houses and brothels? One woman thought this a laudable aim, since men were a degree more perfect than women, and all imitations should be of what was superior. Another insisted that it was better to be a good woman than a defective man,

> for...to have femal bodies, and yet to act Masculine Parts, will be very Preposterous and Unnatural...since we cannot Alter the Nature of our Persons, we should not Alter the Course of our Lives, but...be Acceptable and Pleasing to God and Men, which is to be Modest, Chast, Temperate, Humble, Patient, and Pious, also to be Huswifely, Cleanly, and of few Words, all which will Gain us...Love in this world, and Glory in the Next...

The debate ended on a disappointing note, with a mythic portrait of the pampered aristocratic woman. The last speaker contended that women had more leisure and safety than men and were favoured by Nature as well,

> in Giving us such Beauties, Features, shapes, Gracefull Demeanor, and such Insinuating and Inticing Attractions, as men are forc'd to admire us...and be desirous of us.... They will deliver to our disposals their power, persons, and lives...and what can we desire more, than to be men's Tyrants...and Goddesses....

This rosy picture of feminine privilege bears a suspicious resemblance to Margaret's own situation under Newcastle's uxorious dotage. She was not a true champion of her sex, but an egoist who happened to be of the female gender. The freedom from the limitations of her sex for which she groped in her writings and in her personal 'style' had reference to her own life rather than that of women in general. When balked in her quest for male privileges she adopted a feminist perspective. But instead of wishing to see her female contemporaries raised from their 'dejected' position, her real desire was to shine above all rivals. Indeed her fear of competition extended not only to her contemporaries but even to past ages. She had not read much history, she confessed, 'for fear I should meet with such of my Sex, that have out-done all the glory I can aime at, or hope to attaine'.[133] Her friend Walter Charleton noticed this propensity in Margaret and attempted to gratify it. He assured Margaret that no heroine could compare with her, 'not only in this age, but in all ages past'. He had fancied a resemblance with 'one Sulpicia, who composed a History of Domitian's time...and many other excellent poems...'. But on second thought he decided that 'Your *Graces* statue ought to stand by itself, & at the upper end of the *Gallery of Heroic Women*, & upon a pedestal more advanced than the rest'.[134]

This unique status created problems of identity for Margaret, for Stuart society viewed the sexes as polar opposites in their intellectual as well as physical capacities. Margaret had given some thought to this issue and attempted to suggest that the polarity which her own society imposed upon the two sexes was a false one. Clearly there were good and bad qualities in both sexes, deriving from the training that had been given to each. That these attributes were separable from the nature of men and women had been demonstrated by feminine behaviour in Margaret's own day, for women had adopted men's faults instead of imitating their virtues.

> ...it were very fit and requisit they should be bred up to Masculine Understandings...[and] should practice the Fortitude of Men; But Women now adaies affecting a Masculincy, as despising their own Sex, practise...not the spirits of Men...but their Wilde, Loose, Rude, Rough or foolish affected Behaviour; ...as to talke Impudently, to Swagger, to Swear, to Game, to Drink, to Revell, to make Factions...[135]

Despite this formulation of the masculine and feminine traits that might be selected to make up the perfect woman, Margaret had difficulty in carrying out her ideal. Attracted to the freedom that characterized male behaviour, she made sporadic efforts to imitate it. When not dressed in a theatrical costume (in itself a significant symbol, as Pepys noticed), she experimented with male clothing. Another 'male' liberty was her use of coarse language in her books and conversation.[136]

Thus many of the eccentricities that shocked contemporaries might be attributed to Margaret's inability to make up her mind about the exact gender role, or blend of roles, that she wished to emulate. Since no ideal woman existed whom she might copy, she was compelled to engage in constant improvisation. This tendency to fluctuate between a masculine and feminine point of view is also noticeable in her writings. When representing her own opinion in essays or prefatory epistles, Margaret acceded to male conceptions of female capacities and female roles. Furnished with a disguise in her plays and stories, she allowed submerged feelings and desires to come to the surface, and explored alternatives that her reason repudiated.

Margaret's eccentric aspirations for a 'masculine' fame represented the public side of her egoism. There was a private side as well, expressed in her domestic machinations for financial self-aggrandizement. This aspect of Margaret's character became increasingly prominent in the late 1660s, although it had been evident since her marriage to Newcastle in 1645. In fact the duke's children by his first marriage had suspected Margaret from the start. Their suspicions had some foundation, as their correspondence with Newcastle reveals. All his offspring had sacrificed much of their own income during the Interregnum so that the marquis and his new wife could live in the style to which they were accustomed. At the Restoration, the children's expectations of their father's reciprocation were disappointed, and the cause was ascribed to Margaret's machinations. In 1666 Newcastle reassured his son Henry:

> ...wee are all honeste folkes here and have no unjuste subtle designs...I am confidente you never had an Ill opinion...that I was a foole—or that any had taken a lease off Governinge mee...though I ame verye olde, I doe nott yett dote...[137]

But when the duke and duchess returned from their 1667 London visit, there were ominous signs of Margaret's ascendency. In January 1668 there was an addition to her jointure, including the London mansion at Clerkenwell.[138] By July, Newcastle's daughter Jane and his daughter-in-law Lady Frances Ogle were feeling so aggrieved at the depredations of Margaret's agent Sir Francis Toppe that they discussed the possibility of conspiring against Toppe. Lady Jane complained that Toppe had refused to give her the thousand pounds her father had assigned to her:

> truly I expect nothing hee can keepe from mee, I am of your opinion, hee intends non of my Lords children any good. And am very sorry he should so much wast the Estate as you mention, Mee thinks there might bee sume meanes contrived to hinder him, I would assist in any thing I could.[139]

But Lady Jane died in 1669, and nothing came of the plot.

Meanwhile, Newcastle's own servants were also suffering from Margaret's close attention to the estate accounts. Andrew Clayton, the duke's estate steward, told Newcastle's accountant John Booth what he had inferred about Margaret's plans. First, Clayton believed that she had begun arrangements to rent the entire estate so that she could 'break up the familie and goe to rant at London'. If she was not prevented she would engross the entire rentals into her own hands and 'confound all retainers to the familie'. Secondly, he claimed that Margaret was attempting to add another £2,000 to her jointure, because 'her whole care and studie was nothing more then to inrich her selfe for a second husband, well knowing his Grace could not live long'. Finally, Clayton offered some insights into Margaret's character:

> . . .it was her Graces delight to ruine all p[er]sons that she had to doe with. . .he heard her Grace say the old Countes of Shrewsbury practised the same, and she was a Dutches and consequently a greater p[er]son then a Countes and would out doe her in that kind.[140]

Although Clayton was a biassed witness, and his observations were reported second hand in disadvantageous circumstances, his description does conform to Margaret's behaviour at this period. Clayton himself was by no means an innocent party—in 1668 and 1669 he had accepted bribes to lower a tenant's rent. But he had been frustrated in the performance, 'for that the Duchess did so narrowly of late inspect his Graces affaires, as that he could make no alteration of the Rentall. . .'.[141]

By 1670 Clayton's surmises were proving correct. Margaret's jointure was increased twice in that year.[142] Two days after this latest blow, Clayton hatched a conspiracy with John Booth and Francis Liddell to ruin Margaret's influence with Newcastle. An anonymous letter was dispatched to the duke, accusing Margaret of sexual improprieties with Sir Francis Toppe.[143] The charge was certainly a fabrication, but Toppe was nevertheless a significant choice because he was the agent who carried out Margaret's policies.

Margaret displayed great detective powers on this occasion: the source of the letter was discovered, and two of the conspirators were persuaded to turn crown witnesses against Clayton. Nor had the incident abated Margaret's influence over her husband. A month after John Booth made his 'confession' about the conspiracy, Lord Ogle was lamenting to his friend Sir Thomas Osborne: 'I am...very mallencholly, finding my Father more persuaded by his Wife then I could thinke it possible....'.[144] Meanwhile, Margaret continued to squeeze every last penny out of Newcastle's rentals. Part of the jointure lands bestowed on her in 1670 included waste ground in Sherwood forest, and in the following year it was reported that 'the Duchess of Newcastle...was very severe in punishing those of the Forrest in Nottinghamshire; Taking away all the cattle, y^t were not Branded...'.[145] Although Margaret was still dabbling in science during the early 1670s, her chief energies were poured into estate management on her mother's model.

Whatever Margaret's ultimate plans for her widowhood, they were frustrated by her own death in December 1673, just after Newcastle's eightieth birthday. He was still hale and hearty, and was to live another three years. Newcastle had already arranged for himself and his wife to be buried in Westminster Abbey and had composed the inscription for her tomb:

> ...This Dutches was a wise, wittie and learned Lady, which her many Bookes do well testifie; she was a most Virtuous and a Loving and carefull wife, and was with her Lord all the time of his banishment and miseries, and when he came home never parted from him in his solitary retirements.

Other glowing elegies composed for the occasion were printed in *Letters and Poems in Honour of the Incomparable Princess, Margaret, Dutchess of Newcastle* [1676].

Reactions to Margaret's death, like those to her life, ran to extremes. On the one hand there was toadying flattery from those who were gratified to be patronized by a duke and duchess.

But while some contemporaries voiced disinterested admiration for the duchess's works,[146] her genuine partisans seem to have been a small minority. More typical was the epitaph by John Stansby, who reviled Margaret as

> Shame of her sex, Welbeck's illustrious whore,
> The true man's hate and grief, plague of the poor,
> The great atheistical philosophraster,
> That owns no God, no devil, lord nor master...[147]

Others viewed Margaret's life and work as the product of dementia. Dorothy Osborne thought there were 'many soberer people in Bedlam', and the anonymous author of 'A Session of the Poets' wrote,

> Newcastle and's Horse for entrance next strives,
> Well Stuff'd was his Cloakbag, and so was his Breeches
> And unbutt'ning the place where Nature's Posset-maker lives,
> Pull'd out his Wife's Poems, Plays, Essays and Speeches.
> Whoop, quoth *Apollo*, what a Devil have we here,
> Put up thy Wife's Trumpery, good noble Marquis,
> And home again, home again take thy Career,
> To provide her fresh Straw, and a Chamber that dark is.[148]

Public opinion seems to have agreed with Margaret's nickname: 'Mad Madge of Newcastle'.

Yet a judgement of insanity is always to some degree a social one. How much of the negative reaction which Margaret aroused was a consequence of her personal eccentricities, and what part of it was provoked by her defiance of conventional feminine ideals? Of course from a contemporary perspective the distinction had little meaning, since the very notion of female 'goodness' and even female 'sanity' was inextricably intertwined with women's conventional role.[149] Nevertheless, it is possible to trace a complicated interaction between the duchess and her environment. The immediate effect of Margaret's overweening ambition for fame was to add lustre by contrast to the merits of more retiring female contemporaries. Mary Evelyn caustically compared Margaret's faults with Katharine Philips's virtues, and the funeral elegy for Margaret's step-daughter Lady Jane Cheyne included a tacit reproach to Margaret. The author praised Lady

Jane's 'Poetick spiritt...'

> An Art she knew and practised so well
> her Modesty alone could it Excell
> which by concealing Doubles her Esteem...[150]

But while she was condemned or ridiculed by conventional women like Mary Evelyn and Lucy Hutchinson, Margaret also created feelings of envy which were sometimes transformed into clandestine emulation. Lucy Hutchinson modelled her biography of her husband and her own fragmentary autobiography on that of the Duchess of Newcastle. In fact several female autobiographies written at about this time bear the imprint of the duchess's example: Lady Halkett, Lady Fanshawe, the Countess of Warwick. Although these women did not venture to print their own works, they wrote in the hope that their memoirs would be preserved for posterity. Margaret's effrontery in challenging certain barriers which sustained the polarity of the two sexes may have had a subliminal effect in broadening women's ideas of what constituted conceivable behaviour.

Chapter II

Mary Rich, Countess of Warwick

i. *Mary Boyle: Family and Early Life*

It is a difficult enterprise to assess the influence that aristocratic Stuart parents exerted on the characters of their offspring, for the latter were brought up by nurses, servants or relations. Yet even when the childrearing was delegated to others, certain parents impressed their stamp upon their children by sheer force of personality. Richard Boyle, later first Earl of Cork, was successful in this regard; his numerous sons and daughters copied not so much the man Cork really was, but the myth he created about himself. Some of Cork's qualities were distributed among his twelve offspring who survived to adulthood: his shrewd intelligence, consuming ambition, and obstinate perseverance in any task he set for himself. Other traits that Cork pretended to possess—honesty, piety and charity—also developed in the next generation. This was true of the two youngest in the family, Mary and Robert, the pious lay saint and the empirical scientist. The two grew up distant from Cork's domination in childhood and attained maturity at a time when their father's character, if it had not softened with old age, was at least encrusted with a veneer of pious respectability.

Both Robert and Mary cherished the myth of the Earl of Cork's industrious rectitude, which the latter had enshrined in his own 'True Remembrances', a memoir which one of Cork's biographers has called as 'painstakingly inaccurate' as his son Robert's autobiographical fragment is 'painstakingly accurate'.[1] Mary so venerated her father's memory that she had collected materials for a projected biography of him, a work which never materialized.[2] Luckily for Mary's filial reverence, she was not a good historian. Had she discerned the actual methods of her father's rise she would have been horrified.

In reality Boyle was an unscrupulous adventurer. In 1588 the twenty-one-year-old Boyle arrived in Dublin and bluffed his way into Irish society with no capital except the suit of elegant clothes on his back. Boyle was appointed deputy to the Escheator-general for finding concealed crown lands in Ireland. Within fifteen years he had acquired a fortune in Irish estates by defrauding local landowners, the Established Church, and the crown, meanwhile marrying two heiresses in succession. Despite various reverses, Boyle's rentals by 1614 had reached £4,000 per annum.[3]

Boyle's first wife died in childbirth; his second, Catherine Fenton, bore all his children. Catherine was the only child of Sir Geoffrey Fenton, Principal Secretary of State for Ireland and an old associate of Boyle's in his swindles as deputy Escheator. The match was probably initiated because of its convenience for Boyle and his father-in-law, although some humorous stories which Boyle later circulated among his family alleged its romantic origins.

For whatever motives the match was arranged, it proved a happy one. Catherine was about twenty years her husband's junior; judging from her surviving letters she regarded him with adoration. Boyle showed every sign of being equally devoted to his wife. He was devastated at her death, and in token of his mourning he never remarried.

Although Boyle may have been the busiest man in Ireland, personally managing every one of his numerous holdings, he found time to keep his wife continually pregnant. Of fifteen children born to the couple, five sons and seven daughters lived to adulthood. The births, which occurred at roughly eighteen-month intervals, were set down in Boyle's diary with thanks to God for his wife's safe delivery and a memorandum of the astrological sign. He continued to beget children in the same spirit in which he continued to buy land, with a vision of Protestant hegemony dominated by his own descendants. Boyle's vast holdings could provide land for any number of sons: even his seventh and most famous son, Robert, was allotted a share of landed income. There was cash to purchase titles at a time when the brokerage of honours was a straightforward financial transaction. Boyle himself was knighted on his wedding day, created Baron of Youghal in 1616, and made Viscount Dungarvan and Earl of Cork four years later. In 1627 he noted the payment of £3,000 to Buckingham 'to make Lo. Barry [his son-in-law] Earl of Barrymore, and my sons Lewis and Roger to be ennobled'.[4] Four of his five sons received titles during their father's lifetime.

Daughters were almost as useful as sons in the Earl of Cork's overall strategy. Just as Cork made interest-free loans to relations to tighten his 'connexion', he regarded marriage portions as an investment to cement political alliances. Dowries for eight daughters were as much of a strain on Cork's resources as titles for his sons, but he coped with the need for large cash outlays by advance planning. He began assigning moneys for his daughters' marriage portions just after they were born, and proffered each one to some useful connexion soon afterwards. An indenture dated 1 March 1625 reveals that he had practically used up his supply of seven daughters born to him at the time. The two eldest were married, and matches had been arranged for four of their younger sisters. Only three-and-a-half-month-old Mary lacked a potential husband. But her portion had been fixed: 'unto the La. M., the seventh daughter of the said Earl...the sume of 4000 li...'.[5]

Mary Boyle had been born in Youghal the previous November while her father was in Dublin. The event was recorded in Cork's 'True Remembrances':

My seaveneth daughter named Mary Boyle was borne at yoghall on St. Martyns day being the xj^th daie of November 1624 and Thursdaie, about three of the clock, in thafternoon, the signe in Aries....The god of heaven bless her with all heavenly and earthly blessings and make her frutefull in vertuous and religeous children.[6]

Mary's memories of her early years were vague. She was mistaken about the year as well as the day of her birth and had no recollection of her mother.[7] For her first two years Mary was probably given over to a wet nurse. At age three she was sent away to be cared for by Sir Randall and Lady Cleyton, tenants of her father living on a farm near Cork.[8] Sir Randall was one of the earl's most trusted agents, who served Cork in a variety of financial and personal capacities. Mary was not the first daughter the Cleytons had helped raise; Mary's sister Alice was in their care in 1615. The practice was consistent with the earl's spartan philosophy of childrearing as his son Robert described it:

> his Father, who had a perfect aversion for their Fondnesse, who use to breed their Children so nice and tenderly, that a hot Sun, or a good Shore of Raine as much endangers them as if they were made of Butter or of Sugar; sends him away from home; & committs him to the Care of a Cuntry-nurse...that...Hardships were made easy to him by Custome...[9]

After her mother's death in 1629 Mary remained at the Cleyton household, where she was joined by her sister Margaret. The Cleytons excelled as surrogate parents: Lady Cleyton, Mary recalled, 'neaver haveing had any child of her owne, grew to make as much of me as if she had bene an one mother to me, and tooke great care to have me soburly educated'.[10]

It is not clear what elements comprised Mary's education, except that it emphasized the female requisites of piety and needlework. The latter was evinced by a succession of handkerchiefs, nightcaps and embroidered purses produced each year for New Year's gifts. Mary continued her needlework projects throughout her life, even when as Countess of Warwick she had no necessity to do so. Her religious education—which she later felt had been lax—included her catechism and the Bible, a copy of which was presented to her by her father when she was eight years old. As for secular subjects, the earl did not hire regular tutors for his daughters as he did for his sons. The latter received expensive educations, including Eton and a continental tour to perfect their Latin, French, rhetoric, logic, mathematics, geometry and other subjects.[11] For the earl's daughters, however, the 'foundations of religion and civility' were deemed a sufficient preparation for life.[12] No doubt civility was instilled in Mary by the 'two gentlewomen' and a 'Frenchwoman' who formed part of her retinue in 1628, and who were apparently engaged partly in a tutorial capacity.[13] Certainly Mary learned French, for she devoured romances as a young woman and read her husband a 'French History' later in life. But French and 'civility' were all

that distinguished her as a gentlewoman. Her attainments in her
native language were no better than average for her sex: her
handwriting was the sprawling 'Roman' variety ordinarily learned
by Stuart girls, and her spelling tended to the phonetic. Mary's
brothers, in contrast, were enjoined by their father to cultivate a
small neat hand like their tutor's.[14] In their recreations all the
Boyle children were addicted to plays and romances. The earl
tried to stop his sons from wasting their time on such light
reading. Toward his daughters he exhibited the opposite
attitude, having presented Mary with Sidney's *Arcadia* when she
was twelve.[15]

ii. Courtship and Marriage

In the spring of 1638, Mary was fetched home to her father after
ten years at the Cleyton household. She came unwillingly, having
long since transferred her affections to the Cleytons. The earl had
determined to gather his married and unmarried children around
him to accompany him to England. The trip was occasioned by
his need to block Sir Thomas Wentworth's campaign against
Cork's illegally acquired Irish lands. Cork had tried everything to
stop Wentworth, including bribery, a matrimonial alliance, and
the full force of his Irish connexion, but to no avail. Cork now
had no choice but to go to England in the hope of stopping
Wentworth's mandate at its source. One of Cork's friends, the
Earl of Bristol, had arranged for him to purchase the manor of
Stalbridge in Dorset near Bristol's own country estate. To this
social and geographical half-way point Cork moved his clan in
August, 1638.

As the Boyle family settled into Stalbridge, a marriage treaty
the earl had made for Mary was about to mature. Viscount
Clandeboye, the prospective father-in-law, was an old friend who
had been in collusion with Cork more than thirty years before in
securing Cork's acquisitions of Irish land.[16] Cork had begun his
financial preparations for the marriage years before, making
interest-free loans to relations and associates with the stipulation
that these moneys were assigned to Mary's portion and due when
she became fourteen.[17] The intended groom was a perfect match
by Cork's standards: the only son of a peer (albeit an Irish one),

with an estate settled on him of nearly £8,000 per annum.

According to Mary's autobiography, the pact had been made on condition that the two young people 'likte...when we saw one another'. Nevertheless, it is clear from the earl's behaviour towards Mary's siblings that the clause was merely a formality. Cork always assumed that his children would do as he told them. The consent of his daughters was obtained more easily because of the early age at which he arranged formal espousals for them, often before the legal age of consent. Mary's two eldest sisters had been pre-contracted at the ages of twelve and eleven and were married a year later. The earl's remaining daughters aside from Mary were contracted at even earlier ages.[18]

In using his children as pawns to further his own ends the earl no doubt believed he was acting in their best interests. His practical marriage to Catherine Fenton had been a success, and the earl assumed that his offspring shared his own ambition. An aristocratic connexion was a lifelong investment in status—the only possible 'preferment' to which his daughters could aspire. None of the matches Cork achieved could be faulted in this regard. But unfortunately the personal character of the groom was irrelevant to the earl's matrimonial calculations. As chance would have it, Cork's daughters were all unlucky in this respect. The earl's diary and correspondence are filled with complaints from his maltreated married daughters. Lettice, Cork's favourite child, wrote of her husband, 'to me he is the cruellest man living'. Alice was treated disrespectfully by her spouse. Katherine, the most intelligent of the sisters, was yoked to a drunken lout. Dorothy suffered from her husband's 'unkindness'. Joan was temporarily deserted by her husband.[19] In each case Cork attempted to restore domestic harmony by commanding his son-in-law to rectify his behaviour. But Cork's interference only exacerbated matters, and his daughters spent more time visiting their father than living with their spouses.

Cork's management of his daughters' marriages may explain the rebellious behaviour of his youngest daughter Mary when it was her turn to be confronted with an unappetizing choice. She was nearly fifteen when James Hamilton, heir of Viscount Clandeboye, came to Stalbridge to ask for her hand. The earl must have realized afterwards that it had been a tactical mistake to wait so long to consummate the match. Mary was not an eleven-year-old child to be cowed into submission, but a young woman with a mind of her own. In any case the timing of the marriage ceremony was out of his control. James Hamilton had just returned from the requisite continental tour, as his proud father informed Cork, while gloating in anticipation of a record-breaking marriage settlement:

> ...his mother and I conceave your Lordship to be so Noble and wis as that your Lordship will have in your consideration what such an estate with a sole sonn, May deserve in portion and in congruitie afoord in Joynture, seing your Lordship hath no More daughters nor I Children to bestow...[20]

When he arrived at Stalbridge in mid-August 1639, James Hamilton was warmly welcomed by the earl, who already regarded him as a son-in-law. The young man was directed to make his address to Mary at once, so that the couple could be 'suddenly married'. Mary in turn was commanded to receive him as her future husband. James fulfilled his part of the bargain with dutiful zeal. Either he fell passionately in love with Mary, or he acted the part with vigour, as Mary recalled:

> Mr. Hambletone (possible to obay his father) did designe gaineing me by a very hansome adress, which he made to me, and if he did not to a very high deagre deasemble, I was not displeaseing to him, for he profest a great passion for me.[21]

Unfortunately, she loathed him at first sight. We cannot speculate on the reasons for this antipathy, since Mary refused to supply them, commenting only that 'my aversion for him was exstrordnary, though I could give my father no satesfactory acompte why it was so...' One thing was certain: she was determined not to marry him. Three weeks after his arrival the young man deserted the field, as the earl angrily noted in his diary for 12 August:

> The Lord viscount Clandebiews son and heir Mr James Hamylton...being refuzed in marriadge by my unruly daughter Mary...departed my hows the second of September...

The struggle was not over. Aside from Cork's desire for the

match for its tempting monetary settlement, Mary's refusal placed him in an awkward position. Her rejection of the son of a close friend was humiliating. Moreover the earl's inability to keep his engagement with Viscount Clandeboye diminished his credit in the eyes of the world. Hence he was determined to make his daughter yield.

The earl's authority over his children was not absolute. Throughout the seventeenth century there was an increasing consensus which allowed women a veto in matrimonial affairs. This position was first advocated by the popular conduct books, based on middle-class Puritan interpretations of marriage as a free contract. By the 1630s these liberalizing currents had penetrated other sectors of society, being least influential among the aristocracy. The veto was not unconditional: a woman must have weighty grounds for her refusal. But a veto represented some erosion in the *carte blanche* which parents assumed was implied by the fifth commandment. Some writers even warned that it was sacrilegious to force children into an unwanted match. Although parents could employ all fair means to persuade their children, if these failed they must give up.[22]

There was an ambiguity in the situation created by Mary's unanticipated resistance, since it was not morally clear who ought to give way. While Mary could advance no 'weighty grounds' for her aversion, there seemed no way of budging her as long as she maintained her stance. The earl's efforts to influence his daughter fell into two categories: financial sanctions and social pressure. First, he stopped Mary's allowance of £100 a year. This was of little effect, for Mary simply ran into debt on the strength of future expectations. Secondly, the earl rallied his whole family to help wear down Mary's resistance, as his diary reveals:

21 Nov 1639 My daughter Marie did this day, as she had many ty before, declare a very high aversnes and contradicon to or councels and commands, towching her mariadge with Mr James Hamylton...although myself and all sons and daughters, the Lo Barrymore, Arthure J. and all other her beste frends did moste effectually entreat and persuade her therunto, and I command it...

Mary had only one trump card, the knowledge that no marriage could be consummated without her consent. She must have been aware, too, that time was on her side. Her matrimonial prospects would be equally good for at least another five years. The earl, now past his seventy-third year, was anxious to expedite matters even if it would entail breaking the match and starting over.

This is exactly what Cork began to do. Evidently he had begun bargaining with another prospect soon after Mary's adamant refusal. Cork's diary contains the following entry for 14 December:

> The Lo Deale, and Mr James Maxfield of his Ma[ts] bedchamber, tendred unto me thearle of Annandale his son and heire for a husband to my daughter after she could not be perswaded to marry Mr James Hamylton...But in regard I was engaged by treaty with the Lo Moor I did not accept thereof...

Five weeks later the negotiations with Viscount Moor had borne fruit in a set of marriage articles. It was not Cork's first attempt at a matrimonial alliance with Lord Moor, and Mary represented his last chance to effect a connexion he had long coveted. Nevertheless he engaged in the usual haggling associated with matrimonial negotiations, traces of which appear on the marriage treaty itself.[23]

The portion written on the fair copy was £8,000, but Cork had crossed this out and written 'seaven'. To make up the £1,000 he offered the young couple a house in Dublin. Mary's jointure was fixed at £1,000 per annum, the usual one-to-seven ratio prevalent about this time. Lord Moor had offered the couple £700 per annum maintenance while they lived with him. Cork raised the amount to £1,000. He also altered the income Lord Moor was to give Henry and Mary should they live elsewhere, from £1,000 per annum to £1,250. But neither parent expected the young couple to cohabit immediately after their wedding. Lord Moor was to pay £750 per annum from the jointure rentals to finance Henry's education and to 'maynteyne him nobly abroade...for the bettering of his knowledge'. The remaining £250 a year was assigned to Mary as her allowance. We can assume she would live in Lord Moor's household after the wedding.

The articles contained 'consent' clauses for prospective bridegroom and bride. It is not clear whether this was a feature of all Cork's marriage agreements, or whether he had altered his practice since Mary's refusal of James Hamilton. Perhaps he had learned something about his daughters' propensities since the last occasion on which he had completed a treaty with Viscount Moor ten years previously. This time there was no financial penalty attached to Cork's breaking the match if his daughter should not consent, in contrast to the stipulations attached to the 'unripe match' with one-year-old Margaret.[24] Moreover there was to be no cash down until the wedding day. It is impossible to guess whether the parents or the children broke off this match, because the earl never referred to it again. It was not uncommon for him to arrange a match in order to further a political connexion and later back out of the agreement when his aims had shifted. Whatever its cause, the result of the earl's shifting alliances during 1639–40 was that Mary's tenacity paid off. By June it was evident that she had succeeded in defying her father's commands. Her allowance was restored with back pay and an advance to cover her debts. Moreover, her tactical position had improved; by rejecting matches proffered to her father she had gained the upper hand:

> ...the report that he wold give me a very great portion made him have for me many very great and considerable offres, both of persones of great bearth and fortune but I still continued to have an aversion to maridge, liveing so much at my ease that I was unwilling to Change my Condition, and neaver could bring my selfe to close with any ofred match, but still begd my Father to reafuse all the most advantageous profers, though I was by him much prest to settell my selfe.[25]

Cork and his extended family settled in London for the winter. He had made progress in his campaign to win the favour of the Queen's party, chiefly through marriages arranged between two of his sons and the Queen's impoverished maids of honour. The first match was between Elizabeth Killigrew, a step-daughter of his old friend Sir Thomas Stafford, and Cork's son Francis. As part of the *quid pro quo* Sir Thomas offered Cork his apartments at the Savoy, as well as a Court entrée. The second alliance was between Cork's son Lewis and Elizabeth Fielding, the daughter of Lady Denbigh, who like Lady Stafford was on close terms with the Queen. In the autumn of 1639 the weddings were celebrated with great feasts at Court, whose every detail Cork exultantly set down in his diary. As a result of these alliances the earl was made a member of the Privy Council the following June.[26]

Cork's children were entranced by their new *milieu* and were quick to exploit its possibilities. Just as the elder Staffords had furnished Cork with his initial Court entrée, their daughter Elizabeth Boyle introduced her new siblings by marriage to her friends of both sexes, the adolescent offspring of the nobility. Excessively rich and adequately presentable, the Boyle children were admitted to the diversions of their peers, and soon the private newsletters were commenting upon their escapades. Roger fought an abortive duel about a maid of honour named Mistress Harrison; Lewis sampled the pleasures of the town with unfortunate after-effects which prevented the consummation of his wedding night, as all London learned the next day.[27]

Mary, now under the sway of her sophisticated sister-in-law Elizabeth, was intoxicated with London's diversions. Like most of their female peers, Elizabeth and Mary spent their time perfecting the art of 'exquisite and curious dressing'. The remainder of the day was occupied in

> Readeing Romances, and in Readeing and seeing Playes and in goeing to Court, and hide Park and Spring Garden, and I was so fond of the Court that I had taken a seacret Resolution that if my father dyede and I ware mistres of my selfe I wold become a courtiar...[28]

Whenever they were at home, the two young women were entertained by visits from the young men whom Elizabeth had met during her stint as Maid of Honour.

The Earl of Cork was well-informed about his sons' antics: both Lewis's bout of gonorrhoea and Roger's duel provoked wry comments in Cork's diary. The females under his care were more skilful at concealing their activities. Cork never noticed a drama unfolding under his nose which was to have more serious consequences than his sons' pranks: among the visitors to the Savoy Mary had attracted an admirer whose financial prospects were unsuitable for matrimony.

Charles Rich was a typical young hanger-on at the fringes of Court society. As the second son of the Earl of Warwick, he had

had the breeding of an aristocratic scion, including a tour of the continent and a smattering of Cambridge and the Inns of Court. A motto he wrote in a friend's album during his continental travels flaunts the concerns of a Stuart younger son: 'Vive l'amour, vive la guerre'.[29] Despite his father's example, however, Charles never showed enthusiasm for war as a practical pursuit. 'L'amour' was a different matter. All his life Charles exhibited a passionately emotional temperament. In 1639 he was a witty and handsome young man of twenty-three. He was naturally inclined to direct his passion to a romantic object.

When Mary first became acquainted with Charles late in 1639, he was in love with someone else. Awkwardly for his friendship with the Boyle family, the object of his desire was the same Mistress Harrison upon whom Roger had settled his affections. Charles even served as second to Roger's antagonist in the duel mentioned earlier, and consequently found himself unwelcome at the Savoy. But once Mistress Harrison had rejected both Roger and Charles, the latter resumed his daily visits to the Boyle household. After several months of comradely familiarity with the Boyle children, Charles discovered that he had fallen in love with Mary Boyle.

According to the conduct books, Charles should have obtained the consent of both sets of parents before approaching Mary. The trouble with such honourable behaviour was that it could succeed only when there were no objections to the match. As Charles was aware, there were few grounds to recommend his pretensions to Mary. Although his father was the biggest landowner in Essex, Charles was stinted to an allowance. Even at his father's death he could hope to receive no more than £1,300 or £1,400 a year. The Earl of Cork's reaction to a poverty-stricken younger son could be confidently predicted. At the least hint of matrimonial aspirations he would have forbidden Charles the house. Hence the only course of action open to Charles was the dishonourable one of wooing Mary in secret.

For his secret courtship Charles found an ally in Mary's sister-in-law Elizabeth Boyle. Elizabeth was an old friend who had her own reasons for making mischief. She had felt aggrieved at the Boyle family ever since her husband Francis had been sent to the continent just after the wedding. Meanwhile the prospect of a vicarious romance must have seemed better than none at all. The master-stroke of policy was apparently her idea: Charles was to pretend to flirt with Elizabeth whenever others were present and address his eloquence to Mary when the three of them were alone. Thus Elizabeth served as the chaperone required by convention and drew suspicion away from the real lovers.

The Boyle family were not pleased at Charles' attentions to Elizabeth, but they made no attempt to stop his visits. Meanwhile Mary was becoming entangled. Indeed the plot could not have worked without her connivance, since it was her duty to repulse Charles' advances at the first sign of romantic interest. By failing to discourage him, she had signalled her willingness to consider him as a suitor:

> I was convinced that it was time for me to give him a flat and finall deniall...but when I was upon a readines to open my mouth to utter these wordes, my great kindnes for him stopte it...though I frequently resolved it...which made me begin to give him more hopes of gaineing me then before I had don by anything but my indureing him to com to me after he had declared to me his deasigne in doeing so...[30]

In this sense the feminine passive role in courtship harboured an active component. Although a woman could not initiate a romance, she could command a good deal of control over its progress.

For some months Mary vacillated. She had devoured innumerable plays and romances which portrayed the struggle between 'love and honour', and now she herself was entangled in its throes. In her case the conflicting considerations were more practical than heroic. Primarily there was the terrifying prospect of her father's anger. Confronted with an unsuitable *amour* carried on behind his back, the earl was likely to be roused to a memorable response. Mary also had some of the Boyle ambition and practicality. Having been brought up in the lavish style of the *nouveaux riches*, she was not sure she wished to live within the narrow confines of Charles Rich's £1,300 or £1,400 a year.[31]

Matters reached a crisis when Mary caught measles and was removed to a separate house. Charles Rich continued to visit her, neglecting to keep up the pretence of a flirtation with Elizabeth. Lady Stafford guessed that the whole family had been duped. Holding her daughter responsible for all the mischief, she berated her before going to the Earl of Cork with her suspicions. This proved to be a tactical error, for it gave Elizabeth time to warn Charles that he must secure a firm promise from Mary immediately. While Elizabeth served as look-out, Charles proposed marriage to Mary, and finally secured her promise that she would allow the Earl of Warwick to broach the subject to her father. Charles' position was now immeasurably stronger, since such vows were regarded as binding. Indeed the real role of lovers' vows in the casuistry of youth was to pre-empt the sin of parental disobedience by countering with the apparently more heinous one of breaking a solemn vow.

On the intelligence given him by Lady Stafford, the Earl of Cork exiled Mary to Hampton Court with the command that she was no longer to see young men. 'This he said in general', Mary recalled, 'but named not Mr Rich in particular, which I was glad of' since Charles came to see her there daily. Meanwhile the machinery of negotiations was set in motion. These began haltingly, since Lord Goring (who had been chosen to open the subject) so distressed the earl with his proposals that the latter began to weep and would not allow him to go on. Next Warwick arrived in person with his brother the Earl of Holland, and Cork was obliged to hear them out. Cork still hoped to bully Mary into renouncing her *amour*, and sent his sons Richard and Roger to hector her into submission. Mary had a tactically perfect answer ready. Although she would not marry Mr. Rich without her father's consent, she was resolved 'not to marry any other person in the world'.[32]

The female threat not to marry recurs in a variety of contexts in seventeenth-century struggles between daughters and their families. Like female fantasies of suicide as a species of revenge, the refusal to marry was a form of feminine passivity made active.[33] Sometimes it served as a private consolatory fantasy, as in Dorothy Osborne's darkest moods.[34] In Mary's case it was more of a negotiating position. While technically she had vaunted her obedience by her pledge not to marry without her father's consent, this meant no more than a promise not to elope. In effect the earl had been manoeuvred into a choice between two unpalatable alternatives: Mary as the wife of Charles Rich, or Mary as a spinster. Cork had learned from the James Hamilton affair that she could not be forced to marry against her will. On the other hand he was too fond of his daughter to cut her off for her disobedience.

Mary was also aided by the volatile political situation of early 1641. Although the Earl of Cork professed himself a royalist, his real aim was to emerge on top in Ireland no matter what transpired in England. By 1641 it seemed unwise to leave the Parliamentary opposition out of his calculations: an alliance with leaders like Warwick and Holland, even in the person of a younger son, could prove a hedge against all eventualities. So the earl yielded and settled down to negotiate in earnest.[35]

After ten weeks of bargaining Cork emerged with an agreement almost identical to that which he had negotiated with Viscount Moor. The stipulated portion was £7,000 (which in the event Cork never finished paying). No house in Dublin was offered along with the portion. We can infer that the Earl of Warwick was made responsible for ensuring that there was a roof over the couple's heads. Another victory for Cork was to stipulate that the portion be given to Charles rather than his father, so as to benefit Mary more directly.[36]

Mary's jointure was again fixed at £1,000 per year. The chief difference between the pact with the Earl of Warwick and that with Viscount Moor was that presumably Henry Moor would someday inherit his father's title and estate. Charles Rich was not expected to inherit anything. But given the fact that Mary had become entangled with a younger son, the Earl of Cork had done well for his daughter.

Cork planned to celebrate this new alliance with a large London wedding like the Court feasts that had marked his sons' nuptials. But even in this matter the couple had their own way. Like many young women of the time, Mary had been 'a great enemy allwayes to a publike wedding'.[37] There were two streams of thought which contributed to the contemporary reaction against old-fashioned weddings. Religious scruples against their 'pagan' aspects led to the much simpler civil rites of the Interregnum. But even secular young women like Mary were repelled by the embarrassing popular rituals of wedlock.[38] Charles shared Mary's feelings, and the couple were married privately without their parents' knowledge. The rest of the Boyle family resented Mary's behaviour considerably more than her father did. Except for her favourite sister Lady Ranelagh, the whole group continued to ostracize her for some time after her marriage. Mary had become the *enfant terrible* of the family. Although she had obtained her father's grudging consent to the match, her conduct throughout the affair had contravened all the conventions of female behaviour. Women may have earned the right to a matrimonial veto by the end of the seventeenth century, but writers continued to insist that modesty forbade women from making their own choice.[39]

At the start of their marriage, Charles and Mary were in more straitened circumstances than they had anticipated. Although the Earl of Cork had promised to give Charles £5,000 of the £7,000 portion before he left England, at the time of his departure he had only paid half the promised amount.[40] Meanwhile the Munster rebellion was wreaking havoc upon the Earl of Cork's Irish rents. He had been depending on these rents to pay his debts as well as current expenses, for while in England he had used up all his money buying land. Cork wrote to the Earl of Warwick, '...whereas before this rebellion, my revenue, besides my houses, demesnes, parkes and other royalties did yeald me £50 a day rent, I do vow unto your Lordspp that I have not now 50d a week coming in to me, soe as I feare, I must come a begging to you...'. In March of 1642 Cork was still collecting old debts to bring the total paid to Mary's portion up to £4,100. Money was still owing in 1646, when Charles Rich petitioned Parliament to seize the remainder from the sequestered estate of the new Earl of Cork, Mary's elder brother.[41]

Unable to afford an establishment of their own, Charles and Mary lived with the Earl of Warwick. Among the aristocracy it was common for a young married couple to live as guests of the groom's parents for a few months or even a few years. Because of Charles and Mary's circumstances, the arrangement ended only with the death of the Earl of Warwick seventeen years later. Since friction between in-laws was a common feature of such *ménages*, it is a revealing indication of Mary's obliging temper that she was able to live in harmony with a varied assortment of relations. The Earl of Warwick presented no difficulties, for his good humour was conceded even by his enemies. But his second wife was generally disliked. Originally an alderman's widow, she had become so embroiled in disputes with her snobbish daughter-in-law Lady Rich (*née* Cavendish) that she was 'almost come to a resolution of never living more with any daughter-in-law'. At Mary's arrival at Leighs the countess fled to her daughter's house where, Mary recalled, 'she was resolved to stay till she was by som persone she credited informed wither my humor ware such as wold make hur to live comfortably with mee'.[42] Fortunately the two women lived together affectionately, and Mary later enjoyed the same loving relationship with Warwick's third wife.

Despite their mode of life as part of an 'extended' household, Charles and Mary behaved like a present-day nuclear family. The most striking example of their modern outlook was what appears to have been an effort to practise contraception. Mary became pregnant soon after her marriage and bore a daughter Elizabeth in 1642. A son Charles followed in September 1643. But at that point the couple apparently decided to call a halt.

> ...when I was first married, and had my tow children so fast I feared much haveing To many, and was trobled when I fond my selfe to be with Child so soone out of a proude conceit I had that if I childed so thike it would spoyle what my Great vanety then made me to fancy was Tolerable (at least in my Persone) and out of a Proude opinion too that I had, that If I had many to provide for thay must be poore because of my Lordes small estate...and my husband too was in som measure gilty of the same falte for though he was at as great a rate fond of his to children he had, as any father could be, yet when he had had tow he wold often say he feared he should have so many as wold undoe a youngar Brother...[43]

No hint is offered as to the means of contraception, but the fact remains that no more children were born. Mary's reasons for avoiding pregnancy are noteworthy. She wished to preserve her figure, and with it her sexual appeal. Both Mary and Charles hoped to ensure an adequate income for their offspring by limiting the number who must share it. As Mary pointed out, this did not imply a diminished affection for their children but rather the reverse. Both parents were intensely devoted to their son and daughter. Although Elizabeth was less than fifteen months old when she died, her father had already become deeply attached to the infant, as Mary recalled: 'I was much aflicted, but my husband as pationately so as I ever saw him, he being most extrordnarely fond of hur'.[44] The death of their son just short of his majority was to induce an almost suicidal depression in both parents.

The outbreak of civil war coincided with the couple's first year of married life. Charles did not take a prominent part in the hostilities, unlike his father and elder brother, each of whom became immediately active on opposite sides. We can catch a glimpse of Charles' casual attitude to the debut of the conflict. In August 1642, when the Countess Rivers appealed to Warwick's household for help against a besieging mob, no one could be found at Leighs: the earl was at sea as Lord High Admiral of the Parliamentary fleet, his eldest son Lord Rich had gone to join the King at Oxford and Mr. Charles Rich was 'hunting the stag at Rochford'.[45] The following year Charles sent letters to help recruit troops for Parliament, but there is no record of his having done any fighting. This may have been partly a result of Mary's influence. It is not clear where her sympathies lay at this point, although a few years later she was to become ill at the news of the King's execution. In any case her chief thought was to keep Charles out of the fray, being 'allwayes much averse to his ingageing in the Wares'. Charles was a token Parliamentarian. His father's influence secured him Sir Thomas Peyton's forfeited seat in Parliament beginning in 1645, and Charles was subsequently identified with the Presbyterian axis in local politics. Nevertheless he was not a vociferous partisan. His only recorded activity in Parliament was his petition for the remainder of Mary's portion.

Political rivalries thus had little direct influence upon the couple. But the religious atmosphere at Leighs was impossible to ignore. During the 1630s and 1640s the Earl of Warwick was perhaps the greatest patron of English Puritan divines, placing some of them in the numerous livings held by his family, and extending hospitality to a multitude of others. He had become head of that party, Clarendon wrote, 'by opening his doors, and making his house the randevooze of all the silenced ministers. . .and spending a good part of his estate, of which he was very prodigal, upon them, and by being present with them at their devotions. . .'[46] His household was run according to approved spiritual practices. Warwick was 'very exact in closet duties' as Edmund Calamy affirmed, and

very constant in his morning and evening publick service of God. . .In his conscientious observation of the Lords day. . .in his extraordinary care and diligence in preparing himselfe for the receiving of the Sacrament...[47]

Of course he enforced the same regime on the rest of the household.

When Mary first arrived at Leighs in 1641, she was hostile to the whole spiritual establishment, particularly the Puritan variety. Her chaplain later wrote that Mary had been 'almost frighted with the disadvantageous account' of religion she had previously acquired.[48] Although the Earl of Cork had insisted on the practice of piety for his children, his own brand of Protestantism was a compound of chauvinism, egotism and superstition. It was aptly summed up in his motto 'God's providence is my inheritance', providence being Cork's self-glorifying term for his shrewdly managed good luck. Mary learned her catechism as a child, but as an adolescent her pious manifestations were an outward 'forme of Godlynes' which she affected in order to please her father. As for the 'inward and Spirituall part of it', she later affirmed, 'I was not onely Ignorant of it, but resolved against it, being stedfastly sett against being a Puritan'.[49] It would be interesting to know just how much of the apparent religiosity of Stuart young women was similarly a mere external affectation.

iii. Religious Conversion and the Practice of Piety

At Leighs, the environment of total thought control eventually had its effect on Mary. After five years of daily brainwashing by the most eloquent preachers in England, her resistance was considerably weakened. In 1646 she was worried about her future state and made promises to God of leading a 'new life'. These resolutions were broken as soon as the family returned to Warwick House for the London season. But Mary's accustomed diversions were now accompanied by a sense of guilt.

...though I did indeavour diverting my selfe as formerly, yet God was so mercyfull to me as neaver to sofer me to find my former satesfaction, but still disapoynted my expectationes in every thinge...and though I could not but observe this yet I still went on though I had some inward persuasion that God wold som way or other punich me for my doeing so...[50]

During the mid-1640s there were a number of influences—historical, social, familial and personal—conspiring to precipitate a religious crisis in Mary. In the background there was the nebulous but palpable atmosphere of political turmoil, harbouring the threat of renewed civil strife. The prospect of war exacerbated Mary's fear of death, and such fears were assiduously promoted by the Essex clergy, who cultivated a greater terror of what might come afterwards. At the chapel services at Leighs, Warwick's chaplain Anthony Walker enlarged upon vivid threats of eternal torments. To these clerical exhortations were added the pleas of Mary's brother and sister, Robert Boyle and Lady Katherine Ranelagh. Both Robert and Lady Katherine were caught up in the apocalyptic fervour of these years and seem to have expected that something was about to happen imminently, although it is not clear what. In any case Lady Katherine used every opportunity to communicate her enthusiasm to Mary.[51]

The time was also ripe for conversion in terms of Mary's own stage of life. By their mid-twenties many Stuart women experienced a swing of the pendulum toward piety, as the fading of their beauty, the disappointments of marriage, and the hazards of childbearing altered the value they had placed on secular aspirations.[52] Certainly the first bloom of romance had worn off Mary's marriage by 1647. The change was not in Mary, however, but in Charles. Some time during the mid-1640s he had begun to suffer attacks of gout, an affliction which eventually transformed his entire personality. Even in its first outbreak it was accompanied by moody attacks of rage directed at anyone who happened to be in his hearing. Having sacrificed material benefits to marry Charles for love, Mary felt this change in his temper keenly. Even the eulogistic account of her conversion composed by her chaplain intimated that Charles' behaviour had been one of the chief means God had employed to wean Mary away from the world.[53]

While Mary vacillated, the sudden illness of her only son Charles in 1647 finally brought matters to a crisis. This was the punishment she had been long expecting: 'I was beyond expression strouke at it', she wrote, 'not onely because of my kindnes for him, but because my conscience told me it was for my backeslideing'.[54] The sickbed was the *locus classicus* of conversion. But Stuart casuistry had extended the guilty ramifications of illness from the invalid to include his grieving relations. Contemporary preachers depicted God as practising a kind of holy extortion, afflicting individuals for their sins either in their own person or by the illness or death of those most dear to them. If this were the divine aim then the only hope of saving the surrogate victim lay in immediate reformation. This was the course Mary adopted forthwith.

> Upon this conviction I presently reatired to God and by earnest prayur begd of God to restore my Child; and did ther solemly promise to God if he wold hear my prayur, I wold become a new Creature.[55]

Young Charles suddenly began to recover, 'which made the doctor himself wonder at the sudden amendment he saw in him'. Naturally Mary saw this as a direct answer to her prayers. In consequence she now felt bound to good behaviour for the rest of her life. Like Hannah she had made a bargain for a son, but she herself was the offering on the altar of religion.

Mary's vow to become a 'new creature' entailed a literal as well as a metaphorical transformation. In terms of energy expended, the process of working out one's salvation was much like pursuing a new vocation. So time-consuming was the practice of piety that Frances Widdrington warned her sister to get a firm foundation in godly knowledge while single, for she would never have time to begin it properly once married.[56] Those who followed the counsel of divines and pious friends became involved in a round of devotions which could consume half their waking hours. Public ordinances like attendance at household prayers and Sunday church services were of course essential. But these comprised only a small proportion of the recommended quotidian exercises. The latter ideally included extemporaneous private prayer, a portion of Scripture and books of devotion, several hours of meditation on divine subjects, the examination of one's spiritual condition, the confession of sin, and a record of all the preceding in a daily ledger of spiritual progress.

All these duties required solitude, a commodity of which Mary hitherto had had a small share. Since adolescence she had been surrounded by crowds of company, a mode of life as prevalent among the Stuart aristocracy as in the households of the poor. Most female tasks and diversions were performed in a circle of relations and friends: needlework, visits, card games, music, coach drives, and the other occupations and avocations of the female upper classes. One of Mary's functions as a dependant in the Warwick household was to serve as companion to the relations with whom she lived.[57]

The duties of piety required a re-ordering of these social priorities. Mary's first thought was to get some time alone. With this object in mind she obtained permission from her father-in-law to go down to Leighs by herself in early June, 1648. Expecting to find her husband still in Essex (for he had been sent to Chelmsford with several other members of Parliament to quell a riot there), Mary instead met him on the road near London. Charles and his companions had barely escaped the Chelmsford mob, and they tried to persuade Mary to return with them, fearing that the Essex countryside would shortly be up in arms. But Mary insisted she would go on, declaring there was no danger for her.[58]

A week later, Goring's army halted its march at Leighs in order to seize the contents of the armoury there. The royalists' haul was disappointing, partly because Goring as Mary's friend and relation was too constrained by politeness to search the house for the arms, which the steward had just hidden. Although the soldiers helped themselves to meat, sack and beer, nothing of value was plundered.[59] This circumstance Mary ascribed to the good 'providence' of her own presence there. In any case she was correct in predicting there would be no danger for her. Goring's visit was the last she saw of the military forces during her stay. Although the siege of Colchester continued throughout the summer less than twenty miles away, it had little effect on Leighs, except that neighbourly visiting ceased. With the self-centredness of the new convert, Mary regarded the siege almost as if providence had arranged it to complete her conversion.

Determined, as she wrote, to 'redeem my mispent time', Mary occupied herself continually in devotional exercises. At Leighs she found a spiritual mentor in Warwick's household chaplain, Anthony Walker, who spent a good deal of time teaching Mary how to lead a 'holy life'. Later in the summer Mary's brother Robert came to visit. In harmony with his sister's frame of mind he employed his spare moments writing a treatise on the love of God which he later dedicated to Mary.[60]

When the Earl of Warwick's family arrived at Leighs they noted a surprising change in Mary's behaviour. A serious demeanour had replaced her former gaiety, and she avoided her previous companions whenever possible in order to retire to her religious meditations. When in company, she preferred to converse with the divines who frequented the household. Mary now thought the change in her life sufficiently definitive to warrant writing down 'evidences' of her conversion. These were to be the first in a long series, since as a good Puritan Mary could never feel absolutely sure of her own salvation.[61]

The Warwick household lived in seclusion for much of the next decade. The Earl of Warwick reduced his participation in public affairs after the executions of his brother Holland and the King. This monotonous round of existence during the Protectorate was radically altered for Charles and Mary during the years 1658–9, when three deaths in the family occurred in a space of less than sixteen months. First Robert, Charles' nephew, died without issue in February 1658. The Earl of Warwick succumbed two months later. Mary remembered her father-in-law's death as the most 'smarting grief' she had ever experienced; she mourned him far more than her own father, who had died in 1643. The accession of Lord Rich to the earldom also meant that the couple had to move from Leighs to Mary's own house in Lincoln's Inn Fields. They had hardly been there a year when Charles' elder brother Robert died, leaving three young daughters whose care he entrusted to Mary on his deathbed. Much to his surprise, Charles was now fourth Earl of Warwick. Apparently he was delighted. Referring to the general discontents in England in 1659, a correspondent wrote cynically to Hyde that he saw 'no persons...thoroughly pleased save Ch. Rich now Earle of Warwick'.[62]

Mary, for her part, claimed that she had never desired this advancement:

I had this satesfaction when he came to that honor and Noble estate that I neaver had so much as a wish for it; but on the contrary, hartely prayed for the recovery of them and morned for their deathes for when I maried my husband…it was his persone I maried and cared for not an estate.[63]

The passage implies that her own attitude was unusual for the times. Certainly it presented a contrast to that of Charles' younger brother Hatton Rich, who continually boasted of what he would do when he became Earl of Warwick.[64]

Mary's own protestations should not be taken at face value. They were written in 1672, after a decade spent in the country nursing Charles' gout had buried her hopes of a brilliant social career in the capital. Throughout the 1660s, however, there are hints that the rank of countess had revived her youthful aspirations. Mary was aware of the pitfalls of this resurgence of ambition. 'I entered upon that unexpected change of my condition with much disturbance and fear, lest by having a more plentiful estate, I ought to be drawn to love the glory of the world too well'.[65]

At Leighs it was easy to conquer the urge for glory. For a dozen years Mary had been locked into a devotional routine which left little room for secular desires. A letter she wrote to her friend the Earl of Berkeley (at his request) in 1660 supplying 'Rules for Holy Living' reveals the formulaic quality of her daily exercises, which had long since replaced the spontaneity of her initial conversion.[66] From her first rising to 'bless God' until the final prayer before going to sleep, the day was rigidly programmed with a set of activities designed to keep her mind in a religious frame. From the evidence of the diaries at a later period, we can infer that this regime never altered until her death. Moreover, Mary was kept busy with manorial and neighbourly duties. At Leighs she was a benevolent mistress of the manor: she supervised the running of the household, checked the manorial accounts, and dispensed hospitality, charity and home-made medicines to the entire neighbourhood. One of her chief interests was in overseeing and supplementing the numerous clerical livings that belonged to the estate. After 1662, her charity was also bestowed upon the ejected ministers of the county. Although a conforming Anglican herself, Mary displayed a latitudinarian fellowship with the local clergy of almost all denominations.

But in visits to London Mary's routine was upset and her devotional meditations disturbed by the visits of friends and relations. After several days of dullness in religious duties, she confessed she was 'in company miserably distracted' acknowledging in her diary 'that when thay came to see me thay ware a burthen to me, yet I by sad experience fonde that thay did hendre me in my journey to heaven'.[67] The powerful connexions of her relations, several of whom now occupied important positions at Court, offered a greater temptation. No doubt the most compelling model for emulation was Mary's sister Lady Ranelagh, who managed to combine piety with a brilliant social position and considerable political influence. As Gilbert Burnet wrote of her, 'she made the greatest figure in all the Revolutions of these Kingdoms for above fifty years, of any Woman of her Age...her great Understanding, and the vast Esteem she was in, made all Persons in their several turns of Greatness, desire and value her Friendship'.[68] Could not Mary likewise frequent the arena of the great, so long as she promised not to enjoy herself?

While in London, Mary was brought to Court a number of times by her brother-in-law Manchester, now Lord Chamberlain.[69] Each visit was hedged with prophylactic prayers against the 'temptations of vanity'. Having been 'by all sively received' on 19 March 1667 she was able to 'come home by the mersy of God without haveing my heart at all affected with the court and was much more inclined to pitty ther lives then to envie them'. This being so, one wonders why her contempt for Court life did not discourage her from repeating the experiment. Even in the midst of Court festivities her imagination was crowded with 'mortifying thoughts'. Hearing the trumpet sound at the celebration of St. George's feast, she began to consider 'what if the trompe of God should sonde'—which called to mind 'what Glory I had in that place seen the last King in, and yet out of that very place was he brought to have his heade cut off[f]'.[70] In August the lesson was brought home in a different form when Mary learned that the King had asked Clarendon (her relation by marriage) to resign his office. This unexpected turn of fortune was noted as a 'loude sarmon to me not to put confidence in princes', but it did not put a stop to her Court visits. After attending the Queen before returning to Leighs, Mary avowed in her diary 'that there was much more hapiness in retirement and conversing with God in solitude then In all the pleasures of the Court', a pronouncement in which we can discern a flavour of sour grapes. Mary privately acknowledged to her chaplain that 'her great difficulty...was her love of the pleasures and vanities of the world...', from which God had weaned her by enforced retirement.[71]

Charles did not share his wife's religious scruples which spoiled her pleasure in worldly glory. In the first flush of pride at his accession to the earldom, he hinted at his willingness to play a role in England's affairs, and as Earl of Warwick he was worth courting during the political turmoil of 1659. The previous year Nicholas had dismissed him as a man 'as vertuous and loyall...as his grandfather [sic] the old Rebell Warwick', but the royalists soon discovered that the earl would be favourable to a restored monarchy. Though non-committal at first, by August Warwick had become involved in Booth's uprising.[72]

Warwick's contribution to the restoration of monarchy was little and late. Moreover he was still backing the Presbyterian interest in Essex in the 1660 parliamentary elections, to the disgust of some more zealous royalists. This did not prevent his brother-in-law Lord Manchester (now speaker of the House of Lords) from arranging for Warwick to be made one of the six peers deputed to invite the return of Charles II. And thanks to his friend Monck, Warwick also received the minor sinecure of governor of Landguard Fort. But advancing gout prevented Warwick from following up these honours and interfered with his efforts to attend the House of Lords.[73]

Thus the earldom had come as an ironic preferment to the couple. Charles was prevented by his malady from exploiting its wealth and influence, and Mary felt disqualified by religious scruples from taking pleasure in its social rewards. But Warwick and his wife still had a son to whom they could transfer their frustrated aspirations. In 1662 Lord Rich (as their son Charles was now styled) enhanced his prospects by marrying the only daughter of the Earl of Devonshire. As custom then dictated, Lord Rich was sent off to France three days after the wedding, his wife being too young to live with him. He returned to England sooner than was planned, however, in order to join her in his parents' household.

The happiness of the Warwick *ménage* was short-lived, for the demographic lottery had another irony in store. On 8 May 1664, Lord Rich contracted smallpox. Since his mother had already had the disease, she sent everyone away and took her son to her own house in Lincoln's Inn Fields, where she nursed him herself. Although the doctors held out hopes for his recovery, within eight days he was dead.

When Warwick was told the news, as Mary later recalled, 'he cryed out so terably that his cry was herd a great way; and he was the sadest aflicted persone could possebly be'.[74] He was also extremely anxious about Mary. Anthony Walker recalled that when Warwick's misery was at its height for his son's death, 'he made that the circumflexing Accent of his grief: 'twould kill his wife, which was he said more to him than an hundred sons'. There were grounds for his fear. Mary later confessed that she loved her son so passionately that she would have been willing to 'have dyde ether for him, or with him'.[75]

This was not considered an unusual sentiment under the circumstances. There are numerous examples of Stuart parents who were thought to have perished of grief for their children's sake. Margaret Lucas's sister followed her infant daughter to the grave within months, allegedly from inconsolable grief. The second Earl of Warwick told those at his grandson's funeral 'that if they tarried a little longer, they should carry him down also to be buried with him', a prophecy that proved correct. Alice Hayes recounted the pathetic story of her mother's sacrifice for her:

> I being one Time very weak, and supposed nigh unto Death, the Exercise thereof was so hard to her, That she fell down upon her knees, and prayed the Lord to take her, and spare me; which he did...[76]

Whether grief was the actual cause of death in these cases is not at issue. In the context of Stuart culture it was believed plausible that parents were capable of dying for their offspring.

If any parent was in mortal danger from grief, then Mary was a prime risk. But the species of Protestantism she had embraced did not permit unbridled sorrow. It served simultaneously as a strait-jacket and a support, imposing restraints not only upon the emotions Mary was licensed to express, but even on those she was allowed to feel. Death was the most important occasion on which Christian dogma served as a mediator between objective reality and human belief about reality. To comprehend its power to mould Mary's behaviour, we must distinguish between two contradictory roles which religious teaching performed at this time. First there was the consolatory task of rationalizing the ontological phenomenon of death, by denying the identification of death with dissolution. Second, more tyrannical and opportunistic, was the attempt to exploit the emotional reactions provoked by death, diverting them into channels which served religious discipline. In particular, there was a concerted effort to transform unfocussed grief and anger into pious self-condemnation. The need to reinforce this masochistic inversion becomes comprehensible when it is recalled that death was precisely the occasion when individuals were apt to question life's meaning and God's benevolence. Even among the spiritually sophisticated, unbelief could seize hold when the strokes of demography rained too heavily. After Elizabeth Walker's last surviving child died, she plunged into an atheistic depression.[77] Under such circumstances, casuists could either seize the initiative by persuading mourners to blame themselves instead of God or chance for their misfortunes, or else risk losing all hold over their communicants. Of course this psychological ploy was not imposed upon a resistant population. Guilt feelings were already present, ready to be magnified by religious advisors.[78] This interplay between religious theory and personal psychology will become clearer when we compare Anthony Walker's funeral sermon for Lord Rich with his parents' behaviour afterwards.

The *leitmotif* of Walker's sermon was the phrase 'weep not' (from Luke 7:12–13) signifying the duty of emotional control in the face of death. Walker admitted that there were abundant circumstances to warrant tears: the young man was the only son of a noble family, a youth with many 'natural accomplishments', just married to a noble young lady 'who was not his Bargain, but his Choice'. But the brutal facts of demography made no exceptions for age or class.

The wonder is greater than any man out-lives his Mothers travel, then that he dyes so soon...Most children dye before their Parents, not one of an hundred that are born, lives to be old, and consequently, far the greatest part of men dye young.[79]

And though 'no ayd was wanting, which Able, Skilfull Physitians could afford', the rich were as impotent as the poor in the face of mortal illness. Walker was familiar with these facts from personal experience, for all his numerous offspring were to predecease him.[80]

Having painted a realistically stark picture of the horrors of Stuart mortality, Walker abruptly introduced the consolations of religion. Lord Rich was 'not extinguisht but Removed', presumably to Heaven. For under his mother's intensive supervision during his illness, he had manifested the typical sickbed signs of repentance. He had renounced all his high-flying young friends, remarking 'I now well see, what little good my Feathered-Friends can do me.' Moreover, he had resolved to spend four hours every day in 'Reading, Prayer and Meditation' should he be spared. Walker invoked St. Augustine to set the seal on Mary's spiritual labours: 'a child of so many Prayers (and such Prayers as hers) could not miscarry....'.

Whether or not the survivors were hopeful about the ultimate destination of Lord Rich, their duty remained unquestioning submission to God's will. Walker recalled the oft-invoked Stuart analogy between God's fatherhood and contemporary childrearing practices: if the parents complained, they might 'provoke the Lord to multiply his stripes; as children often suffer more for sullingness and sobbing, then for the first occasion of correction'.[81]

Finally, the parents must accept their son's loss in silence because of the likelihood that their own guilty actions had caused his removal. It was well known that 'only children' were more apt to be struck down than others, because they were 'over-loved', standing 'so betwixt their Parents heart, and Him, He cannot be Lov'd Himself, till they are removed'. Alternatively, the parents' sins might be responsible. We may discern Mary's accents in Walker's quotation: 'But I fear most, that I sinn'd him away, and 'tis for my Transgression, that God hath snatcht him hence'. This was 'an Holy, and a commendable fear', Walker remarked in his sermon. But he cautioned mourners not to be too curious about the workings of providence.

Nevertheless, the main impression both parents carried away from the experience was a morbid sense of guilt for their son's death. So strong was the religious reflex that even Charles succumbed to it, with 'Vowes of God' made 'while the Wound was fresh'.[82] In his case, the impulse was a temporary aberration. But for Mary the trauma was permanent in its effects. In fact we can observe it re-enacted, like some private passion play, on the anniversary of her son's death. The diary entry for 16 May 1667 is entirely taken up with this annual rite:

> May the 16. I kepte it a private fast being the day three yeare upon which my son dide...had...large meditationes upon the siknes and death of my onely childe...his sik bed expressiones...how god was pleased to waken him...then I begane to consider what sines I had comited that should cause God to call them to remembrance and slay my sonn...

It is clear from this entry, and from similar passages on succeeding anniversaries, that Mary had internalized the contemporary religious explanation of her son's death. Indeed she had exaggerated it beyond Walker's worst insinuations. No doubt part of the impetus behind these self-accusations was an attempt to assure herself that her son was an innocent party who had gone to heaven. Sin was the cause of death; someone's sins had provoked God to slay Lord Rich; and consequently Mary preferred to assume that the sins had been her own, since she was still alive to beg for mercy, whereas her son was past praying for. Some women, like Lady Pakington, actually prayed for their dead relations.[83] But Mary was too sophisticated a Protestant to attempt anything of the sort. Hence she transferred as much of the burden to her own back as she was able. And the idea of her own guilt, however horrible, was more satisfying than the psychological anarchy of unfocussed grief. This 'blessed rage for order', so deeply imbued in Stuart perceptions of the world, preferred to turn its terrifying explanations inward against the self, rather than dismiss life's tragedies as meaningless and random.

Being a consistent soul, with an iron discipline unmatched in most of her contemporaries, Mary was determined to follow through with the behavioural consequences of her religious beliefs. This entailed moulding her deportment to the ideal of passive acceptance, an aim in which she was so successful that she amazed all around her. Her chaplain Anthony Walker recalled that 'her behaviour was so submiss, serene and calm, I confess I cannot but judge it scarce imitable...'.[84] We can only speculate about the physical cost of this supernatural calm. Because of a 'great paine' she felt constantly at her heart for months after her son's death, she was advised to drink the waters of Epsom and Tunbridge. The same pattern of physical reaction to the suppression of mental stress recurred during her husband's last years.

In this dejected state, Warwick and his wife set about the incongruous activity of engendering a new heir. Walker's funeral sermon held out hopes of success: 'He that gave him, can give another...A Phoenix may arise out of the ashes...' Their friends agreed. Mary was thirty-nine and Charles about forty-eight years old, not past the age barrier for a conception if heaven deigned to bless their exertions. But their efforts ended in failure. Most likely the cause was Warwick's debilitated condition, for by 1664 gout had invaded most of his body. As a contemporary reported, 'Poore Lord! he lyes continually tormented with the goute, and never stirrs but on crutches when he is at the best ease, the malady leaves such a weaknesse in his limbes'.[85]

But religion suggested to Mary a moral reason for her inability to conceive. It was God's punishment for their previous resistance to the command 'increase and multiply': their efforts to practise birth control early in their marriage.

> I canot but acknowledge a just hand of God in not granting us our petition...and...canot but take notice of Godes with holding that mersy from us when we so much neaded it, being we ware unthankefull for them we had, and durst not trust to his Good providence to provide for more, If He saw it fitt to give them to us.[86]

If Mary's conversion in 1647 was a turning point in her attitude to life, her son's death in 1664 set the seal on her religious quietism. Precisely those of Mary's aims which we would characterize as 'modern' had tragically backfired. As she looked back upon her youth a pattern seemed to emerge. Whenever she had disobeyed Scripture and the social norms, she had been thwarted. She had defied her father (breaking the fifth commandment) in order to marry for love. Now her husband had become her scourge, in a perpetual ill-humour from the pains of gout. In early marriage it seemed prudent to limit the size of their family. Now Mary saw it as a sin which God had punished by depriving them of an heir. The drive for personal fulfilment appeared a snare that left her worse off than before. Hence the remainder of her life was a continual struggle to submit uncomplainingly to God's will, or, as we should call it, the *status quo*.

We have detailed knowledge of the latter part of Mary's life, after most of its dramatic incidents were over. An intimate picture can be gleaned from a religious diary which she began on 25 July 1666. Daily entries were made almost up to the day of her death in April 1678.[87] Although a few books of the diary were subsequently lost, we possess almost a complete record of events and her reactions to them for this period. Since these were years of childless retirement spent mostly in the country, it is tempting to posit a connexion between her monotonous 'leisured' existence and her devotion to the journal. Like her religious exercises, the daily record helped to give a concrete shape and sense of progress to a life which Mary felt to be empty in its externals and composed chiefly of disappointments.

But although childless, Mary was not idle, especially during the last years of her husband's illness, when she nursed him day and night. Most of the burdens of supervising the estate fell on her shoulders, as did the duties of hospitality and charity. After her husband's death Mary served as his executrix, performing all the provisions of his exasperatingly complicated will. Yet she never missed a day of her journal; at the worst, a few successive days were written at one sitting. The reason for this unfailing regularity was that Mary saw it as a duty like her other devotional exercises.[88] Although we do not know why she plunged into her journal without preamble on 25 July 1666, we can be confident about her general motive, the desire to reinforce spiritual discipline. In fact the inhabitants of Leighs had been exhorted for more than twenty years to practise this 'useful duty'. John Beadle preached on the subject at Leighs on 21 July 1644, persuading Warwick's steward Arthur Wilson to begin a spiritual journal. Wilson opened with a summary of Beadle's sermon:

His text was Numbers xxxiii...insisting upon this; That every Christian ought to keep a Record of his owne Actions & Wayes, being full of Dangers & Hazards; that God might have the Glorie...[89]

In 1656 Beadle printed his sermon as *The Journal or Diary of a Thankful Christian*, dedicated to Mary's father-in-law and his wife. Since Mary's own diary follows Beadle's model we may infer that either the book itself or another sermon at Leighs served as her inspiration.[90]

The *raison d'être* for Mary's diary was avowedly religious. Accordingly most of it was devoted to recording her performance of the spiritual exercises which constituted her daily routine. In this respect one day was much like another. She generally rose early, thanking God for allowing her another day. Before getting formally dressed, she went outdoors to a spot called 'the wilderness', a stand of trees forming a private arbour. Here she meditated on a set religious topic for two hours. Back in her closet, she read a portion of the Bible, followed by extemporaneous prayer and a confession of sin. Family prayer in the chapel was next, attended by all the servants. The remainder of the morning was taken up with supervisory household tasks, and the afternoon by social visits of friends and relations. Mary reserved a portion of each afternoon for reading some contemporary book of devotion: Baxter and other divines, Foxe's *Book of Martyrs*, sermon collections, or explanatory essays on miscellaneous topics such as 'The Sacrament' or 'Eternity'. The rest of the day was a mirror image of the morning: family prayers in the chapel before supper, meditation and prayer at night (if Warwick's sickbed requirements allowed it) and a commendation of her soul to God before falling asleep.

Nothing in this daily ritual was original. Every component of the devotional routine was well-established and widely practised throughout the Stuart period. There was an enormous 'culture of devotion' which is accessible to us in its theoretical aspects through countless tracts of advice by Stuart divines and in its practical performance in contemporary diaries, autobiographies, and letters.[91] Although the prescriptive elements were monopolized by the clergy (with a few exceptions),[92] the most dedicated class of lay practitioners were middle- and upper-class females. Some reasons for this apparent imbalance will be suggested below. What is important to grasp is that Mary had no need to create anything. She simply digested some widely-disseminated formulae and cultivated the will to practise them. Indeed one of her clerical friends wrote 'the excellency of a Christian lies chiefly in his will'.[93] Certainly it did not lie in the lay imagination. A comparison of the works that comprised Mary's afternoon reading and the thoughts expressed in her diary suggests that she never produced an original idea of a religious nature, despite her intelligence. When she meditated, her visions corresponded to those described in *Solitude Improved by Divine Meditation* by Nathaniel Ranew (the local minister of Felstead) or to other like-minded authorities such as Joseph Hall or Richard Baxter. Thoughts on eternity resembled those expounded in *A Glimpse of Eternity* by another local cleric, Abraham Cayley; her preparations for the Sacrament were guided by 'Mr. Dykes Book of the Sacrament' [*A Worthy Communicant*, 1642]. The Puritan clergy of the Restoration had devised for their flock a closed and regulated (although endlessly elaborated) system of thought and practice.

The impetus behind publishing this huge bulk of devotional advice was not merely the desire to attract a patron for purposes of preferment. These works sold well because contemporaries felt themselves in need of detailed guidance. In private devotion, an unfettered imagination was a danger rather than a boon. Spiritual diaries commonly complain of 'dullness' or 'wandering thoughts' during prayer.[94] Mary shared this affliction: despite twenty years of discipline she often reported herself 'dull' or 'miserably distracted' for days at a time in private prayer or meditation. Sometimes even a 'good book' failed to rouse her, and she enlisted the help of a chaplain to work herself into the proper frame of mind. Consequently nearly everything she thought and did became formulaic in character.

In addition to the devotional exercises and household tasks that comprised Mary's daily routine, larger periodic rhythms emerge from the diary. Sunday represented the high point of the week, with its two church services and sermons, whose essence Mary extracted by 'praying them over' at home and hearing her young nieces repeat them. The monthly Sacrament was an impressive event, for which Mary prepared the household as much as a week in advance. We can also discern the seasonal repetitions that governed manorial life: Easter, when Mary solemnly renewed her 'covenant' with God; the harvest, whose stages she followed with interest; her Martinmas estate accounts, which like her sins she hated to cast up for fear of finding herself in debt; Christmas, a time of universal hospitality, with large house-parties at Leighs and lavish charity to the poor. Superimposed on these seasonal variations are the more irregular human rhythms of Stuart *rites de passage*: weddings, lyings-in, christenings, sickbed watches, and funerals of relations and neighbours.

All such happenings, whether sacred or profane, tragic or trivial, were set down in Mary's diary or her 'Occasional Meditations' written about the same time. Simultaneously, events were scrutinized in order to disclose their spiritual significance. Indeed this interpretive function was the main purpose of keeping a journal, as John Beadle had summed it up in two complementary precepts:

1. Labour by faith to see and observe God in all things...
2. Labour by faith to see and observe all...good things in God.[95]

The latter dictum often proved difficult for the rebellious Stuart soul, ready to see good in everything *except* God: Baxter confessed that his worst sin was not loving God enough.[96] The corpus of daily devotions was a set of exercises to develop the latter trait. The first of Beadle's precepts, the counsel to discern God's providence in all eventualities, was more congenial to people's inclinations. This is especially the case if we enlarge the concept of providence—as contemporaries did—to include the devil's ubiquitous activities. Spiritual diaries simply channelled and formalized a widespread craving to impose some larger meaning upon the fortuitous accidents of life, a need which bordered on superstition even among the clergy.[97]

In reprocessing the raw material of daily experience spiritual journals performed two intertwining functions: they reinforced religious discipline, and they relieved psychological tension. For the elect were enjoined not only to love God but to seek closer communion with Him. But to carry on a dialogue with a being who did not respond audibly was not easy. Some filled the gap by hearing voices.[98] Others, like Mary, interpreted passages from Scripture as being addressed personally to themselves. A journal as a record of direct divine intervention served as one means of making the conversation with Heaven less one-sided. For example, Mary was able to test empirically whether the Lord answered her prayers and to note when He had done so.

As for the psychological cravings which the diary helped satisfy, these merge so imperceptibly into the religious that it is difficult to disentangle them. As we might expect, their relative proportions were dependent upon external stimuli. We can observe a rough division between two periods covered by the diary. First there are the years 1666–73, dominated by Warwick's worsening illness, provoking blasphemous rages of which his wife bore the brunt in self-imposed silence. During this period Mary especially found that 'the consolationes of God ware not small'. The second division covers Mary's widowhood, when she was the monarch of her little world, with important business to accomplish. Though her external devotions hardly slackened, their emotional quality underwent a metamorphosis. The delicious communion with Heaven which had fed on worldly affliction was now so often beyond her grasp that she was obliged to flail herself into a frenzy of self-loathing for her 'backsliding' in order to recapture it. Mary noted the pattern that connected worldly happiness with religious lapses. In her last recorded 'Occasional Meditation' she compared herself to a boy she had observed. He was only obedient so long as he was beaten, 'being still worst when his father was kindest to him'. In her case, 'when God has bene pleased to take off for som time his fatherly chastisements...I have bene so basely disingenuous as to grow worse by his love...'.[99]

When the diary begins in 1666, God's fatherly chastisements are much in evidence. The main impression to be gleaned from these pages is the precarious quality of Stuart existence. The plague had not quite left the south-east and though Leighs had thus far escaped any deaths from that cause, Mary 'did excedingly adore and admire his mersy that did yet keepe the Plaigue out of my house when that curse was so usely in my husbandes mouth'.[100] Next the Second Dutch War encroached almost to their doorstep. Indeed the diary opens on a note of hysteria, for the noise of guns from the naval battle could be heard at Leighs on 25–26 July. Mary was terrified that the French might prove victorious, cut their throats, and set up Popery in the land. She prayed for assurance of her everlasting condition, 'that what ever becom of my body my S[oul] may be safe'. A month later, she was 'much amazed and troubled' at the news that half London had burnt. The next day was spent fasting, meditating on what she had 'in particular done to provoke God to punich this nation...Deasireing that as my sines had brought fagottes to that fire so I might bring boukets of teares to quench those flames'.[101]

The following May England's prospects appeared at their lowest ebb, as Mary noted the 'dismal news' that the Dutch had 'come as far as Chattorn [Chatham] and set afire some of our great ships'. This judgement, coming on the heels of so many others, elicited a personal campaign of 'seeking God for the nation': Mary spent three days praying 'with great store of tears he would find a way to save us from utter destrouktion'. The result of this spate of acting out Lamentations was that Mary 'did not fear what my enemy could do' [15 June 1667].

The function of the notion of 'divine judgement' as a satisfying explanation of world-historical events is well known.[102] Mary's diary reveals that when occurrences were interpreted in this manner they became susceptible to personal influence even by the most powerless members of the commonweal. By playing Jeremiah, Mary felt she was helping to forestall future judgements. Of course the female sex did not have any monopoly on prayer as a means of influencing global happenings. The government-appointed fast days for the plague, the fire of London, and other disasters were a collective effort to avert future calamities by the spiritual exertions of the community. Men could also resort to more active means of guiding England's destiny. But women were confined to being mere spectators, barring a few notorious exceptions like the Countess of Carlisle, whose unfortunate experiments in political meddling seemed to confirm her sex's incapacity for state affairs.[103] Hence women turned to prayer as their only vehicle for altering the course of history. It is hardly surprising to find female spiritual journals often dominated by vast political designs: Lady Pakington's heavenly entreaties during the Interregnum expressed a blend of religious fervour and partisan politics, and Elizabeth Mordaunt offered the Lord the sum of £5 and a special attendance at sacrament if Sir George Booth and his fellow conspirators would be spared, a debt she duly paid. Some women made a speciality of civil disasters: Elizabeth Bury would retire to her closet to pray the instant she heard of a fire breaking out anywhere, in the hope of stopping its progress.[104] Mary's energetic 'wrastling' with God for aims which ranged from personal to international in scope were a similar effort to transform passive impotence into active intervention.

The judgements of the mid-1660s offered a dramatic exhibition of God's vengeance on a rebellious nation. But as an illustration of life's tenuous quality they formed an occasional descant over the ground bass of illness, accident, and death. Contemporary diaries written from a domestic perspective document the texture of daily existence as a continual round of casualties.[105] During the first two years of Mary's diary, she recorded the deaths of over a dozen relations or friends. Illnesses were more common. Often the entire household was prostrated by an 'ague' while Mary rushed from one sickbed to another. Accidents occurred with sufficient frequency to add to mental stress: 'My Lord told me what preservation we had that night from fire in the laundry' which 'had presently burnt all but that the providence of God wacht over us' [26 March 1667].

Naturally the entire population suffered the strains of life's painful insecurity. But women were in close contact with its depressing *minutiae*. Especially in rural areas, female volunteers were the general practitioners, the chemists, and the nurses who dealt with the most disagreeable aspects of the sickbed. No class lines were drawn: Mary, like many of her female peers, served as doctor not only to her large household of relations and servants, but to the community round about. As her chaplain wrote, the Essex poor resorted to her stillroom as their 'shop for chirurgery and physic'; these medicines were accompanied by personal visits. Then there was the feminine 'illness', the ordeal of childbirth. It was a communal female event in which each onlooker could relive the terror of her own experience:

Aug. 26 1667 ...my Lady Barringtons being in labor...I went directly thiethar...I stayde with her all night she haveing a most terable sharpe labor I was exsidingly afraide of her and with much earnestnes and many teares begde a safe dealivery for her...[106]

Whether or not women's special role in illness and childbirth promoted a more apprehensive attitude to life, it is clear that Mary was deeply moved by the misfortunes around her. Familiarity with suffering did not inure her to it. On the contrary, it heightened her emotional reaction. This was especially true of death, which she perceived almost as a physical pollution or a personification of malignant forces. After Lady Robartes' maid died at Leighs, Mary wrote in her diary, 'the sight of the corpse mightely afected me, and made me consider that death was now entred into my house, and I was mightely moved to consider why God had yet spared me and taken away one much younger' [24 Aug. 1666]. Mary was supposed to meditate upon her latter end as a part of spiritual discipline. But the fact of death made her wonder whether she would be the next victim, and added an obsessive immediacy to her ruminations. 'Jan. 6 [1667] I had the newes brought me that about to oclocke that morneing my Lady Denham dide...and could not thinke of anything that night but death'.

The 'accidents' of life run like a warp thread through the diary, patterning Mary's emotional response. The woof in this depressing pattern was Charles' worsening illness, a major preoccupation of the diary from early 1668 until his death in 1673. If the shocks of the flesh provoked in Mary the fear of death, Charles' rages made her weary of life. Between the two, she was driven into a third realm, the private world of religious consolation.

Warwick attended the House of Lords when sufficiently well to do so, and the chequered pattern of his appearances there tallies with Mary's account of his relapses and recoveries. He was present at irregular intervals from the first session of the House in 1660 until April 1664, just before his son's death of smallpox in May. Warwick's prolonged depression after that event is borne out by the parliamentary records: he did not reappear in the House until October 1667. Warwick did attend its sessions regularly throughout that autumn and winter until 17 February 1668, his last appearance in the House of Lords. From early 1668 until his death in 1673, he was almost continually prostrated by his malady. Most of the time was spent in his bedroom, with ever shorter intervals of comparative relief.

Warwick's disease caused a great physical alteration. In his funeral sermon for the earl, Anthony Walker delineated the striking contrast:

the sprightly Activity, the healthful Vigour, the agile unconfinedness, the strenuous temperature, the hayl Constitution, the graceful Fashion, the amiable Sweetness, and Comely Beauty of his Youth; so Eclips'd, Enfeebl'd, Decayed, Withered, and shrunk into Decrepidness, and a Living Death...the Pains and Sorrows of his Life, outweighing the Pleasures of Living...[107]

The temperamental changes in Warwick were as great. His excruciating pains and frustrating debility had made him bitter and morose. During episodes of gout the smallest provocations called forth unrestrained outbursts of violent temper, accompanied by oaths and insults. 'March 10 [1669]...very melancaly because my Lord had one of the saddest nightes of paine that I remember him ever to have had, no sleep at all, but continually roaring out'.

The oaths were a family habit of the Rich brothers, who violently reacted against their pious education. Even Mary noticed this psychological propensity. In one of her 'Occasional Meditations' she conjectured that those who had had a strong religious education—but not 'sanctified'—were later 'drawne to be the greatest opposers and despisers of Realidgion'.[108] Hatton was the most extreme of the brothers: he boasted that he would send away all the ministers who frequented Leighs as soon as he became Earl of Warwick.[109] His language was remarkably profane: after a dinner party Mary wrote in her diary that Hatton had talked 'like nothing out of Hell could have don...' [15 March 1667].

Charles' feelings about religion were more ambivalent. A part of him was intensely proud of his wife's piety. On one occasion he showed off her holy accomplishments by hiding a minster near her closet to hear the fervent groans that issued from it while she was at prayer. Charles also believed that Mary's saintly discipline gave her a direct line to the Almighty. A diary entry for 15 December 1667 notes: 'After supar my Lord when he was abed not being able to gett any rest bid me pray to God to give him som'. The prayer was successful.

But if Mary's devotions were occasionally useful to Charles, they had practical disadvantages. The hours spent at religious exercises were so much time stolen from companionship with him and he resented it. Indeed most of the dissensions recorded in the diary can be attributed to Charles' irritation at Mary's spiritual preoccupations. Appealing to his husbandly prerogative, Charles waged continual warfare against Mary's heavenly devotions in order to win back her full-time devotion to him. Charles commanded Mary to stay home with him instead of going to the afternoon church service on Sundays, 'much to my troble' as she noted. He wanted her to read history to him in the afternoons rather than her book of sermons. Whenever he felt better he would insist on long coach drives with his wife which prevented her evening prayers, to her intense annoyance. And he was bitterly jealous of the spiritual bonds that united the trio of Boyle siblings, Mary, Robert and Katherine.[110]

More galling than the inconveniences resulting from Mary's pious practices was the fact that they represented a reproach to Charles' own behaviour. Mary made heroic efforts to convert her husband by every means she could devise. She knew from her reading of Baxter of the danger of most people's 'secret infidelity': they believed that their beloved (but unregenerate) relations would *not* be doomed to eternal hellfire. Mary tried not to succumb to this indulgent delusion. She also detested Charles' cursing. After an offensive outburst she recalled that in heaven she would 'never have my soule more grieved at the hearing of the fillthe comenunications of the wicked' [30 Dec. 1669].

No matter how passionately Mary loathed Charles' profanity, it did provide one psychological boon. It offered her a permanent moral handle on him and a dignified reason for feeling aggrieved. Mere bad temper would have given her no scope for protest, for Mary was too proud to admit how much Charles hurt her. Occasionally the urge for self-expression got the better of her, as on one evening when she returned late from a visit:

> ...my Lord fell, without any occasion given by me, into a great pasion with me, which trobled me so much that I fell into a dispute with him wherein I was very pationately affected, and wepte much, and spake unadvisedly...telling him that I was with his unkindnes to me so much trobled that I was weary with my Life, and that my life was a burden to me.... [26 Nov. 1667]

Afterwards, ashamed of this lapse of self-control, she begged God's pardon 'for my shedding so many teares for anything but my sinnes, and for not being content with what his providence was pleased to order for me.'

To dispute with Charles would have been to cast away her last shred of dignity, nor was it likely to improve his behaviour. To defend God's honour was another matter. Mary had been instructed in her devotional readings on the duty to speak out against sin. By casting the conflict into a religious framework, she achieved a meaningful explanation of Charles' sufferings and her own.

Mary had rationalized her previous life as a 'checker worke' of mercies and afflictions, the later shrewdly laid on by providence whenever her recurrent tendency toward backsliding was perceived on high. In an analogy with Stuart childrearing she acknowledged that 'there is not one corection I could have bene without, though thy rods has as it ware drawne blood...'.[111] Charles' retributive role in this grand scheme seemed clear. With an ironic economy of means, providence was utilizing him as Mary's scourge for the great sin of her youth, 'when I by my maredge thought of nothing but haveing a persone for home I had a great pation, and neaver sought God in it, but by maring my husband flatly disobayd His comand, which was given me in His Sacred Oracles, of obaieng my father...'.[112] Judging by the increasing frequency of her lamentations for this lapse of duty, her penitence grew in proportion to Charles' worsening moods. An entry for 12 September 1671 notes 'my disobedience to my dead father, this sinn I did bemone with great plenty of teares, and confest God was righteous in letting me read my sinn in my punichment'. In this year Mary began using the symbol † for Charles in her diary: her husband had literally become her cross.

Nevertheless, after thirty years of marriage Mary still loved her husband too passionately for her supposed spiritual good, thus forcing the Lord to 'have imbitterd the streame that I might com to the fountaine head' [9 Dec. 1671]. Nearly everything reminded Mary of this salutary but painful process. Having plucked a rose and seen it soon wither on her bosom, she compared the wilted flower to

...admired and favorite relationes, and frendes to which we lett out our afectiones to freely, thinking we can neaver lay them to neare our hartes but...God is often so mersyfull...as to throw doune our Idole and his rivall, and to make it...seeme withered in our eyes by having a less blinded passion for that persone...[113]

Since Mary's own 'sanctified afflictions' produced spiritual benefits, she began to hope that Charles' sufferings might likewise serve a purpose, 'that the frute of his punichment might be to take away his sinn, that he might have cause to say, it was good for him he was afflicted'. Gradually the conviction gained on her that Charles' physical torments were sent by providence to prod him to repentance. Naturally she felt obliged to 'presse him to consider what was Godes deasigne in this often and heavily afflicting him with those dredful paines...'.[114]

The concept of earthly pains as an advance warning of hellfire was commonplace.[115] But Mary sometimes felt that the method as applied to Charles verged on cruelty.

> If thou seest fitt by bodily torments to mind us of fleeing eternal ones...mind me that I doe not yeild to my temptation that the Divell would tempt me with som of my relations to thinke thou dealest cruelly because thou torturest ther fraile bodyes...[116]

Usually, however, the diary managed to 'justify God'. Indeed the conviction seems to have become rooted in the Essex neighbourhood that Warwick's gout was a divine punishment for his blasphemous rages. The Reverend Anthony Walker denied the aspersion in his funeral oration for Warwick, 'to satisfie his Memory and Name, against so Unwarrantable and Rude an Impression, as if he were a great Sinner, because a greater sufferer'.[117]

What Charles thought about his own spiritual condition is not clear. Some of his close friends, like the young Earl of Manchester, made a 'mock of sinns' to Mary's great horror. Charles himself vacillated in his religious impulses depending upon his state of physical well-being. At times Mary noted that he had listened patiently to her preaching. On rare occasions he told her he 'was resolved to live bettar'.[118] But sooner or later Warwick returned to his old pattern. As his illness progressed the quarrels became more frequent, their causes increasingly trivial. Sometimes the couple disagreed on money matters, for Mary had larger notions of charity than Charles.[119] At times Charles felt neglected. On 19 July 1671 there was a violent uproar when he decided that Mary had spent too much time with her sister Katherine. During his last years explosions occurred over nothing at all. Once when Charles told Mary he hated the sight of her, she wrote in the margin of her diary as a poignant testimony to the insignificance of the provocation: 'strawberries' [14 July 1673].

As in her response to the death of her son, Mary maintained a stoic silence in the face of this 'sanctified affliction'. Outwardly her behaviour appeared a passive acceptance of her lot. Inwardly there was a continual struggle which deployed every resource of her obstinate, high-spirited, self-assertive character in the arduous pursuit of that elusive goal, resignation to God's will. In this mental combat religion served as her strait-jacket and her support. Mary was conscious of its dual role, begging God that 'when he did strike me with his rod his staff might supporte me, that I might not faint when I was corrected of him' [27 Oct. 1668]. This gruesome metaphor is an appropriate symbol of the interplay between her worldly trials and otherwordly solace.

Among these spiritual consolations, the physical relief of tears should not be underestimated. 'If you can, weep for your sins', Mary told her friend Lord Berkeley, a piece of advice she was not slow to follow, being 'able experimentaly to say that I have had som times the greatest comfortes when I have been able also to say rivers of water have run downe myne eyes for my sinnes'. Reading of Mary Magdalene washing Christ's feet with her tears made Mary 'indeaver to weepe as much as she did'. But a Biblical stimulus was not necessary, since she could divert her personal woes to godly remorse, 'that it may turne all my sorow in to the right chanell, that my teares may noe more be poured out for my friends ill usage of me but...for my crimsone sinnes against thy constant and unmerited goodnes to me'.[120]

In a positive vein, Mary employed her meditations to transform heaven into a personification of whatever was lacking in real life. One aspect of the trinity was always available to serve as friend, counsellor, father, husband, or lover, as circumstances required. The Lord was an ideal confidant, discreet, sympathetic, and accessible at any hour when she needed 'to lay before him all my troble as to a compationate frend' [29 April 1668]. In this respect, divine friendship was much superior to the human variety. Mary told an anecdote of Lady Robartes, who once hurried through her devotions to greet her husband when he arrived home. But she soon perceived that he wanted to be rid of her, 'which made her presently thinke that she was justly punished for her leaveing her God who wold not have bene weary of her converse with him'.[121] Moreover, even perfect human soul mates like Lady Katherine Ranelagh could not remain with Mary all the time. Whenever she sank into depression after a visit from her sister had ended, she reminded herself 'though all my other frends lefte me yet my best frend stayde with me' [15 August 1668].

Prayer was more than a receptacle for painful secrets. It offered the opportunity for a 'peaculior and transcendant' experience of mutual love,[122] a state of mind which it is difficult to characterize, but one which certainly incorporated elements of earthly love. This displacement to a heavenly object was strongly encouraged by the devotional literature of the time. For example Nathaniel Ranew instructed practitioners of the art of divine meditation to imagine Christ as 'a most glorious and delicious Object',

> her Beloved the Lord Christ, his pure Colours, white and Red, his most rare features and exact proportions of every part, his Head, Locks, Eyes, Cheeks, Lips, Hands, Legs, and all his glorious perfections and then adds to sum up all, that he is altogether lovely...[123]

In view of such descriptions, it is hardly remarkable that Mary Penington dreamt of Christ as a 'lovely young man'. Likewise Agnes Beaumont felt no cold when she spent a winter night communing with Christ in the barn: the word '"Beloved" made such melody in my heart as is not to be expressed'.[124] Mary's journal offers numerous examples of the transference of earthly love to a divine object. Undoubtedly her religious milieu helped to promote such feelings. Her diary often notes the intoxicating effect of sermons devoted to 'Christes excellencies'. Mary also culled exhortations from her religious guides. According to Baxter and other divines, the love of God was a crucial sign of salvation, hence Mary periodically examined herself by this criterion. 'I did...try my selfe by som of Mr. Baxteres markes, and I fond that I trewly loved God above heaven and earth' [26 Jan. 1670]. She frequently chose 'love to Christes persone' as her topic for meditation, praying that 'I might more and more be in love with him...and that he wold there give me his loves...' [30 May 1668]. She also quoted Baxter's dictum:

> I fond love was an attractive of love, for whilst I was thinking of Godes great love I fond my heart was warmed with a peaculior and transcendent deagree of love to himselfe. [25 Dec. 1668]

Yet these external promptings do not fully account for the extraordinary ardour which characterizes many passages of the diary. Mary herself apparently recognized an earthly tincture to her more rapturous expressions, for she crossed them out at a later date. Some illustrations follow, with the words she deleted in brackets: 'satisfying pleasure [in warmth of thy love]'; 'fond I [pationately] loved Jeasus for Jeasus sake'; 'had the pleasure of [the warmth] [and fire] with the celestial love'; '[pationately] loveing my blessed saviour'; 'love God [pationately]'.[125] These and similar outpourings were associated with the years 1666–73, when Warwick's ill humour was at its height. The diary contains numerous avowals of Mary's need to find an alternative object for affections which were elsewhere thwarted. In February 1670 she prayed for a heart 'sick of love for Jeasus...being resolved not to have my heart any more torne with the thornes and briars of this world'. On 12 December, musing on 'The unsatesfactoryness of all that I expected solace and satesfaction from' she begged God for 'more love and dealight in him, that he might make up what so ever was wanting in my relationes [i.e., Charles] and that he might be all in all unto me'. On a similar occasion she was 'mightely comforted under my worldly trobles to consider that my maker was my husband' [8 May 1673]. Thus an orthodox doctrine, the tenet that God ought to be loved more than any 'creature', became a psychological crutch.

Another doctrine put to similar use in Mary's meditations was that of heaven, which frequently inspired a train of escapist thoughts. 'My spirit was as it were solacing itself in heaven...while I was one earth...', she wrote in January 1667, and in the paraphrase of Psalm 55 which followed she wished for 'wings like a bird' that she might 'flee away and be with the lord'.

In the journal heaven was pictured alternately as Mary's deliverance from her daily trials and her reward for having endured them. 'Heaven would make amends for all my troubles...', she continually reminded herself; moreover, her 'afflictiones' would worke an exceeding greater weight of glory' [11 August 1672].

As in the anthropomorphic representation of God, we can discern the fertilizing influence of Mary's environment. The diary confirms that she was exposed to innumerable sermons and tracts which confidently described the next world and exhorted the pious to dwell continually on thoughts of it. There was some variation in these descriptions, since contemporaries were apt to stock heaven with whatever they personally lacked on earth. One impoverished cleric whose sermon Mary noted on 9 July 1676 claimed that there would be 'riches, durable riches'. Since Mary's wants were of the emotional kind, her concept of heaven emphasized the affections. During her meditations God assured her that she would spend eternity 'in his fullest love'; she should 'never weep more' and should have 'pleasures forever'.

Thus through the routine of piety Mary constructed a mental world which served as a potent anaesthetic to blot out the pain of the real world. At best it offered moments of transcendent happiness, the 'unspeakable joy' of communion with God. At the worst it prevented her from succumbing to despair. Meditating on the 'benefits of saintefied aflictiones' enabled Mary to 'goe on in my Christian Course with corage and not to be weary and faint'. In fact each one of her 'saintefied aflictiones' was dutifully noted as a 'mercy',

> that I was not drawne by it to a mopeish sadnes, and high disturbing discontent, but...to seake my happynes in my chife Good. [15 Sept. 1672]

Yet there was a price to be paid for this psychological boon. If contemporary doctine transformed worldly afflictions into moral benefits, it also condemned worldly satisfactions as spiritual failings. To this point we have examined the first half of the equation. Warwick's gout, his unkindness, the couple's forced retirement in the country had all been designed for Mary's spiritual benefit. On the other hand, each one of Mary's past attempts at ordinary happiness was 'self-condemned' in daily orgies of self-loathing. Every impulse to deal with her afflictions other than by passive submission was interpreted as a lack of resignation to God's will—one of the most frequent sins for which Mary flailed herself. In an ultimate inversion of normal aspirations, the desire for life itself was classified as evil and irrational:

> I fond my selfe excedingly selfe condemned that I should ever be ether afraide or loath to dye...I was a best [beast] or amost irashanall creature to deasire to live in this place of weepeing rather than to be disolved...with Christ. [30 Nov. 1669]

This doctrine had a conservative effect on women's concept of their domestic role. In theory at least, any form of protest against one's allotted 'relative duties' was interpreted as a rebellion against providence.[126] In this respect female religious quietism conformed to the conservative social conventions of the time, and Mary's behaviour illustrates the success of the system.

Yet in the early 1670s we can begin to see cracks in the mental edifice she had constructed. First, she suffered increasingly frequent attacks of 'spleen'—a kind of physiological protest against her emotional burdens, compounded of headache, 'melancholy', and general prostration. Most attacks occurred the morning after a violent scene with Charles; their incidence increased dramatically during his last years and disappeared altogether when Mary became a widow.[127]

The most interesting manifestation of Mary's rebellion against her self-imposed passivity was the decision to write her autobiography in February 1672. In its origins the impulse was merely another religious duty. On Sunday, 4 February, Mary had been deeply affected by Dr. Woodrooffe's sermon, whose doctrine was that 'it should be the care of a Christian to glorify God'. Mary meditated on the ways she 'might bring glory to God'; on 8 and 9 February she recorded 'some spesialetyes of my one life'.[128] The autobiography does not, however, follow the conventional pattern for a spiritual memoir, which was supposed to confine itself to the writer's religious vicissitudes, punctuated by God's providential intervention. Only a small proportion of the memoir resembles this genre. Once Mary was launched on her project, her ego began to reassert itself: the work is a sensitive recollection of the most significant *secular* incidents in her life. The nearest contemporary model is a secular one, the Duchess of Newcastle's 1656 memoir, 'A True Relation of my Birth, Breeding and Life'.

Like the latter work, Mary's autobiography begins with a proud account of her parentage, notably her father's rise from the 'younger brother of a younger brother' to be Lord Treasurer of Ireland with 'twenty thousand pond a-year coming in'. Nearly a third of the 39-page memoir is a detailed narrative of her courtship: her stubborn refusal of James Hamilton and her clandestine romance with Charles Rich. The events of thirty years before were recollected as vividly as if they had occurred the previous week. At that time Charles had been a 'very cheereful and handsom, well bred and fashioned persone'. Now he lay in bed unable to move, wasted to a skeleton.

Several complications exacerbated Charles' gout, and in 1672 he was rapidly deteriorating both in 'body and soul' as Mary noted in her diary. By this time Mary's outward defences had begun to break down. There were frequent notations of her 'soden eruption of pations' in response to Charles' rages. Usually she was able to hide these 'eruptiones' from the household, 'yet I did softly to my selfe...speake a very ill pationate word [Divel]'.[129] In one incident, after Mary apologized to Charles for 'what he thought I had done amis' when she knew she had 'don no faulte' she was so furious she 'went to rest without comiting my selfe to God' [19–20 Jan. 1673].

iv. Widowhood

Mary had never stopped trying to convert her husband, although he was increasingly unwilling to listen to her. During his final illness, however, he displayed some inclination to penitence; on his deathbed he began a conversion process. But when Warwick died on 24 August 1673 it was not clear that he had shown evidence of salvation. Both Anthony Walker's funeral sermon and Mary's diary entries are silent about Warwick's ultimate fate. Mary's love for her husband had never abated, and her fear that he had met judgement rather than mercy may help explain why his death was such a crushing blow. She had thought her grief for her son so great that it would be impossible to be more afflicted, 'yet I fond I now was so'. For nearly a month after her husband's death Mary could not eat, sleep, or attend to her prayers; she succumbed to 'sithing fits' which apparently were a form of hysteria.[130]

Yet eventually the support of relations, friends and ministers helped Mary to accept her situation. Dr. Woodrooffe preached a private sermon 'in which he did show the unsuccesfullnes and danger of immoderate worldly sorrow', and her religious discipline began to reassert itself. More important, Mary was now sole mistress of Leighs with much business to accomplish. Her first task was to marry off her two remaining nieces, Lady Mary and Lady Essex Rich. The negotiations for Lady Mary's marriage to Henry St. John had been initiated before Warwick's death, and the couple were married a few months later. The matchmaking associated with Lady Essex took place entirely under Mary's management and its details reveal a good deal about the process. Warwick's will had assigned portions of £5,000 apiece for both nieces on condition that they married with Mary's consent. But Mary did allow her nieces a veto. Lady Essex gave a 'flat denial' to Mr. Thomas Vane 'because of his family' although Mary had favoured the match. Aside from expressing her dissatisfaction at the refusal, Mary did not put pressure on Lady Essex.[131]

The next matrimonial prospect was Daniel Finch, son of the Lord Keeper. Since the Finch family was not acquainted with Mary, overtures were conducted through intermediaries and then by letter. The financial negotiations reveal that like her father Mary was a shrewd and obstinate haggler. She persuaded the Lord Keeper to agree to several concessions: the entire portion was to be given to his son and a separate maintenance was provided for Lady Essex. Mary also wangled an additional £5,000 in cash from the Lord Keeper for the couple to buy more land. Only after these matters had been settled was Mr. Daniel Finch permitted to pay his addresses to Lady Essex. Mary had already ascertained 'from all the persones that knew him' that his character was excellent. Unlike her father, Mary's first prerequisite was a moral one. The young men must be 'viceless' and come from families that 'owned religion'.[132] With that condition satisfied she was as eager for an advantageous settlement as any Stuart parent. The fact that women had different roles to play in the courtship process at different stages of life helps explain why conservative attitudes to arranged marriages were so persistent. Even though Mary herself had married for love, she had altered her perspective by the time she was in a position to guide others into matrimony. The 'patriarchal' aspects of arranged marriages were promoted by mothers as well as by fathers.

Once the match between Lady Essex and Mr. Finch had been completed, Mary's next task was to act as executrix of Warwick's complicated will. It was a privilege to be given possession of Warwick's estate, and an honour to be appointed its executrix. Moreover, most of the will's complications seem to have been intended for Mary's gratification. In one of Charles' remorseful moods a few days before his death he had promised Mary 'he wold make me amends for his unkindnes formerly'.[133] He had already signed a will the previous April in which he had given Mary his entire real and personal estate for her life plus one year. After her death, the estate was to be divided between Charles' three nieces, whom Mary loved as if they had been her own daughters, and Mary's three sisters-in-law, who were among her dearest friends. Charles' cousin the Earl of Holland (who succeeded to the title) was given nothing but Warwick House in London.

But Mary's trust was to prove an exasperating task. The conflicting claims of major legatees involved her in complicated negotiations with dozens of interested parties and disinterested advisors for more than three years, during which time she devoted herself continually to the task. Aside from her determination to fulfil every tittle of Charles's will, Mary had resolved to avoid lawsuits or disputes between members of the family. For help with the legal intricacies (of which Mary had had no previous knowledge) she relied on a host of advisors, most of them relations or retainers of the family. Her new nephew Mr. Finch and his father the Lord Keeper were useful with legal counsel; Mary also relied on 'Brother Orrery', 'Brother Burlington' and several cousins with legal training. The trustees appointed by Warwick were constantly consulted. Unfortunately William Jessup, one of the trustees, died in the midst of the negotiations. As a consequence Mary was prevented from selling land to pay Warwick's debts and annuities until she had a special bill passed by Parliament.

The legal impediments, however intricate, were less vexatious than the personal jealousies between the legatees. But personal relations had always been Mary's *forte*, and her resolution of the disputes between her kin was a triumph of diplomacy. Reconciling her three nieces' claims was complicated but relatively painless because of Mary's moral influence on their husbands. Lord Manchester turned out to be Mary's greatest stumbling-block. Although his father had been one of Mary's best friends, the young Lord Manchester was out of sympathy with Mary about religion and other matters.[134] Finally, in order to avoid an irreconcilable quarrel, Mary 'oferd to quit som of my just right for pease sake, which ofar of mine he did at last close with...'. By 16 October 1676 Mary had persuaded every legatee to consent. This she regarded as a providence attributed entirely to God, who had granted her prayers 'that I might fullfil it without haveing any despute with any of his [Charles'] relationes' [16 Oct. 1676]. But Mary's success was owing to three qualities of her own: her quick grasp of the legal intricacies, her skill in diplomacy, and the Boyle pertinacity which she applied to every goal she had set for herself.

During the last years of Mary's life her primary impulse was to employ her increased wealth to expand the charitable activities she had initiated during Charles' lifetime. The local poor, the sick, widows, ejected ministers and those with meagre livings, the 'scolars' of the little school she had established, the town of Braintree, exiled Huguenots—all were recipients of her largesse.[135] Nearly anyone could arouse Mary's sympathy because her charities afforded her deep pleasure. Having relieved a distressed family, Mary noted that 'by seeing the transeporte the neasesutos [necessitous] mother of It was [in] at the seasonablenes of the realife, I fond a very sensible preasent satesfaction'. In his funeral sermon on Mary, Dr. Walker remarked that her only 'fault' had been an excess of charity because of her 'credulous easiness to believe most people good, or at least better than they were'.[136]

Mary's rank, wealth and exemplary life endowed her with strong influence which she attempted to use to convert all and sundry. The servants at Leighs were frequent objects of Mary's exhortations; her 'good counsel' was also offered to neighbours, friends and relations. In June 1676 she talked with her nephew Lord Clifford 'to persuade him from a sin I was much to my grife told he lived in...'; the chastened young man 'promised me reformation'. Mary also used her moral sway as neighbourhood peacemaker to resolve disputes among local families.[137] In fact her authority combined the qualities of a minister and a justice of the peace.

At the same time that Mary's outward zeal was expanding, she noted in her diary that her inward spiritual graces were undergoing an alarming decay. The diary contains frequent references to the 'dangers and folly of backslidinges' and the 'decay of piety'. Reading old diaries from the time of Charles' illness caused Mary to feel 'self-condemned' when she compared her former vigorous love of God to her cold devotions of late [13–23 March 1677]. The need for religious consolation had disappeared and her devotions had become mechanical. More-over her duties as matchmaker and executrix had rekindled her interest in the real world. Mary had even begun to enjoy herself a little, hanging portraits of her relations at Leighs and purchasing 'fine furniture'. Taking stock of her sins from the time of her widowhood, she noted that she was not 'humbled' by her status but

> rather worse, more taken up with the bisnes of the world, and more pleasd with the Glory and Vanety of It... [24 August 1677]

She even paid visits to Court. At Leighs she was engaged in a constant round of sociability. For the memory of her husband she kept up the grand tradition of hospitality, and since she was an excellent hostess her invitations were always reciprocated. An example of this mixture of pious and sociable impulses can be glimpsed in the Reverend Josselin's diary:

> July 2. A choice day of civil concourse mixt with religious at the L. Honywoods whither came the Countesse Dowager of Warwicke and her sister the L. Renula: goodnes and greatnes sweetly mett in them...[138]

A few days later Josselin received a letter from Mary 'writt with her own hand inviting mee to Leez and promising mee a kind welcome...' When Mary died on 12 April 1678 she had attained the status of a saint in the Essex community. Her life offered Anthony Walker abundant material for the model funeral sermon: she was 'the most Illustrious Pattern of Sincere Piety, and Solid Goodness this Age hath produced', as he asserted in the title page to his eulogy.

The interest in Mary's career lies in the interplay between her personal temperament, her female role and the religious *mentalité* which transformed her life. In her youth her aspirations were typical of her secular contemporaries and excluded any interest in religion. The disappointments and demographic accidents of married life induced her to turn to an all-encompassing worldview that provided an explanation for her misfortunes and support in enduring them. Moreoever religion offered the solace of transcendent emotional release during periods of intense unhappiness. The significance of this emotional pattern is that it was closely connected to Mary's dependent role in marriage as wife and mother. Once she became a widow, her independent 'masculine' status obviated the need for otherworldly consolations. Yet the social patterns of piety had become so deeply engrained that they still structured her mental and material world.

Chapter III
Aphra Behn

i. *Early Life, Surinam and Antwerp*

Aphra Behn's origins remain a mystery. So far as we know, she never recorded the details of her birth and parentage.[1] Nor has she been lucky in her biographers.[2] The meagre clues to her past are derived from posthumous accounts that are vague and contradictory. The nearest of these to a first-hand narrative is a note by Colonel Thomas Colepeper probably written soon after Aphra's death:

> Beene the fames female Poet di[e]d 29 April 1689. Her mother was ⟨the⟩[crossed out] Colonell Culpepers nurse & gave him suck for some time, Mrs Been was Borne at Sturry or Canterbury, her name was Johnson, so that she might bee called Ben Johnson, she had also a fayer sister maryed to Capt write their Names were ffranck, & Aphora, was Mr. Beene.[3]

No external evidence confirms this curious story.[4] If Aphra's mother did serve as wet-nurse to the Colepeper household, it was almost certainly an older sibling rather than Aphra herself who was born contemporaneously with Thomas Colepeper in 1637. Although the year of Aphra's birth is nowhere given by her contemporaries, a few scraps of evidence indicate it should be assigned to the late 1640s.[5] Concerning her father, who according to Aphra's own account died on shipboard en route to Surinam in 1663, there is only some dubious Kentish gossip recorded by the Countess of Winchelsea:

> Mrs. Behn was Daughter to a Barber, who liv'd formerly in

Wye...although the account of her life before her *Works* pretends otherwise some persons now alive do testify that to be her original...[6]

The 'account of her life before her *Works*' to which the Countess referred was the anonymous 'Memoirs on the Life of Mrs. Behn', purportedly written by a 'gentlewoman of her acquaintance' and prefixed to the posthumous 1696 edition of Aphra Behn's *Histories and Novels*. The 1696 'Life' arouses considerable suspicion, for aside from its anonymity and sensational style it contains major factual errors. The second edition of 1698 suggests the process by which this 'biography' was composed. Apparently the author wove Aphra's fictional remains into a quasi-biographical narrative eked out with contemporary gossip. Charles Gildon copied parts of the 1696 'Life' for his preface to Aphra's posthumous play *The Younger Brother*; all subsequent biographies of Aphra are ultimately derived from it.[7]

The author of the 1696 'Life' corroborates Colonel Colepeper's assertion that Aphra's 'paternal name' was Johnson, but calls her a 'gentlewoman, by birth, of a good Family in the City of Canterbury', a claim that contradicts other traditions of her origins as the daughter of a wet-nurse or a barber. It would be easy to dismiss the attribution of gentle birth as a gratuitous flourish were it not for Aphra's associations and accomplishments. Her acquaintance at the Court of Charles II apparently had its origin in family connexions. Aphra's knowledge of French and Spanish also suggests the breeding of a gentlewomen.

Since the memoirs shed no light on this puzzle, we must turn to Aphra's own works for clues. Although she remained silent about her earliest years, she let slip a remarkable confession:

I once was design'd an humble Votary in the House of Devotion, but fancying my self not endu'd with an obstinacy of Mind, great enough to secure me from the Efforts and Vanities of the World, I rather chose to deny my self that Content...than to languish (as I have seen some do) in a certain Affliction...[8]

Aphra was secretly a Roman Catholic toward the end of her life,[9] but the preceding passage refers to her youth. While this confession is the only direct revelation of Aphra's connexion with a convent, there are numerous references to nuns and nunneries scattered throughout her plays and novels, and several tales in which a nun is the protagonist. What is so striking about Aphra's portrayals of young women 'design'd for a nun' is that they correspond in specific details.[10] No evidence has yet been found to support the conjecture that Aphra was educated in a continental English nunnery. But such a hypothesis would explain puzzling features of Aphra's upbringing: her excellent education, with its emphasis on continental languages; her associations with the Court and with Catholic families like the Howards, who placed their daughters in English nunneries in Flanders; her detailed knowledge of continental Catholicism and the routine of English continental nunneries.[11]

Aphra's biography as it can be traced in contemporary documents begins in 1663, when she accompanied her family to the English colony of Surinam. Her stay there provided the setting for her novel *Oroonoko*, which she set down a quarter of a century later. The reason for the long voyage was the appointment of Aphra's father to the post of 'Lieutenant-General of six and thirty Islands, besides the Continent of *Surinam*' which the 1696 'Life' attributed to his 'Relation to the Lord Willoughby'.[12] In June 1663, Lord Willoughby received a royal patent as governor of Barbados and the Caribees which granted him various powers including the privilege of appointing his own deputies and officers.[13] One deputy was his friend Sir Robert Harley, appointed Lord Chancellor of Barbados the preceding January. Sir Robert owned three plantations in Surinam, and it is through the reports sent to Sir Robert from his Surinam steward that we can reconstruct Aphra's activities.

Aphra's family arrived in Surinam about December 1663 or January 1664. Her father had 'dy'd at sea, and never arriv'd to possess the Honour design'd him...nor the Advantages he hoped to reap by them'. Aphra and her family continued their voyage to await the arrival of a ship to take them back to England. Apparently they stayed about two months in the colony.[14]

Into this strange new world arrived another curiosity, the slave 'Oroonoko', the protagonist of Aphra's narrative. Aphra's account of him sheds some light on her developing character. Oroonoko had been purchased by Willoughby's steward at

Parham Plantation. According to his own tale he had been a
prince in his native Coromantien. Impressed with his linguistic
accomplishments, Aphra pronounced him fit for any court in
Europe. With characteristic generosity and an exaggerated sense
of her own importance, she promised Oroonoko his freedom as
soon as the Lord Governor should arrive. Thereafter she made a
pet of Oroonoko and his Cormantee wife Imoinda: 'they eat
with me' and 'were scarce an hour in a day from my Lodgings'. A
devout and priggish young lady, Aphra attempted to convert
Oroonoko to 'the knowledge of the true God'; apparently she
was a Roman Catholic at this time, for she told Imoinda 'Stories
of Nuns' while teaching her needlework.[15]

During her sojourn Aphra acquired a sprinkling of Surinam
Negro patois and West Indian slang. She even picked up a few
words of Carib Indian dialect.[16] The effort to penetrate the
idioms of such out-of-the-way tongues was a symptom of
Aphra's lifelong fascination with words, later manifested in the
wealth of obscure and foreign words scattered throughout her
plays and novels. Her interest in languages was one of her
motives for befriending John Treffry, Lord Willoughby's
steward, 'a very good Mathematician, and a Linguist; could speak
French and Spanish. . .'.[17] Apparently Aphra herself was already
advanced in these languages. The dedicatory preface to the first
play she wrote, The Young King, implies that it was begun in
Surinam. Details of plot and dialogue are derived from three
sources: Caldéron's play La Vida es Sueno, a French prose
rendering of this Spanish source by Abbé François de Boisrobert,
and the Eighth Part of Cléopatre by La Calprenede.[18] Aside from
demonstrating Aphra's familiarity with French and Spanish,
these sources suggest that she was addicted to the usual diet of
plays and romances allotted to girls. Aphra was also immersed in
more serious reading. She told Oroonoko 'stories from the Lives
of the Romans', i.e. Plutarch's Lives, one of the few 'historical'
works from the classics accessible to seventeenth-century English
girls.

Aphra's intention of recounting Oroonoko's life obliged her to
omit autobiographical details which she considered extraneous.
But other sources hint at her activities. Apparently Aphra had
acquired a suitor. He was William Scot, eldest son of the regicide
Thomas Scot. A warrant for his arrest dated 5 May 1660 had

forced him to flee England. A report from Deputy Governor Byam to Sir Robert Harley reveals that Scot had been carrying on a flirtation with Aphra in terms of the characters of d'Urfée's *L'Astrée*.[19] Aphra was rechristened 'Astrea' after the heroine of that popular romance, a name which was to stick with her for the rest of her life. It was an apt choice: the 'Astrea' of d'Urfée's romance is a warm and friendly young woman, spontaneously generous, but proud and passionately jealous. William Scot was cast in the role of 'Celadon', Astrea's long-suffering lover. In his case the name was less appropriate. Unlike the virginal young hero of *L'Astrée*, Scot was in his mid-thirties and had been married several times.

Scot's presence in the colony excited apprehension in Deputy Governor Byam, for Scot had naturally allied himself with the Republican planter interest.[20] These factions can be discerned clearly in *Oroonoko*, which is written as though seen through Republican eyes. Byam is cast as the villain and, although Scot does not appear, the hero (aside from Oroonoko himself) is Colonel George Marten, 'brother to the Oliverian'.[21] This is an unexpected point of view, for Aphra was to parade her fanatical royalism two years later. Presumably she was too young to be knowledgeable about politics and had derived her views from Scot.

Eventually a ship bound for England was found, and Byam reported to Harley the departure of Aphra's family, in a report probably written in February 1664. Meanwhile, the arrest warrant had caught up with William Scot, who left the colony shortly after Aphra's departure, as Byam wrote to Harley,

...to advise you of the sympatheticall passion of ye Grand Sheapherd Celedon who is fled after Astrea, beeing resolved to espouse all distresse or felicities of fortune wth her.... Truly the Brethren are much startled that the Governor of the Reformation should Turne Tayle on the day of battle.[22]

Scot did not pursue Aphra to England, but instead sailed directly to Holland, where he joined Colonel Bampfield's English regiment. Little is known about Aphra herself over the next two years. It has been assumed that she was married on her return from Surinam to an otherwise unidentified Mr. Behn, whom the

'Life' described as a 'Merchant of this City, tho' of Dutch extraction'. Aphra herself never mentioned husband or marriage; all that is known is that by 1666 she was signing her name 'A. Behn'. Presumably she became a widow soon after her marriage. It is tempting to infer from her silence that the match was not a happy one. The theme of forced marriage takes on the dimensions of an obsession in her works. Her first play to be staged was *The Forc'd Marriage; or, the Jealous Bridegroom*, and one of her most successful adaptations was a modernization of Wilkins' *Miseries of Enforced Marriage*. The plays themselves bristle with anti-matrimonial sentiment. This was a fashionable pose in Restoration drama, but Aphra's stories contain even more vehement condemnations of forced marriage and matrimony *per se*. In the autobiographical confession in which Aphra recalled her failure to become a nun, she mentioned another form of parental compulsion:

> ...I could wish, for the prevention of abundance of Mischiefs and Miseries, that Nunneries and Marriages were not to be enter'd into, 'till the Maid, so destin'd, were of a mature Age to make her own Choice; and that Parents would not make use of their justly assum'd Authority to compel their Children, neither to the one or the other.[23]

Had Aphra resisted a nunnery only to be forced into wedlock? A passionate invective against marriage was voiced by one of her heroines, concluding, 'Who is't loves less than those that Marry? and where Love is not, there is Hate and Loathing at best, Disgust, Disquiet, Noise and Repentance...'.[24] It is also significant that Aphra never remarried. Judging from the passionate animus of her anti-matrimonial diatribes, her first taste of marriage may have made her wary of repeating the experience.

Aside from Aphra's probable marriage in 1664 and her widowhood a year or two later, little can be inferred about her life during these years. She may have been presented at Court upon her return from Surinam, as the 1696 'Life' claimed. At any rate by 1666 the King had made her acquaintance.[25] Two courtiers are associated with Aphra's family at this time: an unidentified friend referred to as 'Sir Thomas', and Thomas

Killigrew. We know of Killigrew's acquaintance with Aphra by 1666 because he decided to employ her in Lord Arlington's secret service as an agent in Flanders. The mission for which she was chosen, 'Unusual with my Sex, or to my Years', as she later wrote,[26] was to persuade her quondam suitor William Scot to become an informer for the English crown. Scot had made overtures to Arlington in June of 1665, volunteering to give details of an English uprising, but had been 'prevented by som body'.[27] Apparently it was Killigrew's idea to send a contact who would not have the appearance of an English agent and so reveal Scot's betrayal of his fellow Republicans.

At first sight Aphra was ideally suited for the task. Aside from her previous association with Scot, she possessed a precocious intelligence and a good command of languages. But Aphra was still unworldly. Internal evidence from the Antwerp correspondence corroborates her assertion that she was unusually young. Aphra herself was defensive about her youth. In an outburst to Killigrew she protested, 'how great a Child soever I am in other matters: I shall mind dilligently wt I am now about...'.[28]

Aphra set off for Antwerp toward the end of July 1666, accompanied by her brother and a pair of servants. On her arrival she wrote to Scot; two weeks later their first meeting took place in a jolting coach, a romantic rendezvous which was to set the tone for the rest of their collaboration.[29] Aphra had already chosen the code names 'Astrea' and 'Celadon' for herself and Scot, no doubt in recollection of their flirtation in Surinam. This was the first hint of Aphra's intention of exploiting Scot's presumed attraction for her. Her aim was intimated in her reports to Major Halsall at Whitehall and later exaggerated to the point of burlesque in a fictionalized treatment of the whole episode which was posthumously printed in the 1698 edition of the 'Life'. In the latter, Scot is recognizable as the thirty-two-year-old Vander Albert, 'who before the War, in her Husband's time, had been in love with her in England, and on which she grounded the Success of her Negotiations...'. A comparison of the 1698 'Life' with Aphra's 1666 letters reveals close correspondences between the two. The fictional Vander Albert,

as soon as he knew of her Arrival at Antwerp...made a short Voyage to meet her, with all the Love his Nature was capable of...and after a Repetition of all his former Professions for his Service, press'd her extreamly to let him by some signal means give undeniable Proofs of the Vehemence and Sincerity of his Passion; for which he would ask no Reward, till he had by long and faithful Services convinc'd her that he deserv'd it.[30]

In her initial report to Halsall, Aphra admitted she had found Scot 'very shy' but later he became 'extremely willing'...'no thing being more seemingly passionate...then himself...he will perish he says or do me som service...'. Scot undoubtedly exaggerated the pose of love-besotted servant in order to gain Aphra's trust. Indeed his behaviour suggests that he may have been playing a role altogether.[31]

Aphra gave Halsall a perspicacious sketch of Scot's character: '...he has wit enough & is cuning enough & knows as well how to fflatter as any man...'. But it never occurred to Aphra that she herself might prove the object of Scot's wiles. Although she had been warned by more experienced English agents to judge Scot by his deeds, she accepted him at face value: '...he expresses him self very hansomly: & I beleeve him in all things'...'he will trust no body but me'...'he scruples not to communicate all things to me...'. Occasionally there is a glimpse of Scot's own romantic rhetoric: '...though I can deny ASTREA nothing: I would have HER not yet mention his name...yet I put all in to yr hands & discretion'.[32]

Aphra's credulity arose not from feminine vanity but from an overwhelming desire to succeed in her mission. 'I am very confident that no person in the world could have drawne him to a resolution of yt kind, besides my self', she told Arlington, forgetting Scot's overtures before her arrival. Having 'converted' Scot, she had a vested interest in her protégé and was afraid he might backslide if not rewarded: 'he will grow Cold if you do not Conferme a little of all I had in charge to promise him'.[33]

Aphra found herself trapped between two adversaries, for Major Halsall took a different view of Scot's motives. A reply by Scot suggests that Halsall had accused Scot of being 'suspicious' and having 'scruples'.[34] Halsall's neglect of the affair was so extreme that Aphra could not even persuade him to reply to her dispatches enclosing Scot's intelligence. She herself wrote rambling, emotional letters by every post. Although her reports display a keen intelligence, they are full of youthful errors not found in later examples of her autograph. Her garrulity was to serve her well in her career as a Grub-street writer, but it must have exasperated Halsall's clerks, who had to make précis of her dispatches.

Meanwhile Aphra was running into debt, thanks to her lavish generosity to Scot. As she explained to her employers, 'ye stats not paying him he is fforced all ye time he stays from Holand to be on my charge...'. During the Second Dutch War, crown agents were more likely to lose money than earn it, as Scot already knew, and Aphra soon found out: 'his Majtys friends heare do all complaine upon the slenderness of theire rewards...'. But Aphra viewed the promised reward to Scot as a debt of honour. A month after her arrival she had pawned her rings in order to pay him. Her debts finally precipitated an open quarrel with her employers. In default of any answer from Halsall, she began appealing to Thomas Killigrew, 'because twas from you as well as any I receavd my buseness...'.[35] To Killigrew Aphra sent a certain 'Mr. Piers' to fetch an additional £50 requested for expenses. Apparently dissatisfaction with Aphra's naiveté had been growing at Whitehall, for Killigrew seized upon the pretext that Piers was too 'mean' a fellow for the errand and berated Aphra's entire conduct of affairs. Killigrew also told everyone at Court about her 'ill management'. A glimpse of Aphra's relationship with her mother appears in Aphra's defensive reply to Killigrew, in which she explained that she had no one to send aside from Piers

> ...except Sir Thomas...my mother was not so ffitt being a woman: & posibly I should be loath to have her have it, for another reason...

For Aphra the worst blow was the news that she had suffered in the King's opinion: 'they tell me his Majty is displeased that I have imployd so base a ffellow...'. Her postscript dramatically reiterated her concern:

> for christ his sake Sr let me receave no Ill opinion from his Maj:ty who would give my poore life to serve him in never so little a degree...[36]

Meanwhile Scot's intelligence was improving but it was too
late to win the confidence of Whitehall. On 12/22 September
1666, Scot gave an early account of the Dutch plan to sail up the
Thames:

> their is one thomas woodman formerly a Capt...for the
> parlimt...hee undertakes to sincke shipps, and block upp the river of
> thames, to hinder trade and soe make the people muteny...[37]

Hallsall's clerk noted the information, but nothing was done.
Most likely its significance was also lost on Aphra at the time.
But years after Scot's forewarning had been proved correct,
Aphra took irate satisfaction in the knowledge that she had
warned Whitehall. Her resentful recollection mixed together the
Thames plot, insinuations of Arlington's treasonable connexion
with the Dutch, and the mortifying incident of Mr. Piers:

> The latter end of the year 1666...Albert informs her, that Cornelius
> de Wit,...had with de Ruyter propos'd to the States, to sail up the
> River of Thames, and destroy the English Ships in their
> Harbours...you may depend on it, my charming Astrea...we have
> that good correspondence with some Ministers about the King,
> that...we look on it as a Thing of neither Danger nor Difficulty....
>
> But all the particular Circumstances she gave, nor the consequence of
> it...could gain Credit enough to her Intelligence, to make any
> tolerable Preparations against it: And all the Encouragement she met
> with, was to be laugh'd at by the Minister she wrote to; and her
> Letter shew'd, by Way of Contempt, to some who ought not to
> have been let into the Secret...[38]

Aphra probably continued to send dispatches throughout
October. Finally her finances were so desperate that she appealed
directly to Lord Arlington. Forcefully listing her grievances, she
concluded with a reproach to his intelligence staff:

> ...I promis'd him all wt I had in charge to do: wch because he saw no
> effects off: he knew not what to think...I sent to yr Lp...not
> missing a post...to give him som incouragt but...I never could get
> that nor a poore answer of all I sent...in fine My Lord; you had bin
> servd more effectuall, had those promises been keep'd...[39]

Aphra also mentioned that Scot now lay in a debtor's prison, and she herself was in 'extreame want & nessesity', with debts in excess of £100.

Although Arlington's reply informed Aphra that Scot was not to expect any more money, she ventured another appeal 'for on 100 pd more, of wch my friend [Scot] shall have part', reminding Arlington,

> I neither petitioned ffor nor desird ye place I now have nor voyage I have taken…& I am all most killd wth ye griefe I have to be so Ill though[t] on…& if I com not now by this convoy I must stay this too months or more…

Whether Aphra received the £100 she had requested is not clear. Certainly Arlington did not send sufficient funds to pay her debts, for she later borrowed money to discharge them. It seems she missed her convoy as well.[40]

ii. *London* Milieu

Aphra's activities on her return to England can be inferred from the contents of a miscellany entitled *Covent Garden Drolery* [sic] which she published in 1672.[41] As its name implies, it drew most of its material from the theatre, containing prologues and epilogues from plays that were staged between 1667 and 1672. Apparently Aphra had begun haunting the Court and theatres and other fashionable amusements on her return to London in the spring of 1667. Whatever her Court connexions they enabled her to attend exclusive performances of amateur theatricals there.[42] Aphra was gathering acquaintances in both the aristocratic and theatrical worlds. At about this time she became friendly with the 'theatrical' Howards. After her return from Surinam she had donated a feathered costume 'infinitely admired by persons of quality' for Sir Robert Howard's play *The Indian Queen*.[43] By 1668 Aphra had met Dryden, the play's co-author and Sir Robert's brother-in-law. *Covent Garden Drolery* contains fourteen pieces by Dryden composed for performances staged between 1668 and 1672. Many of these received their first publication in Aphra's miscellany. She had also become acquainted with the actors and actresses of the Theatre Royal, who bestowed prologues, epilogues and poetry upon her.

Aphra herself had begun her play *The Young King* in Surinam some years before. A dedicatory preface addressed to 'Philaster' informs us that this tragicomedy was Aphra's 'youthful sally of my Pen, this first Essay of my Infant-Poetry...'. When she wrote this dedication, Aphra expected her play to be performed shortly. She had chosen Philaster for her patron 'since she knew she cou'd not appear upon the too-critical English stage without making choice of some Noble Patronage...'. Aphra's first work to be given a commercial première was not *The Young King*, however, but *The Forc'd Marriage*, which was staged in 1670.

When was the dedication to *The Young King* written? Although the identity of 'Philaster' is a mystery, the name itself was taken from the hero of Beaumont and Fletcher's popular play. *Philaster, or Love Lies a Bleeding* was frequently performed during the 1667–8 theatre season, a possible clue to the year in which Aphra wrote her preface, as it was her habit to introduce titles of current productions into her writing. An early date is also suggested by the diffident style of the preface, in contrast to Aphra's breezy impudence of the early 1670s.

Apparently Aphra had good reason for hawking her juvenilia in 1668: she was in desperate need of money. The year before, she had settled her debts in Antwerp by borrowing a lump sum from one Edward Butler. By the end of 1668 the debt amounted to £150, and Edward Butler was becoming importunate about the repayment of the loan. Aphra had been put off with promises from Killigrew and King Charles. She now addressed a petition to the King, explaining that 'after more then two yeares suffering' she was again applying to him, 'wch nothing but an Execution against her this next terme could have made her doe.' But the King displayed forgetful indifference; Aphra's next petition informed him that Edward Butler had given her a week's time to pay the £150, 'which Mr. Halsall and Mr. Killigrew knowes is soe justly due'. Still the royal bureaucracy failed to come to the rescue. The next document in the State Papers is an hysterical note from Aphra to Killigrew written the eve before she was to be taken to prison.

...I have cryed my self dead & could find in my hart to break through all & get to ye king & never rise till he weare pleased to pay this, but I am sicke & weake & unfitt for yt or a Prison...

The note concludes with characteristic defiance: 'Sr if I have not the money to night you must send me som thing to keepe me in Prison for I will not starve'.[44]

Aphra had promised to send her mother to the King with a 'pitition', and this is the next (and last) document in the series.

...after long waiting on Mr. Killigrew for ye 150 l due to Edward Butler...& being at last ordered to go to my Lord Arlington (whom he said had order from yor Matie to pay it) his Lo[rdshi]pp said, he had neither monies nor orders. And Mr. Butler being out of all patience, hath taken his Revenge in arresting yor Pet...

It was written in gaol, for it begged the King to order Mr. Butler his money 'yt I may not p[er]ish here'.[45]

The King's memory must have been jogged by this dramatic appeal.[46] Still, even with the debt paid, Aphra's circumstances could not have been affluent. If *The Young King* was offered to the theatre at this time, it may have been as a commercial venture.

In addition to a financial incentive, Aphra had an impressive example of feminine theatrical success to inspire her in 1668. Early in February, the leaders of Court society staged an amateur performance of Katharine Philips's translation of *Horace*. The production was literally dazzling: Lady Castlemaine wore jewels to the value of over £40,000 for the occasion, as Evelyn noted with disgust.[47] Both as a social and a theatrical event the performance must have made a deep impression on Aphra.

To add to its dignity, there was a valedictory air about *Horace*. Its authoress had died four years earlier, having translated all but the last act. Katharine Philips had established her poetic reputation during the 1650s and 1660s with two translations of French tragedies and a series of poems on friendship. During her lifetime her fame was enhanced by a cult of French classicism which she propagated among her noble acquaintance; it was sealed by her death of smallpox in 1664 at the age of 32.[48] Contemporaries thought her the foremost female poet of her age, a judgement recorded in Edward Phillips' *Theatrum*

Poetarum in 1674 and repeated in Langbaine's *Account of the English Dramatic Poets* a quarter of a century later. Aphra regarded Katharine Philips as her prime rival, although the style of their poetry, to say nothing of their lives, was radically different.

Horace enjoyed a fashionable success; Pepys saw the commercial version in 1669 and though he thought it a 'silly tragedy', the play had a reasonable run. Apparently its favourable reception implanted the idea of writing a play in more than one female mind. Elizabeth Cottington mentioned in a letter to her uncle Walter Aston that Herbert Aston had gone to see *Horace*, and this led to other theatrical gossip:

> Wee ar in expectation still of Mr. Draidens play. Ther is a bowld woman hath oferd one: my cosen Aston can give you a better account of her then I can. Some verses I have seen which ar not ill; that is commentation enouf: she will think so too, I believe, when it comes upon the stage. I shall tremble for the poor woman exposed among the critticks...[49]

The editor of the *Tixall Letters* assumed that this mysterious authoress was Aphra Behn, but a verse epistle found in *Tixall Poetry* strongly suggests that the 'bowld woman' was Mrs. Frances Boothby, a relation of the Aston family. Nothing is known of her except that her tragedy *Marcelia: or The Treacherous Friend* was performed at the Theatre Royal in 1669, thus making her the first Englishwoman to attempt a commercial production of an original play.

It was not a promising beginning. A verse letter directed to a niece of Walter Aston, entitled 'To my honored Cosen Mrs Somerset on the Unjust Censure past upon my Poore Marcelia' is the lament of the authoress on the failure of her play:

> But why this furious hurricane did rise
> Where by detracting zeale I'm made a sacrifice
> I cannot reach; for sure a woman's pen
> Is not (like comets) ominous to men...[50]

Neither Frances Boothby nor her 'Poore Marcelia' was heard of again. Another female playwright, Elizabeth Polwhele, wrote two plays intended for performance at about this time, but their fate

is even more obscure than that of Mrs. Boothby's *Marcelia*.[51]
Apparently the novelty of the playwright's sex was not in itself
sufficient to ensure success. It was not yet clear whether women
writing for the stage laboured under a disadvantage.

Aphra must have been working on her second play by this
time. *The Forc'd Marriage; or, The Jealous Bridegroom* was given
its première in September, 1670. Its prologue was cautious:

> ...To day one of their Party ventures out,
> Not with design to conquer, but to scout.
> Discourage but this first attempt, and then
> They'll hardly dare to sally out again...

The play itself, like Aphra's drama *The Young King*, is a pastoral
tragicomedy of a type fasionable in the 1660s. It shows the
influence of Fletcher and Shakespeare, Aphra's favourite 'ancient'
playwrights. A noteworthy feature is the violence of its 'forced
marriage' plot, a combination of *Othello* and *The Winter's Tale*.
Alcippus strangles his unwilling bride Erminia in a fit of jealousy.
When she later reappears, unaccountably alive, the marriage is
annulled, and the two couples rearrange themselves according to
true preference. Aphra was attracted to old-fashioned jealousy
and forced-marriage tragedies, but she infused a modern spirit
into these works by granting her heroines divorces instead of
letting them die of grief, murder or suicide.

Although it was not crafted with the competence of Aphra's
later manner, *The Forc'd Marriage* was a promising first effort.
The prompter John Downes recalled that it was 'a good play and
lasted six days'.[52] Success must have been gratifying to Aphra in
financial terms. She would have earned the playhouse receipts for
the third day, and something for the printed version, which
appeared in 1671. Aphra forbore a dedication: the title page
carried the epigraph 'Va mons enfant, prends ta fortune'. The
motto and the lack of a noble dedication imply that she was
determined to be independent and was now buoyantly optimistic
about it.

Aphra's play was also mentioned by Downes as the occasion of
Thomas Otway's sole acting stint. Another playwright involved
in the première of *The Forc'd Marriage* was Edward Ravenscraft,
who seems to have written its prologue. He was to become a

successful writer of farces; at this time he was a young lawyer with literary inclinations. Aphra had already befriended a number of the men who were to become the most prominent playwrights and critics of the 1670s and 1680s. Her acquaintance with Dryden has been mentioned. She may have met Wycherley at about this time, as he is represented by a lyric in *Covent Garden Drolery*. Rochester was another acquaintance. In a poem written after his death, Aphra mentioned his early encouragement of her poetic career:

> With the same wonted Grace my Muse it prais'd
> With the same Goodness did my Faults Correct;
> And Careful of the Fame himself first rais'd,
> Obligingly it School'd my loose Neglect...[53]

Aphra's ability to form professional friendships with men was to be a key asset in promoting her success as a commercial playwright. The good will of influential amateurs was crucial during the initial stages of a theatrical career. Self-proclaimed critics like Rochester and other Court wits held enormous sway over popular opinion when a play was premièred. Their verdict deflated Edward Howard's literary pretensions and ensured that Wycherley's *Plain Dealer* was acclaimed a success when no one knew what to think of it.[54] The recommendation of an established playwright or a noble amateur might be necessary before a manuscript was read by a theatrical company in the first place.

The friendships Aphra formed during these years were not the product of foresight or self-interest, but the result of her irrepressibly sociable nature. A large measure of innocent flirtatiousness aided her initial entrée into literary society. 'The Trial of the Poets for the Bays', a satire written years later, hints at the double allure of Aphra's talent and feminine charm when she first appeared upon the literary scene.

> The poetess Aphra next show'd her sweet face
> And swore by her poetry and her black ace
> The laurel by a double right was her own
> For the plays she had writ and the conquests she'd won...[55]

Many of Aphra's earliest poems are of an occasional nature, and they help form a picture of her private life during the late 1660s and 1670s. A poem entitled 'Our Cabal' (in joking reference to the King's Privy Councillors) offers verse portraits of nine young men and four young women who belonged to Aphra's inner circle.[56] Unfortunately we cannot be certain who these bosom companions were, because their identities are indicated only by initial letters and pastoral sobriquets like 'Amyntas', 'Lycidas', and so on.

The latter practice, which Aphra adopted for her poetry and intimate correspondence, was fashionable among upper-class youth during the Interregnum and Restoration. Women were especially fond of the affectation: Katharine Philips renamed herself and all her epistolary acquaintance, a practice which henceforth became *de rigueur* for aspiring poetesses. Aside from sounding romantic to a generation enamoured of Sidney and Spenser, these pastoral nicknames helped to conceal flirtations from the gossiping world.

Nevertheless, we can tentatively attach names to a few of the portraits in 'Our Cabal'. 'Mr. Je.B.' is apparently Jeffrey Boys, a young Gray's Inn lawyer whose friendly intimacy with Aphra is revealed by references to her found in a diary he kept in 1671.[57] 'Mr. N.R.V.' or 'Philocles' is probably Nathaniel Reymes Vernatti, a friend of Jeffrey Boys who succumbed to marriage in 1673. 'Mr. J.H.' or 'Lycidas' has been assumed to be John Hoyle, another Gray's Inn lawyer. Like Jeffrey Boys, he was a younger brother of an established gentry family. At least one female friend can be identified from another work. This was Carola Harsnett, daughter of Sir Roger Harsnett; Aphra addressed a verse epistle to her some time before Carola (aged eighteen) married Sir Samuel Morland in 1670.[58] If Aphra's own social background was like that of her companions, then she was of minor gentry stock just as the author of the 1696 'Life' claimed.

Even this small sample of Aphra's male friends contains a preponderance of lawyers. There were many others, like her fellow-playwrights Edward Ravenscraft and Thomas D'Urfey, and her friend James Wright, a theatre enthusiast who contributed lyrics to her miscellanies and plays. Even in Aphra's later years, handsome young lawyers were added to her coterie. This predilection for the legal profession is easy to explain: those who frequented the Inns of Court were the most eligible men-about-town of the gentry. More sophisticated than college students, they had the leisure and the education to ape the habits of the Court wits. The phrase 'Gray's Inn Wit' was proverbial as early as 1673, when Rochester ridiculed one of the species in a satire. Later in the century, the group was described by James Wright:

> ...the younger sparks of the Inns of Court...adorn all their studies with the poets, and fill their heads with Lampoons, Songs, and Burlesque...instead of Cook upon Littleton...Assignations Billet-deux etc. fill up their tablets....[59]

Young barristers shared a number of interests with fashionable young women like Aphra. Her friend Jeffrey Boys displayed the same enthusiasms, including a fondness for French romances and plays and a taste for music.[60] Although not a regular theatre-goer like Aphra, Jeffrey did see her play *The Forc'd Marriage*. During the spring and summer months, Jeffrey's diary chronicled a succession of holiday excursions like that commemorated by Aphra's poem 'Our Cabal'. He was learning to dance, too, like Aphra's hero Truman in her anonymous play *Woman Turn'd Bully* [1675]. Both Jeffrey and Aphra were habitués of the gala holiday entertainments at the Inns of Court which included masques and dancing. These dances and holiday outings were one sign of the permissive social life enjoyed by Restoration youth. Their romantic possibilities are suggested by one of Aphra's early poems which relates how she became acquainted with 'Mr. J.H.':

> ...in the taking forth to Dance,
> The Lovely Swain became my Chance.
> To whom much Passion he did Vow,
> And much his Eyes and Sighs did show
> And both imploy'd with so much Art
> I strove in vain to guard my Heart...[61]

Although called 'Amyntas' in this and other poems, 'Mr. J.H.' is almost certainly John Hoyle, the same young man referred to as 'Lycidas' in 'Our Cabal' as well as in eight posthumously printed letters written by Aphra. The initials alone do not warrant the inference, since Aphra knew at least half-a-dozen men who could satisfy this criterion, from the Hon. James

Howard to the dishonourable Joseph Haines. Nor can we put uncritical trust in contemporary gossip which insisted on an intimate connexion between Aphra and Hoyle.[62] But gossip is corroborated by the fact that Aphra described both 'Mr. J.H.—Amyntas' and 'Mr. J.H.—Lysidas' as bisexual, a propensity which can be documented in the life of John Hoyle. Hoyle followed the conventional younger son's career of Cambridge and the Inns of Court, becoming a 'learned advocate' of the Inner Temple. The posthumous catalogue of his library reveals a man of eclectic taste, including everything from *The Practice of Piety* to *Le Putanisme d'Amsterdame avec figures*. Toward the latter part of his life Hoyle was indiscreet about his sexual preferences. Tried for buggery with a poulterer in 1687, he was let off with an *Ignoramus*, evoking satirical comparison with the *Ignoramus* verdict bestowed upon Shaftesbury. For, among Hoyle's defects—'an Atheist, a Sodomite professed, a corrupter of youth, & a Blasphemer of Christ' as Bulstrode catalogued them—Hoyle was an 'Old Oliverian' like Aphra's former suitor William Scot.[63]

When Aphra first met him, Hoyle was equitable about his sexual preferences. Although he left behind him a long trail of broken hearts, his behaviour only increased his attraction for Aphra and her friends, who 'whilst his falsehood we wou'd blame...wouds't commend and praise the same'. His dual sexual allegiance, 'too amorous for a swain to a swain', was noted dispassionately by Aphra. In 'To Amintas. Upon reading the Lives of some of the Romans' Aphra drew on her knowledge of Plutarch to imagine how Amyntas might have changed the course of ancient history. Sophonisba, Massanissa, Cleopatra, Lucretia, even Sextus and Caesar would have fallen in love with him, 'for neither sex can here thy fetters shun'.[64] The portrait which emerges is that of an arrogant and tantalizingly attractive young man.

> ...*Lysidas*, that haughty Swain
> With many Beauties in a Train,
> All sighing for the Swain, whilst he
> Barely returns Civility...

Aphra's involvement with Hoyle can be speculatively traced in a succession of poems about 'Mr. J.H.' which chronicle a typical Restoration flirtation. They first describe his unremitting pursuit, while Aphra feigns coldness. Later, the poems celebrate their mutual love and Aphra's triumph over her rivals. Finally, they reveal his desertion of her for another conquest.[65] Aphra's posthumously printed letters to 'Lycidas', while they conform to the outlines suggested by the poems, disclose a more complicated relationship.

When first published in 1696 at the end of the posthumous *Histories and Novels*, these eight 'Love-Letters to a Gentleman' were alleged to have been 'printed from the Original Letters'.[66] While there is no reason to trust the word of the publisher, Sam Briscoe, the letters do display internal evidence of Aphra's authorship. Not only are they in her distinctive style throughout; they contain favourite phrases which crop up elsewhere in her works.[67] Nor is it likely that Aphra wrote them as fiction. The quotidian details, the odd gaps and unexplained allusions, indicate that these were genuine notes sent to an intimate friend.

Unfortunately the letters contain no useful clues as to when they were written. The setting is London, where Aphra met with her friends in the evenings. She emerges as a social butterfly, living up to her nickname as the adored and sought-after Astrea. Indeed life copies art in Letter I, for Aphra has 'banished' Lycidas but now revokes her decree: 'The Date of Banishment is already out, and I could have wished you had been so good-natur'd as to have disobeyed me'. Yet the two continue to quarrel in subsequent letters just like the adolescent characters of *L'Astrée*. The cause of this childish pique is soon apparent. Aphra is fond of flirtation and Lycidas is jealous. Her defensive replies reveal that he continually reproves her for her flighty behaviour. To vindicate herself, Aphra has been obliged to make a 'Resolution...of seeing no Man till I saw your face again'. In the next letter Aphra boasts, 'I have been very good ever since I saw thee, and have been a writing, and have seen no Face of Man, or other Body, save my own People'. This was hardly an example of virtue, for she had seen Lycidas that same evening.

We next learn that Lycidas has drawn up a lawyer-like code to regulate their relations. Aphra begins Letter VI: 'Since you, my dearest Lycidas, have prescrib'd me Laws and Rules, how I shall behave myself to please and gain you, and that one of these is not

Lying or dissembling...'. Later she comments, 'Your articles I have read over, and do not like them; you have broke one, even before you have sworn or seal'd'em; that is, they are wrote with reserve'. That Aphra resented these limits upon her freedom is suggested by a strikingly similar passage in the fictional *Amours of Philander and Silvia*, probably written years later.

> ...Philander having reduced Silvia to the very brink of Despair, and finding by her Passionate Importunity, that he could make his Peace with her on any term of Advantage to himself: resolved to draw such Articles of Agreement, as should wholly subdue her to him...the conditions were, that...she should give herself entirely to his possession, and quit the very Conversation of all those he had but an Apprehension would disturb his Repose...so that she bends like a slave for a little empire over him; and to purchase the Vanity of retaining him, suffers herself to be absolutely undone.[68]

At this stage we find her chafing at the bit. She warns Lycidas she 'would fain be us'd well; if not, I will march off'.

The proviso against 'lying and dissembling' provokes an interesting defence from Aphra: 'you need not have caution'd me, who so naturally hate those little Arts of my Sex...'. Aphra did resent one important aspect of conventional female behaviour: the obligation to conceal her feelings. In these letters she shows herself well aware of her propensities. 'Nor dare I...tell all the little Secrets of my Soul; why I write them, I can give no account; tis but fooling myself, perhaps, into an Undoing'. We can trace the progress of mutual affection in these notes, from 'complaisance' through friendship, esteem, hypothetical love and finally, passionate protestations of eternal love. At each stage, Aphra confesses more of her true feelings than a modest young woman was supposed to do, provoking repeated 'censures' and 'wise reproofs' from Lycidas. The 'friendly smile or kiss' which she bestowed upon her acquaintances was a manifestation of the same propensities. For Aphra, to feel an emotion was to express it directly.

But Lycidas was a 'scrupulous' young man who harboured old-fashioned expectations about feminine behaviour. He thought her exaggerated professions insincere. In Letter VII she writes, 'Tho' you think it Use...I find my heart swell with Disdain at this minute, for my being ready to make Asseverations of the contrary, and to assure you I do not, nor never did love, or talk at the rate I do to you since I was born'. Apparently echoing his complaints, she continues, 'Why, my lovely Dear, should I flatter you? Or, why make more Words of my tenderness, than another Woman, that loves as well, would do, as you once said?' Although their relations appear to have been free of physical intimacy, Lycidas is suspicious of her exuberant affection, even when it is directed at him. Letter VI exclaims,

> ...for God's Sake, do not misinterpret my Excess of Fondness; and if I forget myself, let the Check you give be sufficient to make me desist. Believe me...'tis more out of humour and Jest, than any inclination on my Side; for I could sit eternally with you, without that Part of Disturbance: Fear me not, for you are (from that) as safe as in Heaven itself.

Ultimately these passionate displays caused Lycidas to lose interest. He had already shown signs of being a trophy-hunter. In Letter IV: 'You would not be in Love for all the World, yet wish I were so...why should you believe that necessary for me, that will be so very incommode for you?' The last letter (VIII) details his neglect:

> ...witness your passing by the End of the Street where I live, and squandring away your time at any Coffee-house, rather than allow me what you know in your Soul is the greatest Blessing of my Life...I died, I fainted, and panted for an Hour of what you lavish'd out, regardless of me, and without so much as thinking of me!...

Apparently Lycidas' waning interest induced Aphra to stop writing. In Letter VIII we find him 'Taking it unkindly' that she has not written. Aphra points to his neglect, then adds, 'yet if I...behave myself rudely, as I have done, you say, these two or three Days—then, Oh Astrea! where is your Profession? Your Love so boasted?...' Evidently the least sign from him has destroyed all her resolves.

> ...I cannot disobey you, because I would not, tho 'twere better much for both I had been forever silent...Whatever Resolutions I make in the Absence of my Lovely Friend, one single Sight turns me all Woman, and all his...

She concludes her letter by asking to see him 'as soon as possible (you say Thursday)...'. Like her character Silvia, whose unstable temperament was delineated by Aphra in *The Amours of Philander and Silvia*, Aphra here seems incapable of either concealing or mastering her emotions.

iii. Career as a Playwright

Among the incidental details disclosed by 'Love-Letters to a Gentleman' is the fact that Aphra was spending her time writing. Judging from the dates of composition of her first five plays, we can infer that she had already established a working routine early in the 1670s. She was to become one of the most prolific of Restoration authors; her plays were issued at an average rate of one a year for twenty years.[69] From the start Aphra exploited her ability to write rapidly. *The Forc'd Marriage* was followed five months later by *The Amorous Prince*. In style and atmosphere it is similar to her two previous efforts. An unprinted pastoral entitled *The Wavering Nymph* (adapted from Randolph's *Amyntas, or the Impossible Dowry*) should be assigned to this period as well.

This romantic vein was terminated by the Duke of Buckingham's parody, *The Rehearsal*, in December 1671. If Buckingham's satire did not cause the demise of the old-fashioned romantic tragicomedy, it warned Aphra that the genre was no longer in vogue. Indeed *The Amorous Prince* was one of the targets singled out for attack in *The Rehearsal*, probably because of Aphra's association with the Dryden-Howard coterie. In any case, Aphra wrote no more Arcadian plays. By 1672 she was at work on two intrigue comedies. She printed *Covent Garden Drolery* [sic] the same year, showing herself to be an acute judge of literary trends. This was one among a flood of 'drolleries' that appeared in 1671 and the years immediately following. But it was more successful than most of these, as can be inferred from its re-issue within the year, as well as an envious comment it provoked from the editor of the *Bristol Drollery* (1674). Aside from the theatrical material already mentioned, *Covent Garden Drolery* contains light poems and songs, including at least four pieces by Aphra herself. One of these lyrics, 'I led my Silvia to a grove', was transformed the following year into 'Amyntas led me to a grove' for its inclusion in Aphra's new play *The Dutch Lover*. The song's theme of sexual seduction was to occupy Aphra in a diversity of forms:

> ...A many Kisses he did give
> And I return'd the same
> Which made me willing to receive
> That which I dare not name....

The song attained immediate and lasting popularity, but the play was not so lucky. Based on a pseudo-Spanish novel entitled 'The History of Don Fenise', its plot awkwardly combined a brother-sister incest motif with a sub-plot involving a farcical 'Dutch Lover', whose discomfiture was meant to gratify anti-Dutch feeling aroused by the Third Dutch War. Everything went wrong with the production, as Aphra indignantly related in her preface to the printed version. The play was 'Hugely injur'd in the acting', the costumes were a disappointment, and even the epilogue promised by a friend failed to materialize.

More significant are the indications of opposition towards Aphra because of her sex, as her preface complained:

> ...that day 'twas Acted first, there comes me into the Pit, a long, lither, phlegmatick, white, ill-favour'd wretched Fop.... This thing...opening that which serves it for a mouth, out issued such a noise as this to those that sate about it, that they were to expect a woful Play, God damn him, for it was a womans.

But in her five-page prefatory vindication, Aphra addressed only half a sentence to the debate on women, 'waving the examination why women having equal education with men, were not as capable of knowledge of whatsoever sort as they...'. Instead of defending female abilities, she chose to deflate the value of dramatic art. Plays were 'intended for the exercising of men's passions not their understandings', and it was ridiculous to expect that they could reform men's manners or morals:

> ...for that I may appeal to general experiment, if those who are the most assiduous disciples of the Stage, do not make the fondest and lewdest Crew about this town...

The true function of the theatre as Aphra defined it was simple entertainment. Hence women could write as well as men, for plays had 'no room for that which is men's great advantage over women, that is Learning'. Aphra offered the example of Shakespeare, 'who was not guilty of much more of this than often falls to women's share'. As for the modern poets,

> except our most unimitable Laureat, I dare to say I know of none that write at such a formidable rate, but that a woman may well hope to reach their greatest hights.

Thus in a bold stroke Aphra dismissed the entire neo-classical tradition which so dominated the imagination of her literary peers.[70] A more specific target is discernible, the neo-Jonsonians with their 'Musty rules of Unity, and God knows what else besides', which 'if they meant anything, they are enough intelligible, and as practible by a woman...'.

We can recognize in this full-scale war on her detractors Aphra's characteristic defiance in response to failure. Nevertheless, the fiasco of *The Dutch Lover* must have been mortifying. Aphra's consolatory poem to Edward Howard on the failure of his play *The New Utopia* vividly depicts the 'whistle and rude hiss' of a hostile audience. It could not have been easy to take the advice she had offered him:

> Consider and consult your wit
> Despise those ills you must indure
> And raise your scorne as great as it
> Be confident and then secure
>   And let your rich-fraught pen
>   Adventure out again...[71]

In fact her own career was temporarily balked. During 1672 a comedy entitled *The Woman Turn'd Bully* was at least half-way finished, yet it was not staged until 1675.[72] Moreover, when *The Woman Turn'd Bully* did appear, it was brought out anonymously. The plot and its Inns of Court setting came from an obscure comedy, *Ram Alley or Merry Tricks*. But Aphra made the play her own, particularly in her treatment of the heroine Betty Goodfield, 'an aery young lady...come up to London...in mans apparel; she personates a town gallant and discourses out of plays'. Easily recognizable as the young Aphra Behn, Betty Goodfield is an example of Aphra's favourite female character: the bold, witty young woman who disguises herself and runs wild, fighting duels, making assignations, and occasionally proposing marriage. It hardly mattered what, so long as her behaviour was out of harmony with the code of female respectability.[73]

The Woman Turn'd Bully made little stir.[74] But Aphra had protected herself through anonymity, and she was now back in her stride. In the next two years she produced five plays. Two were anonymous adaptations, but these underline her determination to make a living from the theatre. Heroic ranting tragedy was fashionable during the mid-1670s, and Aphra tried her hand at it with *Abdelazar, or the Moor's Revenge* (1676), whose plot was borrowed from the anonymous *Lust's Dominion*. *Abdelazar* received its première just after that of Otway's tragedy *Don Carlos*, an immense success which temporarily made his fortune.[75] Aphra had probably seen her friend's manuscript beforehand; she tried to imitate it, even copying Otway's device of using a little girl to speak the epilogue.

Contemporaries noticed that this was not the only instance of Aphra's borrowing, and like nearly all her subsequent plays, *Abdelazar* was branded with the charge of plagiarism. The accusation was well-founded, as Aphra freely admitted in a letter to a friend.

> In your last, you inform'd me, that the World treated me as a Plagiery, and, I must confess, not with Injustice...I have sent you the Garden from whence I gather'd, and I hope you will not think me vain, if I say, I have weeded and improv'd it.[76]

To the world at large Aphra sometimes denied her thefts. Alternatively, she complained that her rivals were equally guilty but failed to get caught, being 'not more expert in stealing than in the Art of Concealing'. Langbaine's numerous examples of unacknowledged borrowings support Aphra's charge that no Restoration dramatist was free of the taint.[77] Yet she was more shameless than most, at various times trying every kind of plagiarism including the line for line copying of dialogue. Her financial exigencies did not allow her the luxury of crafting a few original plays. Instead she constructed competent ones as quickly as the Duke's House could take them. Having the advantage of wide reading, she lacked the imagination to produce a constant stream of original plots. Hence she functioned more like an editor than a playwright, fitting obscure English and continental sources to Restoration taste. In this, her career resembled that of her friend Edward Ravenscraft, that 'politick plagiary' as Langbaine called him. The chief difference between the two was that Ravenscraft always specialized in farce, whereas Aphra sank into it by degrees.

In conformity with current taste, Aphra's work became slightly bawdier with each successive production. In *The Town-Fopp* (1676) she converted the depressing plot of Wilkins' *Miseries of Enforced Marriage* into a lively comedy. Through the legally improbable expedient of allowing the 'enforced' couple a divorce,[78] the deserted heroine was able to marry her lover instead of expiring from grief as in Wilkins' original. Although the play contains racy dialogue and Hogarthian scenes involving London prostitutes, it is firmly grounded in a moral framework. In the midst of his debaucheries the hero Bellmour exclaims,

> Gods! what an odious thing meer Coupling is!
> A thing which every sensual Animal
> Can do as well as we...[79]

Soon after *The Town-Fopp*, Aphra produced anonymous adaptations of two Caroline comedies. Brome's *Mad Couple Well Matched* became *The Debauchee* (1677), and Shirley's revision of Middleton's *No Wit, No Help Like a Woman* appeared as *The Counterfeit Bridegroom* (1677). Scenes were pruned and the dialogue was translated into Restoration idiom: 'drab' became 'whore'. Aside from adding a bawdy drinking scene to each play, Aphra did not exercise her originality in these hasty pieces produced for pecuniary motives.

Aphra's next adaptation was a more creative effort. Her source for *The Rover* (1677) was the play *Thomaso*, an interminable semi-autobiographical fantasy by Thomas Killigrew, her old friend and employer. Although Aphra retained Killigrew's plot, his characters, and many of his best lines, the play was transformed from a closet piece into a fast-paced comedy. Aphra

added one major character, impudent Hellena, an improved
version of Betty Goodfield of *The Woman Turn'd Bully*. Like
most Behn heroines, Hellena masquerades in disguise, taking
advantage of her incognito to propose marriage to Willmore
'rather than put your Modesty to the blush, by asking me....'.
Thus she puts into practice the philosophy she has just
expounded to her older sister:

> *Florinda*...who will like thee well enough to have thee, that hears
> what a mad Wench thou art?
> *Hellena* Like me! I don't intend every he that likes me shall have me,
> but he that I like...[80]

Although Hellena is an original creation infused with Aphra's
own spirit, the other characters were left as Killigrew created
them, notably Thomaso, now called Willmore—'The Rover'.
Willmore is a stud bull in human form, with the habit of
assaulting anything in petticoats. 'Thou know'st there's but one
way for a Woman to oblige me', he explains. His amorous
solicitations are expressed in alimentary analogies: 'Oh, I long to
come first to the Banquet of Love! and such a swinging Appetite
I bring'.[81]

The Rover was brought on stage anonymously. To avoid
discovery, Aphra resorted to her old ploy of concealing her sex
behind the pronoun 'he' in the prologue. If it was her intention
to fool the misogynist faction among the critics, she
accomplished her aim, for *The Rover* was a hit. Its dashing
portrayal of the exiled royalists made it a favourite of the King
and the Duke of York, and the latter requested a sequel, which
was dedicated to him in 1681. Besides being presented at Court,
The Rover became a permanent repertory piece, with
performances well into the eighteenth century.

Despite its popularity, the play appeared without a name on
the title page when it was first printed. It has been suggested that
Aphra concealed her identity because she had 'no desire to impair
the success of her play with the imputation of a woman's
authorship'.[82] But *The Rover* had long since established itself.
Why did Aphra persist in anonymity?

A postscript to the first issue suggests one reason. It informs
readers that *The Rover* had been delayed in the press because of a

report about town that it was merely 'Thomaso alter'd...which made the Booksellers fear some trouble from the Proprietor of that Admirable Play...'. There are also hints that Aphra was ashamed of the play. Willmore was the only amoral hero she created. Unlike the most Epicurean of her other male leads, he lacks the smallest tincture of sentiment to justify his animal passions.

Whatever Aphra's true feelings about *The Rover*, she overcame her scruples during the middle of the press run, adding her name to the title page of the third issue. At the same time a feminist slant was added to the postscript directed at the critics 'who are naturally so kind to any that pretend to usurp their Dominion, *especially of our sex*'.

The contemptuous prologue to Aphra's next play, *Sir Patient Fancy*, summarized the lessons she had gleaned from the popularity of *The Rover*:

> We write not Now, as th'Ancient Poets writ,
> For your Applause of Nature, Sense and Wit;
> But, like good Tradesmen, what's in fashion vent,
> And Cozen you, to give ye all Content...
> Who at the vast Expence of Wit would treat,
> That might so cheaply please the Appetite?...
> And if this chance to please you, by that rule,
> He that writes Wit is much the greater Fool.

So much for her opinion of her recent triumph. The epilogue renewed hostilities mentioned in *The Rover's* postscript, with new jibes for the anti-feminist critics and neo-Jonsonians. It echoed Aphra's preface to *The Dutch Lover*, except that her defence of women now assumed an aggressive tone.

> I here, and there, o'erheard a Coxcomb cry,
> Ah, Rott it—'tis a Woman's Comedy...
> Why in this Age has Heaven allow'd you more
> And Women less of Wit than hertofore?
> We once were fam'd in Story, and could write
> Equal to men; cou'd Govern, nay, cou'd fight...

But Aphra had miscalculated the degree of licence allowable in the play itself, and ironically the same sex on whose behalf she had just launched her first forthright defence now pronounced her comedy unfit for feminine ears.

Aphra complained in her preface that her sex alone had provoked the accusation against her.

> I printed this Play with all the impatient haste one ought to do, who would be vindicated from the most unjust and silly aspersion, Woman could invent to cast on Woman; and which only my being a Woman has procured me: *That it was Baudy*, the least and most Excusable fault in the Men writers, to whose Plays they all crowd, as if they came to no other end than to hear what they condemn in this: *But from a Woman it was unnaturall...*

Was Aphra correct in claiming she was attacked for indelicacy solely because she was a woman? A glance at the reception given to bawdy plays written by her male peers suggests that this was not the case. Aphra's friend Ravenscraft, for example, was so taken to task by the ladies for his popular farce *The London Cuckolds* (1681) that he offered the chaste *Dame Dobson* as a 'Recantation Play'. Otway met with the same fate for his comedy *The Souldiers Fortune*: 'Says a Lady...Fogh! Oh Sherru! 'tis so filthy, so bawdy, no modest Woman ought to be seen at it; Let me dye, it has made me sick...'.[83]

It is possible that Aphra was vulnerable to greater censure for smaller lapses than those committed by men. Certainly her *personal* reputation was to suffer proportionately more because of her sex. But at this stage, the real problem was not her gender but her pecuniary exigencies, as she admitted in her preface:

> Nor does it's loss of Fame with the Ladies do it much hurt [i.e. in box-office receipts], though they ought to have had good Nature and justice enough to have attributed all its faults to the Authors unhappiness, who is forced to write for bread...and consequently ought to write to please...an Age which has given severall proofs it was by this way of writing to be obliged, though it is a way too cheap for men of wit...a way which even I despise as much below me...

Like all the 'trading poets', Aphra aimed for a full house. The success of *The Rover* had proven that the way to ensure a full house was to write bawdy farce. She might be attacked for literary whoredom as a result, but at least she would not starve.

Sir Patient Fancy provoked another group in the audience. The title character was meant to portray Sir Patience Ward, the ultra-Protestant Whig alderman soon to be elected Lord Mayor. Aphra did not carry the personal satire very far. But she did get in a few barbs, like the suggestion made by Sir Patient to 'accuse 'em for *French* papishes, that had a design to fire the City...'. The jibe was also a symptom that the political temperature had begun to rise long before Titus Oates made his allegations of a 'Popish Plot'.

iv. Politics and Grub Street

Both by sentiment and by interest, Aphra was aligned to the Tory faction in the ensuing struggle. She had been long associated with the Court: it was more than a decade since the naive young woman had written to Killigrew from Antwerp that she would give her life to serve the King. More recently, royal patronage for her plays had supplied material grounds for allegiance. But like other Tory poets Aphra remained quiet during the hysteria that characterized the first two years of the Popish Plot. Her initial reaction was annoyance at the disruption to town life, with its adverse effect on box-office revenues. In January 1679, a few months after Oates had made his accusations, the prologue to her play *The Feign'd Curtizans* complained,

> The devil take this cursed plotting Age,
> 'T has ruin'd all our Plots upon the Stage:
> Suspicions, New Elections, Jealousies,
> Fresh Informations, New discoveries
> Do so employ the busie fearful Town
> Our honest calling here is useless grown...

Aside from some veiled references to the Duke of York's forced exile to Flanders, Aphra left the field to the Whigs, who were busy exploiting the wave of anti-Catholic feeling. Elkanah Settle's *Pope Joan* (1679) was the most notorious success in this genre, but even Dryden temporarily succumbed with *The Spanish Friar* (early November 1680). Apparently this unexpected betrayal roused Aphra's fighting instinct, for a few weeks after the première of *The Spanish Friar* she entered the fray, railing at Dryden and Settle in her epilogue to *The Second Part of The Rover* (late November 1680). In the prologue Aphra elaborated on the Tories' favourite charge that the Whigs wished to 'play the old game over again' (i.e., the Civil War), a battle cry she was to repeat on every possible occasion. The same doctrine was elaborated in her dedication to the Duke of York, with a history of 'this again gathering faction'

> who make their needless and self-created fears, an occasion to Play the old Game o're again; whil'st the Politick self-interested and malitious few betray the unconsidering Rest, with the delicious sounds of Liberty and Publick Good; that lucky Cant which so few years since so miserably reduc'd all the Noble, Brave, and Honest, to the Obedience of the ill-gotten Power,...of the Rabble.

This passionate outburst inaugurated a decade of zealous Tory propaganda. Aphra's printed works adapted a full range of literary forms for the purpose. Prologues and epilogues offered a running commentary on current happenings. *The Roundheads* applied the lesson of past history, and *The City-Heiress* satirized current events. Scandalous chronicles threw discredit upon Whig leaders,[84] while Pindaric odes deified the royal family. Manuscript satires, squibs and songs were circulated. What has survived in print represents only a portion of the whole. In a mock 'recantation' forming a prologue to her farce *The False Count* (1681) Aphra summarized her activities:

> 'Twas long she did maintain the Royal Cause
> Argu'd, Disputed, rail'd with great Applause
> Writ Madrigals and Dogerel on the Times
> And charg'd you all with your Fore-fathers crimes...

These early 'Madrigals and Doggerel' were probably circulated anonymously in manuscript and are no longer identifiable as Aphra's work, although we do possess political satires and songs composed by her at a later period.

In part this frenetic activity was an expression of Aphra's habit of following the fashion. Her prologue to *The Second Part of The Rover* reported:

> Poets have caught too the Disease o'th'Age
> That pest, Of not being quiet when they're Well
> That restless Feaver, in the Brethren Zeal...

Aphra exulted in a good fight, especially if it entailed sticking her neck out like one of her 'bully' heroines. It was as much out of mischievous impudence as patriotic fervour that she reported what the Whigs were allegedly saying about her play *The Roundheads*: '*what, to name us...she deserves to be swing'd....*'.[85]

Aphra's satisfaction was doubtless enhanced by the rewards which the Court bestowed upon her for her propaganda efforts. How much she was paid is impossible to determine. A verse letter to Thomas Creech written in 1684 mentions a royal subsidy.

> From *Whitehall* Sir, as I was coming,
> His Sacred Majesty from Dunning
> Who oft in Debt is, truth to tell
> For Tory Farce, or Doggerell...[86]

By 1682 the playhouse audience was of Tory sympathies. It was now good business to indulge in polemics which a year or two before would have been dangerous.

The foregoing are only the most superficial aspects of Aphra's motivation; behind them lay a personal concern. There are strong hints that she had never abandoned Catholicism, but adhered to it secretly while conforming outwardly to the Established Church. Her hatred for those who tried to blame the Fire of London on the Catholics, her sympathetic portrayal of Catholic ritual in plays and stories, and her dogmatic support for James are tell-tale signs. Aphra confidently declared that the Plot was a Whig fabrication.[87] Most telling of all was her reaction to the trial of Viscount Stafford, whom she portrayed as a martyr comparable to Christ. To the Earl of Arundel, the only Howard peer who did not vote to convict his unpopular cousin, she wrote,

A thousand times I have wept for fear that Impudence and Malice wou'd...stain your Noble and ever-Loyal Family...and as often for joy, to see how undauntedly both the Illustrious Duke your Father, and your Self, stem'd the raging Torrent that threatned...May

Heaven and Earth bless you for your pious and resolute bravery of
Mind, and heroick Honesty, when you cry'd, *Not Guilty*...[88]

In the light of this secret bias, Aphra's outbursts throughout the
1680s become more comprehensible.

Aphra's earliest treatment of political themes appeared in her
comedy *The Roundheads, or The Good Old Cause* (c. December
1681). An adaptation of Tatham's *The Rump* (1660), *The
Roundheads* offered a graphic illustration of the Tories' equation
of civil war and Whig policies. The few changes introduced by
Aphra gave the play a peculiarly feminine twist. She added a 'love
interest' in the form of two Cavaliers who pursue the affections
of Lady Lambert and Lady Desborough. As a result, the drama
shifts its focus from the narrative of the last days of the
Interregnum to a farcical exposition of harem politics—'The dear
mystery of jilting' as Lady Lambert calls it.

> Kings are deposed, Kingdoms ruled...
> By Jilting all the Universe is fool'd...

Lady Lambert thus enjoyed a greater share in state affairs. But
Aphra portrayed her more negatively than Tatham had done. In
The Rump, Lady Lambert is proud but harmless; in *The
Roundheads* her Machiavellian ambitions have a sinister air.

In later works Aphra continued to portray feminine political
interference in a negative light. It may therefore seem odd that
she saw nothing unnatural in her own role as Tory advocate. In
part this could be rationalized because of the distinction between
the male realm of action and the female realm of speech. Aphra's
epilogue to *The Roundheads* invoked the proverb that 'Words
are women, deeds are men':

> For since I cannot fight, I will not fail,
> To exercise my Talent, that's to rail...

But this was only a token disclaimer. If anything, Aphra
exaggerated the effect of her propaganda, persuading herself it
was as important as those struggles being waged in the real world.
Her dedication prefixed to *The Roundheads* asserted

...'tis as easily seen at a new Play how the Royal Interest thrives, as at a City Election, how the *Good Old Cause* is carried on; as a Noble Peer lately said, *Tho the Tories have got the better of us at the Play, we carried it in the City by many Voyces, God be praysed!*

The preface jumbled together more Tory history and political theory, especially Aphra's *idée fixe* that the Whigs 'wou'd be at the same game their forefathers played'. Her lengthy dedications thus began to assume the features of a political tract. Because of her daring references to the Duke of Monmouth, they were almost as dangerous.

Aphra's second political comedy, *The City-Heiress* (1682) brought affairs up to date with a satire on Shaftesbury. By now this was a cliché in the theatre, and Aphra had little to add. *The City-Heiress* was a success, and Aphra dedicated the comedy to Henry Howard, Earl of Arundel, making one of her ironically prophetic remarks:

> ...no doubt on't, so long as the Royal Cause has such Patrons as your Lordship, such vigorous and noble Supporters, his Majesty will be great, secure and quiet...

Seven years later, as Duke of Norfolk, he was to take his place in the Privy Council of William III.

Meanwhile, the popular success of Aphra's political plays led her to infer that 'honesty is in fashion again'. In her preface to *The Roundheads* Aphra had confidently proclaimed, 'Now we may pray for the King and his Royal Brother, defend his Cause, and assert his Right, without the fear of a taste of the Old Sequestration call'd a *Fine*. . .'. But Aphra had been treading close to the line that separated loyalty from *scandalum magnatum*; in her next exploit she stepped over it.

In August 1682, an anonymous play entitled *Romulus and Hersilia* received its première at the Theatre Royal, with prologue and epilogue by Aphra Behn. The prologue offered the usual catalogue of charges against the Whigs. But the epilogue, spoken by Lady Slingsby in the character of Tarpeia, could be applied only to the Duke of Monmouth:

> ...of all Treasons, mine was most accurst;
> Rebelling 'gainst a King and Father first.
> A Sin, which Heav'n nor Man can e're forgive;

Nor could I Act it with the face to live...

A month before, Dryden and Lee's play *The Duke of Guise* had been prohibited from being performed because it vilified the Duke of Monmouth. Aphra was now taken into custody along with Lady Slingsby by warrant of the Lord Chamberlain. The author of *Juvenalis Redivivus* gloated:

> Sappho with her wondrous empty shew
> A Torie faith, yet shan't unpunished go...

Yet Aphra did wiggle out of custody. A comment in one of her dedications suggests that she was let off with a warning: 'I have only just escaped fleaing by the Rebels in order to starve more securely in my native Province of Poetry'.[89]

Nevertheless, the epilogue for *Romulus and Hersilia* was Aphra's last political piece to be presented on stage.[90] An event which had nothing to do with politics was now responsible for silencing nearly all the established playwrights over the next few years. This was the amalgamation of the King's and Duke's companies into the United Company, which began acting under Betterton's direction in November, 1682. Betterton's first aim was to retrench expenses by refraining from accepting new plays. In his preface to *The Treacherous Brother* (1690), George Powell recalled,

> The time was, upon the uniting of the two Theatres, that the reviveing of the old stock of Plays, so ingrost the study of the House, that the Poets lay dorment; and a New Play cou'd hardly get admittance, amongst the more precious pieces of Antiquity...

All the playwrights suffered from this ban. Aphra was luckier than most, since two of her plays completed before King Charles' death were presented in 1686 and 1687. Meanwhile, she lost not only her accustomed revenue but her credit as well. In a letter probably written in 1683, Aphra explained to her publisher Jacob Tonson,

> I have been wthout getting so long yt I am just on ye poynt of breaking, espesiall since a body has no creditt at ye Playhouse for money as we usd to have, fifty or 60 deepe, or more...[91]

Apparently the regular playwrights had been regarded as 'King's servants' like the theatre personnel, and were able to survive between windfalls from box-office receipts by running up a cushion of debt. Tom Brown opined that 'poets ought to be poor, and those that disdain the station, can have no true title to the honour'.[92] Evidence from the Restoration confirms his dictum. The poets' mode of life contributed to their plight, for they copied the leisured ideals of their patrons. Their notion of good fellowship consisted mainly of coffee-house gossip and 'drinking to engender wit', to which convivial pursuit Aphra was no stranger.

> Because it being cold, you know,
> We warm'd it with a Glass—or so...

As the actor John Bowman told Oldys, 'Mrs Behn was the first Person he ever knew or heard of who made the liquor called Milk Punch'.[93] An habitué of all the town amusements, Aphra was not the saving sort. Her tendencies to extravagance were an expression of generosity toward her friends rather than self-indulgence. Aphra was what is vulgarly termed an 'easy touch'. Thomas Wilkes related that when Otway was starving in a garret, a month before his death, 'He now had no resource left but to apply to Mrs. Behn for the loan of five pounds...which she generously advanced...'. Her generosity is underlined by the fact that Aphra herself asked Jacob Tonson to stand surety for a loan of six pounds a few months later.[94]

This corporate feeling among the poetic fraternity was established long before the adversity of the 1680s. For over a decade, Aphra and her friends had been in the habit of reading their manuscripts to each other before exposing a work to the public. The practice is mentioned in 1673, in the preface to *The Dutch Lover*. On one occasion, Aphra became annoyed with Otway for giving an insincere opinion of the manuscript of *Abdelazar*:

> ...that Mr. Otway shou'd say, my Sex wou'd not prevent my being pull'd to pieces by the Criticks, is something odd, since...he may very well remember when last I saw him, I receiv'd more than ordinary Encomiums on my *Abdelazar*.[95]

Supplying prologues and epilogues was another form of
cooperative exchange. Aphra's 'Letter to a brother of the pen in
tribulation' jokingly reproved a fellow poet for nursing a case of
pox when she 'wanted a prologue to a play'. Collaboration
sometimes went farther. Aphra was offered *Le Malade
Imaginaire*, 'translated by a gentleman infinitely to advantage',
which she turned into *Sir Patient Fancy*.[96]

During the 1680s cooperation reached its acme in a series of
joint literary projects. Aphra's publisher Jacob Tonson (better
known as Dryden's publisher and later as secretary of the Kit-Kat
club) coordinated the miscellanies and translations that were
churned out by the best talent of the age. In a letter from Aphra
to Tonson we can observe him composing differences among the
querulous writers in his charge, helping Aphra to some 'honour'
related to Dryden, and receiving instructions about printing her
first collection of poems. Tonson's shop, located at the corner of
Fleet Street and Chancery Lane, served as a general rendezvous
for Aphra and her friends. In a verse letter to Thomas Creech,
Aphra mentioned that she had meant to leave a note for him at
Tonson's.

> And Billet Deux in Pocket lay,
> To drop as Coach should Jolt that way...

A list of 'Lodgers and Inmates' of St. Bride's Parish drawn up the
winter of 1683–4 reveals that Aphra had lodgings in the house of
a 'Mr. Coggins' just around the corner from Tonson's shop, in
New Street. The neighbourhood was a bohemian section of
town, stocked with poets, actors and actresses, men-about-town
living in chambers at the Inns of Court, a multitude of
booksellers, and a tavern or coffee-house at almost every door.[97]

In this lively setting Tonson fostered a variety of literary
endeavours, the germ of the Grub-street activities of the next
century. Some projects were on a massive scale, like the new
translation of Plutarch's *Lives* edited by Dryden (1683) for which
Tonson herded together forty translators. The new edition of
Plutarch serves as a reminder of two facts. First, translation was
the primary resource of poets in adversity.

> Since Betterton of late so thrifty's grown

Revives old Plays, or wisely acts his own...
Those who with nine months toil had spoiled a Play
In hopes of eating at a full third day...
Have left stage-practice, chang'd their old vocations
Atoning for bad plays, with worse translations...[98]

Secondly, the classics were the works most in demand by the book-buying public of the 1680s. Here Aphra was at a disadvantage, for she knew neither Latin nor Greek.

Aphra felt the lack keenly apart from commercial considerations. Since childhood she had devoured the classical authors available in English or French. Plutarch's *Lives* and Ovid's works were favourites which she re-read often, judging from frequent references in her plays and poetry. When Thomas Creech's translation of *De Rerum Natura* of Lucretius appeared in 1682, Aphra addressed a tribute to the author with special reference to the disabilities of her sex:

'Till now I curst my Sex and Education,
And more the scanted Customs of the Nation:
Permitting not the Female Sex to tread
The Mighty Paths of Learned Heroes Dead...
    The Fulsom Gingle of the Times
Is all we are allow'd to Understand, or Hear....[99]

Such a display of resentment was rare for Aphra. The 'learned lady' was a ridiculous figure in Restoration England, and Aphra avoided the slightest appearance of ambition in that direction. Although she seems to have known some Latin tags, she quoted them in English when writing under her own name.[100] Sometimes she herself satirized female learning, using sections from *Les Femmes Savantes* for *Sir Patient Fancy*. Perhaps in compensation, there were insults directed at the 'vain young coxcombs' who came up to town from the universities and tried to impress her with their recently acquired pedantry.[101] Still, the tribute to Creech reveals a mixture of jealousy and longing:

...Thou by this Translation dost advance
Our Knowledge from the State of Ignorance
And Equallst Us to Man! Oh how shall We
Enough Adore, or Sacrifice enough to Thee!...

Of course Creech's translations did not make Aphra equal to
men with respect to the translating projects of the Restoration.
It is a measure of the acceptance Aphra had won among the
'trading poets' that they nevertheless invited her to join their
collective translations of Latin works. The first of these involving
Aphra, an edition of Ovid's *Heröides* edited by Dryden (1680),
boasted a list of contributors that reads like a roll call of the
literary 'gang'. Headed by Dryden and his patron Lord
Mulgrave, it included Otway, Settle, Tate, Flatman, Rhymer, Sir
Carr Scroope, and half-a-dozen poetasters. Aphra was assigned
the letter of the Nymph Oenone to Paris. Contemporaries noted
something ludicrous about Aphra in the role of Ovid's
translator. In his 'Satyr on the Modern Translators' Prior
castigated her 'not for abusing Ovid's verse but Sands'.[102] But
Dryden handsomely covered for Aphra in his preface to the
Heröides:

> ...That of Oenone to Paris is in Mr. Cowley's way of imitation only.
> I was desired to say that the author who is of the Fair Sex
> understood not Latine. But if she does not, I am afraid she has given
> us occasion to be ashamed who do.

There was some truth to the compliment. Those who
commissioned Aphra for these tasks did so not only for
friendship's sake, but in the knowledge that her pseudo-
translations exhibited a flair lacking in scholarly but pedestrian
authors. She could imitate anything and did so with panache.
Even when Aphra translated French, she rarely produced a literal
version. Contemporary models of 'imitation' or 'paraphrase' gave
her considerable freedom to infuse her own spirit into her
translations.[103]

The advantages of Aphra's ignorance of Latin can be seen in
her version of the lyric 'Lydia, bella puella candida', a piece
attempted by several minor Restoration poets including Aphra's
friend Charles Cotton.[104] Cotton's literal translation does not
even scan:

> Lidia, thou lovely maid whose white
> the milk and lily does outvie....

The same disregard for metre continues to the end.

> Thy bosome's killing-white then shade
> Hide that temptation from mine eye;
> See'st not I languish, cruel Maid!
> Wilt thou then go, and let me die?

Aphra's version begins with a false rhyme, but at least it scans:

> Lydia, Lovely Maid, more fair
> Than Milk or whitest Lilies are....[105]

In contrast to Cotton's stilted lines, Aphra's verse builds with unflagging energy to a climactic conclusion:

> Shut thy Bosome, white as Snow,
> Whence *Arabian* perfumes flow;
> Hide it from my Raptur'd Touch
> I have gaz'd—and kist too much...
> Cruel Maid—on Malice bent,
> Seest thou not my Languishment?
> *Lydia*!—Oh I faint!—I die!
> With thy Beauties Luxury.

It is not a first-rate poem, but its flowing rhythms and suggestive overtones appealed to Restoration readers.

Translation was the basis of another source of literary income, the miscellany. A book-length translation was taxing and time-consuming, hence the poets invented a quicker expedient. The main work of translation comprised only a part of the volume, the rest being filled up with short translations, poems, lyrics and satires by the author and his friends. It is no coincidence that the years 1684 and 1685, the worst years for new plays, saw the flowering of this patchwork genre. Dryden and Tate issued miscellanies in 1684, and Aphra was not far behind with her collection of *Poems on Several Occasions with a Voyage to the Isle of Love* (1684). The 'Voyage' was Aphra's translation of a poetic fantasy by the contemporary Frenchman, Paul Tallement. Aphra found that a French poem served as well as a Latin classic, particularly since she had the business sense to specialize in works about love. The remainder of *Poems on Several Occasions* was filled out with her own poems of miscellaneous date and subject, some of them composed ten or fifteen years before.

The following year saw the publication of another miscellany edited by Aphra, crowned with her translation of 395 maxims of La Rochefoucauld. Having virtually exhausted her own store of poetry, she called upon her friends, who furnished songs, poems, short translations from Ovid, Catullus, Horace, and other staples of contemporary taste. Otway donated a song, and Nahum Tate, a political satire. Some of the Court wits were represented by songs, and Aphra persuaded a few female friends to print their verse. But most of the contributions were supplied by the lawyers and university youth who paid court to Aphra. Tom Brown, in one of his 'Letters from the Dead to the Living' written long after Aphra's death, recalled:

> You were the young poets' Venus; to you they paid their devotion as a goddess, and their first adventure when they adjourned from the university to the town was to solicit your favours...[106]

Although this was meant to be insulting, Tom Brown was himself one of the callow youths fresh from college who sought Aphra's friendship during the 1680s. He appears in unrecognizable guise in Aphra's 1685 *Miscellany*, with his offerings of bathetic lyrics like 'Friendship' and 'The Parting', in odd contrast to the coarse alcoholic effusions of later years:

> Our Lambs have gaz'd
> And stood amaz'd
> To see this pitch of Love; for living thus
> Our very Flocks learnt innocence of us....

Numerous young men visited Aphra, many of them with loftier careers in prospect. Thomas Creech had recently been made famous by his *Lucretius*; John Adams of King's College Cambridge became a professor of theology; Peter Weston was to become an eminent barrister; Thomas Sprat was already Dean of Westminster and Bishop of Rochester. Aphra's admirers also comprised ordinary country curates, commissioned officers, physicians, young noblemen, women of various degrees, and unclassifiable eccentrics like Thomas Tryon, the vegetarian mystic and 'Pythagorean'.

During the 1680s Aphra presided over an informal salon. Her

reputation for repartee lived after her.[107] Oldys had been informed that 'she had a ready command of pertinent expressions, and was of a fancy pregnant and fluent...'.

> I am told, moreover, by one who knew her, that she had a happy vein in determining any disputes or controversies that might arise in company; having such agreeable repartees at hand upon all occasions, and so much discretion in the timing of them, that she played them off like winning cards.[108]

Charles Gildon, who used to visit Aphra late in the 1680s, also testified to her conversational powers:

> ...Mrs. Behn, in the nicest Metaphysical points, would Argue with judgment, and extreamly happy distinctions; she would, with an engaging Air, enforce her Notions, with all the Justness of the most able Philosopher, tho not with his Majestical Roughness....[109]

Apparently Aphra entertained her friends while she worked, for Gildon saw her write *Oroonoko* 'and keep her turn in Discoursing with several then present in the Room'.

Gildon was one of the next generation of literary men who came to sit at Aphra's feet, just as she had sat at the feet of Dryden and Rochester. Another admirer was Thomas Southerne, who built a successful dramatic career on the plots he pillaged from Aphra's novels. The young George Granville (later Lord Lansdowne) was both protégé and patron. Like many other friends he addressed adulatory verses to Aphra:

> Where'er you look, with every glance you kill,
> Whene'er you write, you triumph with your quill....[110]

The genre was well established by this time, since more than a dozen complimentary verses can be found prefixed to *Poems on Several Occasions* and *The Lover's Watch*. We can even count two feminine examples. One, not published by Aphra, was by 'Ephelia', a poetess of mediocre talents; another, printed in *Lycidus*, was a Pindaric on Aphra's Coronation poem. Aphra herself had long ceased to take seriously these

> ...praises of my face and Eyes,
> My verse, and all those usual flatteries
>   To me as common as the Air;...
> All which as things of course are writ
> And less to shew esteem than wit....[111]

By now she was sufficiently well known to be pestered with
attentions which she viewed with a mixture of amusement and
annoyance.

v. Fame and Notoriety

Perhaps, as Tom Brown later insinuated, these legions of aspiring
coxcombs were drawn to Aphra by the personal notoriety she
had begun to acquire along with the fame of her works and her
conversation. In 1682, even before the publication of her more
suggestive prose works, it was already questionable whether a
woman of virtuous reputation could safely befriend Aphra. In
that year the poetess Anne Wharton began a protracted dispute
with her spiritual advisor, Gilbert Burnet, on the subject of
Aphra Behn. Aphra had written an elegy on the death of the Earl
of Rochester which Mrs. Wharton, a cousin of the earl, had
admired. In a tentative gesture of friendship, she addressed a
poem to Aphra praising the elegy:

> You prais'd him living, whom you dead bemoan
> And now your tears afresh his laurel crown.
> It is this flight of yours excites my art,
> Weak as it is, to take your muse's part....[112]

The two women offer a striking contrast. Anne Wharton was
'reserved, severe, and the very reverse of gaiety and gallantry'.[113]
Trapped in a loveless marriage with the profligate Thomas
Wharton, she sought consolation in literature and piety. Burnet
ruled her with a heavy hand: when she broached the idea of
separating from her husband, Burnet threatened never to see her
again.

It is a downright rejecting the yoke of God, and rebelling against his
providence...one must lay doune both religion, vertue, and prudence

in the moment, that one takes up such a resolution, unless they are
really in danger of their lives....

He also took her to task, somewhat more reasonably, for being
shy about showing her poetry and for failing to correct her first
drafts. 'You want yet one of the pleasantest and most
entertaining parts of Poetry; for a criticall reviewing and mending
what one has writ, is a very noble diversion...'.[114] In her
pampered isolation she was typical of the talented female
amateur, too genteel to subject her poetry to publicity or
criticism, except the polite praise of her social inferiors.

Despite the gulf between them, Anne Wharton and Aphra
Behn were attracted to each other. Both loved poetry, and each
recognized the other's talent. But Anne Wharton could not
approach Aphra without administering a moral rebuke tagged on
to her praise:

> May yours excel the matchless Sappho's name;
> May you have all her wit without her shame...
> Scorn meaner themes, declining low desire,
> And bid your muse maintain a vestal fire....[115]

Aphra was touched by the fact that Anne Wharton had written
to her and replied in her usual exaggerated manner, 'Enough kind
heaven! to purpose I have liv'd...'. But she ignored the moral
reflections. Utilizing the conceit that Rochester had been reborn
in his cousin, Aphra recalled that Rochester too had 'School'd
my loose Neglect'.[116] It is impossible to imagine Rochester
counselling Aphra to avoid the shame of Sappho; no doubt the
'loose neglect' was Aphra's resort to false rhymes and short-cuts
to restore the metre. Moreover, in a silent insult to Burnet,
Aphra failed to mention the latter's famous deathbed conversion
of Rochester, a triumph of Burnet's career.

When Burnet learned of Aphra's verse reply he warned his
disciple:

> Some of Mrs. Behn's songs are very tender, but she is so abominably
> vile a woman, and rallies not only all Religion, but all vertue in so
> odious and obscene a manner, that I am...heartily sorry she has writ
> anything in your commendation....

Apparently he encountered resistance, since he later clarified his position:

> ...there are some errors in women, that are never to be forgiven to that degree, as to allow those of a severe vertue to hold any correspondence with them. And so many grosse obscenities as fell from her come under that qualification....[117]

It is significant that Burnet was unable to name any improprieties in Aphra's behaviour. This may explain the fact that Mrs. Wharton continued to defy her advisor. A poem she wrote some time after February 1684 was printed in Aphra's collection *Lycidus*. Rochester again formed the link: Mrs. Wharton's poem praised Thomas Wolseley for his prologue to the second day of Rochester's posthumous play *Valentinian*, premièred in February 1684. Aphra herself had composed the first day's prologue. Her *Poems on Several Occasions* had just been printed, as had an anonymous *roman à clef* entitled *Love Letters between a Nobleman and his Sister*. Although the volume bore only her initials, contemporaries guessed its author and perceived that the work described the scandalous elopement of the Whig chief, Forde Grey, Lord Warke, with his sister-in-law Henrietta Berkeley. These works offered a large field for biographical speculation about Aphra herself. *Love Letters between a Nobleman and his Sister* contained quasi-pornographic elements; some of the poems were apparently autobiographical and others were suffused with libertine ideas. Perhaps it was for this reason that attacks on Aphra's reputation began to assume a public form. But except for some venomous remarks in Prior's 'Satyr on the Modern Translators', most of the *ad feminam* attacks on Aphra during this period can be traced to one author, a minor poetaster named Robert Gould. A domestic servant who had filled 'various stations...unfit to name', Gould was consumed with a raging desire to be a poet. He was patronized by the Earls of Dorset and Abingdon; however both noblemen asked him to abandon his versifying 'with the very name of poet'. But Gould could not desist; his rejection by his contemporaries seems to have spurred him on. Most of his energies were channelled into coarse satires against those who failed to appreciate his talents: women, the theatrical world, professional poets, fashionable society, and ultimately mankind.[118]

Since Aphra belonged to all these categories, her career aroused in Gould a frenzy of jealousy expressed in gross satire. But his jibes were often so misinformed as to be pointless. 'The Female Laureate' (1684), Gould's first known diatribe against Aphra, jeered at her for celebrating the Earl of Mulgrave's passion for Princess Anne. Aphra had indeed written a poem on that subject entitled 'Bajazet to Gloriana', but it was a satire *against* Mulgrave, certainly not a commissioned work for a patron, as Gould suggested.[119]

Gould's ludicrous errors cast suspicion upon biographical allegations against Aphra that are not confirmed by other sources. None of Gould's insinuations about Aphra's morals is supported by external evidence. The remark that Aphra and her fellow poetess 'Ephelia' prostituted themselves for sixpence a time can be dismissed:

> ...Hackney writers, when their verse did fail
> To get'em Brandy, Bread and Cheese, and Ale,
> Their wants by Prostitution were supply'd,
> Shew but a Tester, you might up and ride:
> For *punk* and *Poetess* agree so Pat,
> You cannot well be *This* and not be *That*.[120]

The same can be said of some even more colourful aspersions contained in 'The Description of a Poetress', almost certainly by Gould as well:

> ...The Upper Galleries she dayly plies
> With Whitaker and Boyle as dayly lies...
> From thence she ranges to the common stews
> Where she as freely buggers with the Jews...[121]

Although Gould's allegations are of limited use for biographical purposes, they point to the raw material that served to blacken Aphra's reputation. 'The Female Laureate' opens with a quotation from Aphra's paraphrase entitled 'The Golden Age', which introduced *Poems on Several Occasions*. Gould wrote:

> The Nymphs she says were free, no nice disdain
> Forbad their Joys, or gave their Lovers pain

He continued with a paraphrase of Aphra's description:

> Ten thousand wanton Cupids you might view
> That Scatter'd Leacherous darts where e're they flew
> Here you might see expecting Virgins Lye
> And straight young swains those Virgins Lust supply....[122]

Gould was on target in citing 'The Golden Age', an Epicurean fantasy which illustrates Aphra's flirtation with libertine ideas. The source of the poem (which reached Aphra in a French translation) is the first chorus 'O bella éte de l'oro' from Tasso's *Aminta*, a popular work in seventeenth-century France and England. When Henry Reynolds translated the *Aminta* into English in 1628, he found Tasso's phrase 's'ei piace, ei lice' (that which pleases is permitted) so offensive that he omitted it.[123] But Aphra not only retained Tasso's 'pleasure principle', the core of Stuart Epicurean philosophy; her version was twice the length of the original in order to dilate upon every hint contained in the chorus. Gould's paraphrase may have been blunt, but it did not distort her meaning.

Nor was 'The Golden Age' an isolated example of Aphra's association with libertine or 'Epicurean' currents of thought. Her writings show a familiarity with all her contemporaries who had earned a place in the clergy's black book. As early as 1673 she had characterized Hobbes as 'ill-natured but prettily ingenius'.[124] The Earl of Rochester remained her idol. Her elegy declared,

> Large was his Fame, but short his Glorious Race,
> Like young *Lucretius* liv'd and dy'd apace.[125]

The comparison was not fortuitous. Creech's translation of Lucretius (1682) served as a banner waved by the libertines, as Prior's 'Satyr on the Modern Translators' noted:

> This [Creech's *Lucretius*] pleas'd the Genius of the
>   vicious Town;
> The Wits confirm'd his Labours with renown,
> And swore the early Atheist for their own.

This was true of wits in Aphra's circle like John Hoyle, 'sodomite...atheist...blasphemer of Christ', who was

> A Wit uncommon, and Facetious,
> A great admirer of *Lucretius*....[126]

Aphra also read continental writers of the same tradition, including Montaigne, whose *Essais* were translated by her friend Charles Cotton in 1685, the year that she printed the cynical maxims of La Rochefoucauld. In her prefatory essay to the maxims, significantly called 'Seneca Unmasqued', she defended the proposition that pure virtue is an impossibility.

Aphra's later writings display another strain of thought allied with Epicureanism, the primitive naturalism that often accompanied it in seventeenth-century Europe. Although the purest expression of this creed is found in *Oroonoko*, naturalism also exerted a strong influence upon Aphra's literary theories. Years before, in *The Young King*, she had written,

> How much more charming are the works of Nature
> Than the Productions of laborious Art.

The thought was later echoed in verses which Pope appropriated:

> Wit is no more than Nature well exprest;
>   And he fatigues and toyles in vain
> With Rigid Labours, breaks his Brain
>   That has Familiar Thought in lofty Numbers drest.[127]

In the preface to 'Seneca Unmasqued', the doctrine was given an aristocratic twist and associated with the prince of Epicureans, Rochester:

> I always prefer that unstudied, and undesigned way of writing...as that of the late Lord Rochester and present Lord Mulgrave...and if there be Art, it lies so delicately veiled under natural expressions, as 'tis not at all discernable...and doubtless the real Beauty of Poetry is, when Art disguises her self under natural appearances....

Were these strands of influence merely a literary affectation, a penchant for whatever seemed fashionably outrageous? Or was Aphra a cynical expositor of libertine principles in word and deed, as Gould insisted? The question is not an easy one to resolve. It was not just the allure of fashion but Aphra's whole temperament that rendered her susceptible to Epicurean influence. For Aphra was an aesthete of refined sensibility who lived for that transcendent state of consciousness induced by works of art, religious ecstasy, and especially the transports of love. Susceptible to each of these aesthetic stimuli by itself, Aphra evoked their intensified effect in combination. 'To Lysander at the Musick Meeting' describes feelings of infatuation heightened by the power of music.

> One Charme might have secur'd a Victory,
> Both, rais'd the Pleasure even to Extasie....

Poetry also pandered to the senses, and even painting could fulfil the same function, as a scene in *The Amours of Philander and Silvia* reveals.[128] Later in the same work Aphra offered a baroque apotheosis of all these elements, with an account of a ceremony in a Flemish cathedral:

> All I could see around me, all I heard, was ravishing and heav'nly; the scene of Glory, and the dazzling Altar; the noble paintings, and the numerous Lamps; the awfulness, the Musick, and the Order, made me conceive my self above the Stars....[129]

Despite the heavenly apparatus that dominates this passage, Aphra's interest centred on love, not religion, as the source of transcendent feelings. Even while attempting a paraphrase of the Lord's prayer, she was reminded of love by the words 'trespasses' and 'temptation':

> Of all my Crimes, the breach of all thy Laws
> Love, soft bewitching Love! has been the cause;...[130]

Aphra was fond of saying that her soul was 'composed entirely of love'. Sometimes she suggested that love comprised women's peculiar vocation, as Fanny remarks in *Sir Patient Fancy*:

> ...I have heard you say, *Women were born to no other end than to love*: And 'tis fit I should learn to live and die in my calling....

Elsewhere, the importance of love assumed both a universal and an autobiographical application. 'Who can be happy without love?' Aphra asked in her preface to *Love Letters between a Nobleman and his Sister*,

> for me I never numbred those dull days amongst those of my life, in which I had not my Soul fill'd with that soft passion. To Love! why 'tis the only secret in nature that restores Life to all the felicities and charms of living;...I... have even prefer'd all the torments of Love, before dully living without it.

That these torments were extreme is revealed in a passage which describes the griefs of despairing lovers, 'where the most easie Moments are, those, wherein one resolves to kill ones self, and the happiest Thought is Damnation'. Yet Aphra preferred this to no feeling at all,

> For when the mind so cool is grown
> As neither Love nor Hate to own,
> The Life but dully lingers on.[131]

But if we ask what Aphra meant by love, we are far from finding a consistent answer. In her youth she had been bred on romances imbued with the neo-Platonic ideal of the pure union of two souls. This influence dominated her 'Arcadian' plays and shaped the comedies of the mid- to late-1670s. Marriage was the goal of her upper-class heroines in these middle plays, whatever indelicate tricks they carried out to achieve their aim. But in the works of the 1680s Aphra stood at the crossroads of romantic love and libertine sensuality. Contemporaries were perhaps correct in attributing biographical significance to this fact, for Aphra's efforts to harmonize the two discordant philosophies in her writings mirrored a parallel struggle in her life.

We possess an autobiographical confession on this subject in Aphra's Pindaric poem 'On Desire'.[132] It was unusual for a woman to write a poem about female sexual desire in the 1680s. Even more astonishing was Aphra's effrontery in publishing it under her own name. As her character Silvia exclaimed, 'To wish was such a Fault, as is a Crime unpardonable to own; to shew Desire is such a Sin in Virtue as must deserve Reproach from all the World...'.[133] Her sensations led Aphra to draw cynical conclusions about the rest of her sex. Apparently their boasted chastity was either an accident or a ruse:

...when you do resist the pressing youth,
'Tis want of dear desire, to thaw the Virgin Ice...
While to th'admiring crow'd you nice are found;
Some dear, some secret, youth that gives the wound
Informs you, all your virtu's but a cheat...
Your modesty a necessary bait
To gain the dull repute of being wise...

Ironically, Aphra had arrived by a different route at the same conclusion as her scabrous detractor, Robert Gould. She inferred that all women were susceptible to sexual desire, whereas Gould wrote of women,

Their guilt's as great who any ills wou'd do,
As their's who freely do those ills pursue:
That they would have it so their Crime assures;
Thus if they durst, all women wou'd be Whores.[134]

In her poem 'On Desire', Aphra associated her newly discovered sexual feelings with a young man whose identity she hid under the sobriquet 'Lysander'. Although no one has established his identity, his character and the chronological limits of his involvement with Aphra can be deduced. The first mention of Lysander occurs inadvertently in *Love Letters between a Nobleman and his Sister, Part I* (composed in 1682-3). Moreover, a letter in the same volume is a prose version of the poem 'On Desire', and other letters duplicate the content of poems which Aphra addressed to the real Lysander.[135] Hence we can conjecture that Aphra's infatuation was contemporaneous with the composition of *Love Letters between a Nobleman and his Sister*. It continued at least until 1685, when she addressed her preface for 'Seneca Unmasqued' to Lysander and worked his name into several of the translated maxims. Lysander was the opposite of John Hoyle, the only one of Aphra's amours identifiable by name. The preface informs us that Lysander is a virtuous and serious young man: 'his grave silence, and scarcity of speaking...gives me an occasion to run into the other Extream of talking all, purely to prevent a dumb Entertainment, for which I have many times met with wise Reproofs...'. Lysander is a typical Restoration 'Stoic'.

But he is not stoical in all respects: 'You should be a Lover',

Aphra teases him, 'if one will believe you or your Complexion', the latter term referring to a sexually susceptible constitution. This quality created difficulties to which Aphra alludes in several poems. In 'To Lysander, who made some Verses on a Discourse of Loves Fire', Aphra reproaches him for seeking an outlet for the sexual desires which she herself had aroused but was forbidden to satisfy:

> 'Tis true, when Cities are on Fire,
> Men never wait for Christal Springs;
> But to the Neighb'ring Pools retire...
> Though Honour does your Wish deny,
> Honour! the Foe to your Repose;
> Yet 'tis more Noble far to dye,
> Then break Loves known and Sacred Laws....[136]

Another poem, 'To Lysander on some Verses he writ, and asking more for his heart than 'twas worth', is more explicit. Lysander has been attempting to circumscribe Aphra's flirtatious behaviour.

> Is't not enough, I gave you Heart for Heart,
> But I must add my Lips and Eies;
> I must no friendly Smile or Kiss impart;
> But you must *Dun* me with Advice....[137]

Meanwhile, he has used 'Adraste' for sexual purposes, but Aphra does not dare 'blame the happy licenc'd Thief: That does my Dear-bought Pleasures steal...'

> Whilst like a Glimering Taper still I burn,
> And waste my self in my own flame,
> Adraste takes the welcome rich return;
> And leaves me all the hopeless Pain.

We do not know how Aphra and Lysander managed to resolve their dilemma. But both agree that Aphra's 'honour' must be preserved despite their mutual desires.

The vast quantity of quasi-pornographic writing that issued from Aphra's pen at this time may have been a by-product of her self-denial. *Love Letters between a Nobleman and his Sister* offers scene after scene of seduction, provocatively anticipated, sensually delineated, and then recollected in anxiety:

> What tho' I lay extended on my Bed, undrest, unapprehensive of my Fate, my Bosom loose and easie of Access, my Garments ready, thin and wantonly put on, as if they would with little Force submit to the fond straying Hand: What then, Philander, must you take the Advantage?

The Voyage to the Isle of Love culminates in a neo-Spenserian 'Bower of Bliss', provoking a back-handed tribute to Aphra's powers of suggestion by her friend Creech:

> In the same Trance with the young pair we lie,
> And in their amorous Ecstasies we die.

We can consider Aphra's diatribes against honour in 'The Golden Age' and 'Voyage to the Isle of Love' more as expressions of personal resentment than a libertine credo.

> Oh cursed Honour! thou who first didst damn
> A Woman to the Sin of shame;
> Honour! that robs't us of our Gust...
> Thou base Debaucher of the generous heart,
> That teachest all our Looks and Actions Art....[138]

The libertines had laid the groundwork for Aphra's verbal war against feminine 'honour'. The term itself was much debased compared with its usage half a century earlier, partly because of Epicurean assaults on it, like that of Rochester:

> Consider real honour, then:
> You'll find hers cannot be the same.
> 'Tis noble confidence in men;
> In women, mean mistrustful shame.[139]

It was assumed that feminine honour always entailed deception. For marriageable young ladies, this was part of a game that was well understood by both sides. Elizabeth Malet's verses to Rochester describe the game:

> Think not, Thyrsis, I will e'er
> By my love my empire lose.
> You grow constant through despair:
> Kindness you would soon abuse.
> Though you still possess my heart,
> Scorn and rigor I must feign;
> There remains no other art
> Your love, fond fugitive, to gain.[140]

Neither her honour nor her strategy could be faulted, and in due course Elizabeth secured Rochester in the bonds of matrimony.

Aphra despised this play-acting. Not that she was averse to stretching the truth on occasion. But the compulsion to talk about her emotions, to 'make more words...than another Woman, that loves as well, would do', caused her to view the game of honour as a degrading restraint. Aphra saw a good deal of justice in the Epicurean critique of female honour. Men's sexuality was direct and natural in its expression, but women were constrained to be

> so contradictory...to our selves...We are a sort of aiery Clouds, whose Lightning flash out one way, and the Thunder another. Our Words and Thoughts can ne'er agree.[141]

No wonder men conquered with such ease, her character Silvia complained, 'when we are only safe by the mean Arts of base Dissimulation, an Ill as shameful as that to which we fall'.[142] Women, Aphra suggested, were forced to be unnatural creatures.

The flaw in the libertine position became clear to Aphra thanks to the revelations of her friend 'Alexis'. After reading Montaigne's essays, he informed Aphra that Montaigne had correctly described the nature of male sensuality. Alexis confessed that he invariably lost interest in any woman he had managed to seduce.[143] This provoked a lament from Aphra, 'To Alexis in Answer to his Poem against Fruition'.

> Ah hapless sex! who bear no charms,
> But what like lightning flash and are no more...
> While all our joys are stinted to the space
> Of one betraying interview,

With one surrender to the eager will
We're short-liv'd nothing, or a real ill...

Although perhaps tempted by the idea of the sensual expression of love outside marriage, Aphra rejected promiscuity. 'Broken vows' made love a sin, she wrote in the 'Epistle of Oenone to Paris'. Nor was inconstancy 'natural' to women, as it apparently was to men. 'Women are by Nature more Constant...than Men', she wrote in a short story, 'and did not their first Lovers teach them the trick of Change, they would be *Doves*...and, like *Indian* Wives, would leap alive into the Graves of their deceased Lovers, and be buried quick with'em'.[144]

For Aphra this difference implied that men and women harboured conflicting interests in the realm of sexuality. Hence the aggressive battle of wills so common in her works:

Her Pride in her denyal lies,
And mine is in my Victories.[145]

The model of 'natural' relations between the sexes was not the Golden Age of Tasso, but the pandemic warfare of Hobbes.

The wits of the Restoration had substituted guile for primitive force,[146] and guile is the most salient trait displayed by Aphra's libertine heroes: Wilding of *The City Heiress*, Lycidus of 'Lycidus, or the Lover in Fashion', Philander of *Love Letters Between a Nobleman and his Sister*, Willmore of *The Rover*. All are Hobbesians in their motives and behaviour. Inconstant in other things, they are true only to their appetites: 'them I can never quit; but you most easily', as Wilding tells Lady Galliard. From this perspective, women's deceptions did not appear so culpable,

there being a thousand little Actions of their lives liable to Censure and reproach, which they would willingly excuse and colour over with little Falsities; but in a man, whose most inconstant actions pass oftentimes for innocent Gallantries...whom Custom has favoured with an Allowance to commit any Vice and boast it...'tis not so brave.[147]

Thus Aphra reached an impasse, for she was at odds with both warring sectors of Restoration society. There were the hypocritical prudes who damned her plays,

> ...whose knack of Cant
> Boasts of Virtues that they want:
> Cry *Faugh*—at Words and Actions Innocent,
> And make that naughty that was never meant....

On the other hand there were the rakes whom she compared to a stream overflowing banks of ravaged flowers:

> ...fickle *Swains*, who invade
> First this, then that deceiv'd, and yielding *Maid*...
> So the [soild] flow'rs their rifled Beauties hung,
> While the triumphant Ravisher passes on.[148]

Only in her paraphrase 'The Golden Age' was the synthesis achieved between romantic love and Epicurean sensuality, with a magical proviso ensuring eternal constancy:

> The Lovers thus, thus uncontroul'ed did meet,
> Thus all their Joyes and Vows of Love repeat:
>   Joyes which were everlasting, ever new
>   And every Vow inviolably true.

From this perspective Aphra's baroque description is not a libertine creed but a private vision of pre-lapsarian paradise,

> Beneath who's boughs the Snakes securely dwelt,
> Not doing harm, nor harm from others felt;
> With whom the Nymphs did Innocently play,
> No Spightful Venom in the wantons lay;
> But to the touch were Soft, and to the sight were Gay.[149]

The innocent snake naturally evokes the image of the Serpent before the Fall. But more importantly, the snake is here—as in two other poems by Aphra—a potent symbol of male sexuality, rendered harmless to women in this Eden that existed nowhere in Aphra's world.[150]

vi. Last Years

There was a poignant irony in these visions of 'joys which were everlasting, ever new'. Women aged quickly in the seventeenth century, and Aphra found herself approaching the time of life when feminine amours were consigned not to song but to satire. We can presume that by 1685 she had reached or passed her mid-thirties.[151] In one of Aphra's novels, Lady Henrietta Wentworth was represented as already old at thirty, and obliged to fortify her charms with a love philtre. While admirers continued to praise Aphra's beauty, Prior's sneering reference to 'the ruin of her face' in 1685 was an ominous sign. Although women of the town aged more rapidly in satire than in real life, Aphra could foresee the time, as her character Silvia was told, when she would 'hear people say, she was once charming, once a Beauty: Is anything more grating, Madam?'[152]

More devastating to female beauty than satire was the effect of illness, like that which transformed Nell Gwyn into 'one of the wrinkled rout' in her thirties. It is not clear what combination of ailments attacked Aphra about 1685 or 1686, but it is certain that she was continually ill from 1686 until her death in 1689. In retrospect it seemed to a contemporary tragically fitting that Aphra's physical decline should correspond to the political fortunes of her patron James II.[153]

But in 1685 the political portents appeared favourable, as Aphra proclaimed in her 'Pindarick on the Death of Our Late Sovereign: with An Ancient Prophecy on his Present Majesty'. Capable of exaggeration while commending her friends' mediocrities, Aphra exceeded herself in hyperbole when describing royalty. The Pindaric and the Coronation Poem which followed it compared Charles, James, and his consort Mary to so many pagan and Christian gods that she gives the impression of a befuddled polytheist. The rapid transition from dead King to living monarch which so offended Johnson in Dryden's *Threnodia Augustalis* was even more pronounced in Aphra's Pindaric. The defeat of the Duke of Monmouth's rebellion a few months later seemed another happy sign for Aphra, who mentioned her pleasure at 'our late victory and the growing glories of my King' in her dedicatory preface to the second part of *Love Letters between a Nobleman and his Sister*

(1685). The third part of these chronicles offered a thinly disguised narrative of the events leading up to Monmouth's execution. Since the latter, now safely dead, was viewed with sympathy, Aphra blamed the conspiracy on the ambitions of his mistress Lady Henrietta Wentworth (Hermione) and her evil counsellor Fergus (Fergusano).

Even before this account was out of the press, Aphra perceived that her royal patron was going to uphold his reputation for being a fool. We can follow the progress of her despair from 1686 until the end of her life, thanks to the preservation of a manuscript commonplace book comprised mainly of political satires which she kept during these years. The volume, a folio of more than 300 pages, bears the title 'Astrea's Book for Songs and Satyrs—1686' in Aphra's autograph; a punning friend scrawled 'Behn's and Bacon' on the same page. The satires cover the years 1682–8 in chronological order; they were copied into the book in a number of hands aside from that of Aphra.[154] The volume contains at least one original composition by Aphra herself, a lengthy satire on James' 1686 Hounslow Heath encampment entitled 'Caesar's Ghost'. The poem portrays Charles II risen from the dead to survey the summer encampment and its personnel. While showing veneration for James himself, it subjects every aspect of the encampment to ridicule.[155]

Sufficiently anti-Stuart to be included in *The Muses Farewell to Popery and Slavery* (1690) after Aphra's death, the piece reveals her disillusion with James' sagacity. Additional signs of anxiety are evident in the commonplace book, stemming from the reaction to Dryden's conversion to Catholicism in 1686. All available satires on the Poet Laureate were copied by Aphra. One of these, 'On Mr. Dryden, Renegade', has been posthumously assigned to her, but the attribution is certainly mistaken.[156] Aphra considered making a public disclosure of her Catholicism two years later; the satires against Dryden were a reminder of the price to be paid. Her disapproval of these squibs is shown by her marginal annotations upon one of them, 'A Heroic Scene: Enter Oliver's Porter, Fiddler and Poet in Bedlam', an attack on Dryden and her friend Roger L'Estrange.[157] Although she entertained doubts about Dryden's past allegiance to James, Aphra was abusive to the author of the satire, defending both Dryden and L'Estrange against his aspersions. Her own secret concern was betrayed by her marginal note on the satirist's suggestion that L'Estrange planned to turn Roman Catholic: 'a sly knave, ye poet, and a plaguey guess'.

Meanwhile, Aphra was in severe financial straits. Her income is very difficult to calculate, but it is possible to make a rough guess at her earnings. It has been estimated that a full house at the Dorset Garden Theatre yielded about £95, and the Duke's Company took in an average of less than £50 a night.[158] Aphra's plays were produced at a rate of about one a year and were received with variable success. We can assume that her income from plays reached an upper limit of £100 in any one year and was probably closer to £50. The dedication of the printed version would bring about ten guineas. This major source of income from plays was now gone. Aphra's miscellanies of 1684 and 1685 had brought only about £20 or £25 each. In August 1685, Tonson stood surety to her for a loan of six pounds from Zachary Baggs, the theatre's treasurer. 'I do here by impowre Mr Zachary Baggs in case the said debt is not fully discharged before Michaelmas next, to stop what money he shall here after have in his hands of mine upon ye playing my first play....'.[159] The Duke of Norfolk was Aphra's titular patron throughout the 1680s, but apparently his help did not rescue her from insolvency.[160] She must have been relieved to see her comedy *The Luckey Chance* receive a successful première in April 1686.

Like previous comedies, the play provoked 'the old never failing scandal—that 'tis not fit for the Ladys'. As before, the accusations elicited a lengthy prefatory vindication from Aphra, mostly an elaboration of previous claims that her sex alone had provoked discriminatory treatment. In an attempt to prove this, she listed a variety of popular plays with scenes allegedly more indelicate than her own.

If I should repeat the Words exprest in these scenes I mention, I might justly be charg'd with course ill Manners...yet they so naturally fall into the places they are design'd for, and so are proper for the Business, that there is not the least Fault to be found with them; though...those things in any of mine wou'd damn the whole piece...such Masculine strokes in me, must not be allow'd...one thing I will venture to say, though against my Nature, because it has Vanity in it: That had the Plays I have writ come forth under any

Mans Name, and never known to have been mine; I appeal to all unbyast Judges...if they had not said that Person had made as many good Comedies, as any one Man that has writ in our Age; but a Devil on't the Woman damns the Poet.

Aphra no longer appealed to pecuniary reasons as an excuse, 'for I am not content to write for a Third day only'. She realized that her personal reputation was being destroyed by aspersions of bawdry, so she felt obliged to defend herself on that score. 'I hope the better Judges will take no offence...knowing my Conversation not at all addicted to the Indecensys alledged...'. There is no reason to disbelieve Aphra. Her posthumous biographer wrote, 'I knew her intimately, and never saw ought unbecoming the just Modesty of our Sex, tho' more gay and free than the Folly of the Precise will allow'.[161] But the 'biographical fallacy' had damaged her reputation past retrieve. She concluded her preface defiantly:

All I ask, is the Priviledge for my Masculine Part the Poet in me...to tread in those successful Paths my Predecessors have so long thriv'd in...If I must not, because of my Sex, have this Freedom, but that you will usurp all to your selves; I lay down my Quill, and you shall hear no more of me...I value Fame as much as if I had been born a *hero*; and if you rob me of that, I can retire from the ungrateful World, and scorn its fickle Favours.

To contemporaries this request to exercise the privileges of both sexes seemed incongruous, if not monstrous. Both friends and foes increasingly saw Aphra as a mixture of male and female. Her admirers praised this androgynous quality:

With all the thought and vigour of our sex
The moving softness of your own you mix...

But to a satirist in 1688, Aphra was a mongrel combining the worst features of both sexes:

...since her Works had neither Witt enough for a Man, nor Modesty enough for a Woman, she was to be look'd on as an Hermaphrodite, & consequently not fit to enjoy the benefits & Priviledges of either Sex....[162]

She had achieved the fame of a professional poet, but at the cost of her personal repute as a woman.

Aphra's next comedy, *The Emperor of the Moon* (1687) was free of bawdry. An unabashed farce, it attained even more popularity than *The Luckey Chance*. But a play a year was now insufficient to keep Aphra from poverty, even with the occasional aid of noble patronage. Her illness must have entailed increasing expense. Aphra seems to have been under the care of Dr. Peter Bellon, a fashionable physician and *littérateur*. The notation, 'Dr. Bellon next doore to the Gold Bottle in Salisbury Streete neare Salysbury house in the Strand' appears at the back of her manuscript 'Book for Songs and Satyrs', along with other important addresses such as that of her printer. Dr. Bellon had studied with Sir Thomas Mayerne and had been employed as chemist by Charles II and the Duke of Buckingham, so his fees would have been high.[163]

In a satire of 1687-8, Gould mocked Aphra's increasing illness:

> Doth that lewd Harlot, that Poetick Quean...
> Mend for reproof, others set up in spight,
> To flux, take glisters, vomits, purge and write.
> Long with a Sciatica she's beside lame,
> Her limbs distortur'd, Nerves shrunk up with pain,
> And therefore I'll all sharp reflections shun,
> Poverty, Poetry, Pox, are plagues enough for one.[164]

Except for the imputation of 'pox', the remainder was true. In a letter to Waller's daughter-in-law written late in 1687, Aphra apologized for her 'yll writing...with a lame hand scarce able to hold a pen'. She excused the elegy on Waller which she had enclosed. 'I can only say I am very ill and have been dying this twelve month, that they want those Graces & that spirritt wch possible I might have drest em in had my health & dulling vapors permitted me...'. The elegy is not dispirited, but it does begin with a melancholy reference to her own condition:

> How, to thy Sacred Memory, shall I bring
> (Worthy thy Fame) a grateful Offering?
> I, who by Toils of Sickness, am become
> Almost as near as thou art to a Tomb?[165]

The verses also mention the 'low ebb' of neglect into which poetry had fallen. A few months earlier, Aphra had referred to her poverty and that of her fellow poets:

> The Muses that melodious cheerful Quire
> Whom Misery could nere untune, nor tire
> But chirp in Rags, and ev'n in Dungeons sing...[166]

Nevertheless, Aphra wrote at a furious pace until her death, turning out a prodigious number of translations and tales. The saccharine *Lovers Watch* appeared in 1686, with a dedication to young Peter Weston. Aphra praised his freedom from the vices of the 'roving Wits of the mad Town,...that wretched unthinking Number, who pride themselves in their mean Victories over little Hearts...'. Aphra's contempt for the libertines was chronicled in *Lycidus, or the Lover in Fashion* (licensed 1687), a free translation of the second part of Tallement's *Voyage à L'Isle d'Amour*. The same spirit of disillusion characterizes *The Amours of Philander and Silvia* (1687), the third and final part of *Love Letters between a Nobleman and his Sister*. In the same year Aphra produced a piece of fulsome flattery on the Duke of Albemarle's voyage to Jamaica. She also supplied couplets for a new edition of *Aesop's Fables* (1687). Many of these couplets had nothing to do with Aesop's original, being Aphra's musings on recent political events such as Monmouth's Rebellion. Others bore a personal application:

> Tho wrackt with various paines yet life does please
> Much more than death, which all our pressures ease.[167]

The year 1688 was also a prolific one. Ranging farther afield for works to be translated, Aphra chose two popular books by Fontenelle, *A Discovery of New Worlds* and *A History of Oracles, or, Cheats of the Pagan Priests*. *A Discovery of New Worlds* was introduced by a thoughtful essay on the difficulties of translation, the new Copernican science, and the relation of the latter to the Bible. Although Aphra described herself as a 'new beginner' to science, her reading in Descartes had enabled her to correct one of Fontenelle's errors concerning the height of the earth's atmosphere. Yet her justification for producing a scientific translation was a modest one: 'the Authors introducing a Woman as one of the speakers...were further Motives for me...for I thought an Englishwoman might adventure to translate anything, a French Woman might be supposed to have spoken'. Aphra boldly plunged into the Copernican controversy, arguing in its favour against clerical detractors. By no means a deist, Aphra faulted Fontenelle because 'he ascribes all to Nature, and says not a Word of God Almighty...so that one would almost take him to be a Pagan'. Nevertheless, she was attracted by modern Biblical interpretations which distinguished between matters of faith, and 'other things...relating to Astronomy, Geometry, Chronology, or other liberal Sciences...':

the design of the Bible was not to instruct Mankind in Astronomy, Geometry, or chronology, but...to lead us to Eternal life...through the whole Bible, when anything of that kind is questioned, the Expressions are always turned to fit our Capacities...and the Common Acceptances of things to the Vulgar.[168]

Early in 1688, while Aphra was still ruminating on such past outrages as the Popish Plot and Monmouth's Rebellion,[169] news spread throughout the country which lent a different complexion to her thoughts. The announcement of the Queen's pregnancy, unexpected by all and undesired by most, filled Aphra with such joy that she wrote 'A Congratulatory Poem to her Most Sacred Majesty' even before the Queen had been brought to childbed. Aphra was ready for the birth on 10 June with a 'Congratulatory Poem to the King's Most Sacred Majesty on the Happy Birth of the Prince of Wales', which displayed her extravagant optimism. Likening the birth to that of Christ, Aphra recklessly predicted that the new Prince would 'thoroughly purge the Floor or Land...Then all one Faith, at least one Soul shall be'. England would again be a Catholic country.

A note affixed to the poem announced that 'On Wednesday next will be Published the most Ingenius, and long Expected History of Oroonoko' With *Oroonoko* in the press, Aphra had decided to take an opportunity of a dedication to the Catholic Lord Maitland to reveal her true religious sympathies. She wrote of the future Jacobite,

Where is it amongst all our Nobility we shall
find so great a Champion for the Catholick Church?
With what Divine Knowledge have you writ in Defence
of the Faith!

Thus read the dedication in the uncorrected sheets of the first
issue. But either Aphra had second thoughts, or her printer
exercised his prerogative, for these lines were deleted from all
other copies of *Oroonoko*.[170] It is easy to see why Aphra agreed
to the deletion. Even her 'Congratulatory Poem', written
immediately after the birth, betrayed an awareness that the
Prince's legitimacy was widely questioned. Aphra possessed
numerous satires on the subject copied into her manuscript
'Book for Songs and Satyrs': 'The Miracle. How the Dutches of
Modene being in Heaven pray'd the Virgin Mary that the queen
might have a son And how Our Lady sent the Angell Gabrill
with her Smok Upon wch the Queen Conceived'; 'Loretta and
Winifred or The new way of getting Children by prayers and
presents'; 'Tom Tyler or the The Nurse'; 'The Prince of
Darkness...'. Her collection of songs against the Declaration of
Indulgence and the trial of the seven bishops was equally
comprehensive, and indicative of the popular mood.[171] Aware of
James' lamentable sense of strategy, Aphra now perceived that
her brief hopes for Catholicism had been vain, even with a
Catholic Prince of Wales.

There was no longer anything to hope for, and nothing to do
but write. Aphra's finest stories date from these months:
'Oroonoko', 'The Fair Jilt', 'Agnes de Castro', 'The Fair Vow-
breaker', 'The Lucky Mistake'. One of her last commissions was
considered a special honour. Tate asked her to versify 'Of Trees',
the sixth book of Cowley's Latin work *Of Plants*. No doubt
Tate offered her a prose translation of the Latin. Aphra's version
is an odd mixture of politics and poetry, for she freely
interpolated whatever was on her mind. At the passage on 'the
laurel', she inserted a personal aside which echoed her first
mention in a satire:

I by a double right, thy Bounties claim
Both from my Sex, and in *Apollo's* name
Let me with *Sappho*, and *Orinda* be

> Oh ever sacred Nymph, adorn'd by thee;
> And give my Verses Immortality.[172]

By late autumn, Aphra had ceased to keep up her commonplace 'Book for Songs and Satyrs'. After William's invasion a friend added an epigram on the event:

> When Jacob stole the Flow'r of every Flock
> From his old Syre: His very Gods he took.
> Our Tyrant stript his father of the Throne
> But left his Gods: 'Tis plain that he has none.[173]

Some time in early 1689 Burnet inquired after Aphra, hoping to enlist her talents on behalf of William. But Aphra refused.

> What must I suffer when I cannot pay
> Your Goodness, your own generous way?
> And make my stubborn Muse your Just Commands obey.
>
> My muse that would endeavour fain to glide
> With the fair prosperous Gale, and the full driving Tide,
> But Loyalty Commands with Pious Force...
> The Brieze that wafts the Crowding Nations o're,
> Leaves me unpity'd far behind
> On the Forsaken Barren Shore...[174]

Although she would have nothing to do with William, Aphra did address a 'Congratulatory Poem to her Sacred Majesty Queen Mary, upon her arrival in England':

> Sullen with stubborn Loyalty she lay
> And saw the world its eager Homage pay...
> But Oh! What Human Fortitude can be
> Sufficient to Resist a Deity?

To James she explained her dilemma:

> ...Great Lord, of all my Vows, permit
> My Muse who never fail'd obedience yet
> To pay her Tribute at Marias Feet
> Maria so divine a part of You
> Let me be Just, but Just with Honour too.

Both as a poem and a political act it was a failure.

We do not know whether Aphra would have reconciled herself to the new order of things, for she died on 16 April, five days after the coronation of William and Mary. She was buried in Westminster Abbey, with 'two Wretched Verses for her Epitaph, who had her self Wrote so many good':[175]

> Here lies a Proof that Wit can never be
> Defence enough against Mortality.

Her death did not pass without notice. A few days after Aphra's burial, a 'pindaric' written by a 'young Lady of Quality' appeared in broadside. Its main burden was the loss Aphra's death represented for the rest of her sex.

> Of her own sex, not one is found
> Who dares her Laurel wear
> Withheld by Impotence or Fear;
> With her it withers on the Ground...[176]

The 1696 'Life' similarly noted Aphra's singularity:

The reader must remember that there are few Astreas arise in our age, and till such a One does appear, all our Endeavours in Encomiums on the last, must be vain and impotent.

That Aphra was unique for her time seems obvious without the testimony of contemporaries. How her unusual qualities evolved cannot be explained because so many pieces are missing from her biography. We can perceive the outlines of her character, but do not know how it was formed or what effect special circumstances such as her Catholicism may have had on her education or her outlook on life. Nevertheless, although we cannot supply the original impetus for Aphra's career, we can place it in its social context.

The Stuart ideal represented the feminine virtues as an organic whole: modesty, chastity, obedience and silence were deeply interrelated. The various facets of Aphra's life represent an inversion of this ideal. Instead of modesty she was known for her 'confidence' or 'impudence', her ambition for a 'masculine' fame, and the notoriety of her works and life. Of her physical chastity it is impossible to judge, but her public confession of sexual desire was equivalent to promiscuity in the eyes of contemporaries. For silence she substituted loquacity in her conversation and her works, and for passive obedience to a husband, the psychological and economic independence of a *feme sole* who earned her living in the male domain of professional writing.

This expression of an 'inverse' of conventional femininity did not arise *ex nihilo*, but in relation to a specific *milieu*, the Restoration Court. The Court supplied a context for Aphra in two senses, economic opportunity and an alternative morality. Pepys lamented that the excesses of the Court all stemmed from 'idleness, and having nothing else to employ their great spirits upon'.[177] Yet the idleness of the courtiers created work for others: actors and actresses, musicians, artists, courtesans and 'trading poets' like Aphra. The Court also fostered a unique moral atmosphere. Whereas the Puritans had attempted to create a single moral standard based on chastity for both sexes, the Court offered an inverted single standard in which both sexes were promiscuous. This experiment in sexual licence was short-lived, limited to a small sub-culture, and strongly condemned by society at large. Yet it offered the only philosophical challenge to the dominant ideology which restricted love and sex to the confines of marriage. Indeed the Court wits insisted that love and marriage were inimical. Tom Brown wrote a poem to a lady explaining that he would not marry her because he loved her.[178]

Amidst this milieu Aphra formed her friendships with actresses, courtesans, and fellow poets. The professionalism that characterized Aphra's career distinguished her from her competitors among the closet poetesses, women like Anne Wharton, Anne Killigrew and the Countess of Winchelsea. Their talent had not been polished by open competition but fed only on itself. If we were to subtract from Aphra's writings everything which she produced in the hope of earning money, we should be left with one romantic play, some occasional poetry, and half-a-dozen short tales, a corpus comparable in quantity and quality to that of Anne Wharton or the Countess of Winchelsea.

The poetesses whose rank had fitted them with an adequate education had nothing to gain by setting up as 'trading poets'. Judged by an amateur female standard they were showered with praise, but had they been subjected to the impartial criticism of the marketplace they would have been relegated to the lowest rank of minor poets, where modern anthologies have placed them. It was not mere modesty that motivated their fear of publicity and criticism. The Countess of Winchelsea wrote out two plays in fair copy, but prefaced them with the warning: 'a more terrible injury cannot be offer'd me, then to...permit them ever to be represented'.[179] There was also the question of subject matter. Aphra's worldly experience had been wide, and it was further enlarged by reading. Her favourite works presented a broad canvas of life: Shakespeare, Cervantes, Rabelais, Plutarch. Even so, her first plays remained within the puerile Arcadian tradition. Her forays into more audacious topics were spurred on by financial necessity, but held back by well-founded fears about her reputation. Her best-selling works were those that did the greatest damage to her 'honour' as a woman, *The Rover* and *Love Letters Between a Nobleman and his Sister*. In this respect it was inconceivable that the closet poetesses could imitate Aphra. A verse letter addressed to Anne Wharton illustrates the point:

> When counterfeit Astrea's lustful Rage
> Joyns to Debauch the too Effem'nate Age...
> Tis time for you with all your Wealth of Thought
> Forth from your lov'd Retirement to be brought...
> You best can tell the charms of vertu'ous Joy
> Despising *Venus* with her Wanton boy...[180]

Although Aphra's personal reputation declined after her death, her literary influence was felt by the next generation of female authors. Mrs. Pix, Trotter and Centlivre, the triumvirate of female playwrights who emerged at the end of the seventeenth century, all looked on Aphra's corpus for plots and a boost to their morale. Aside from expressing her admiration for the 'genius' of Mrs. Behn, Susanna Centlivre took on Aphra's *nom de plume*, 'Astrea'. The name, as well as what it represented, had begun a new tradition of female professionalism.

Epilogue

What can individual biographies tell us about the limits of women's mental world in the seventeenth century? At first sight, the diversity of the three lives chronicled here seems to suggest a good deal of latitude, since not all women followed the model of appropriate behaviour imposed on them by a traditional society. But an analysis of the patterns that lie behind this diversity reveals that even the most flagrant defiance of convention fell within a narrowly defined framework. Women sometimes expressed resentment at the limited role assigned to them, and in rare cases they sought a wider field for their ambitions. What they did not challenge was the whole complex of cultural axioms about gender, with its implicit assumption that the two sexes were polar opposites with two sets of mutually contradictory traits. Intellectual and moral as well as physiological qualities were linked to either one sex or the other, and consequently those who tried to enlarge the female sphere found themselves justifying their encroachment on forbidden male territory. Even at the height of her personal rebellion, Aphra Behn did not question the polarity of gender as it was defined by her contemporaries. Instead she appealed for a special dispensation for rare creatures like herself, the intellectual 'hermaphrodites' of her society: 'All I ask, is the Priviledge for my Masculine Part the Poet in me...'.[1]

Most women did not venture beyond the traditional virtues assigned to their sex: 'to be Modest, Chast, Temperate, Humble, Patient and Pious; also to be Huswifely, Cleanly, and of few words...' as the Duchess of Newcastle expressed it.[2] This conservative propensity has elicited little comment, for historians have presumed that the inertia of custom adequately explains women's acceptance of their lot. But the Duchess of Newcastle pinpointed the fallacy inherent in this assumption when she asked why women should be so different from the rest of creation:

> every Creature naturally desires and strives...to be superiour, and not inferiour...and are unwilling to obey...even the Beasts of the Field, the Birds of the Air, and the Fishes in the Sea...only Women...for women are so far from indeavouring to get power, as they voluntarily give away what they have.[3]

Of course this proto-Darwinian comparison was not an accurate description of feminine endeavours in every sphere, for women behaved exactly like their husbands and brothers with respect to *class* ambitions. Seventeenth-century proverbs and satires depict women as obsessed with social advancement; within the limits of their own sphere they betrayed the same eagerness as their male counterparts to achieve 'preferment' for themselves and their children.[4] Women's avidity for class mobility thus stands in contrast to their indifference, or indeed hostility, to 'gender' mobility. Appeals by English women for the same privileges as men (whether political, legal, educational or sexual) were so unusual at this time that those, like the Duchess of Newcastle, who openly acknowledged such aspirations were liable to be pronounced insane.[5]

One explanation suggested by contemporaries for women's willingness to endure their subject status was the belief that feminine subordination was merely nominal, not real. Writers of conduct books noted (and deplored) the disparity between their own ideal of orderly hierarchy and 'the opinion of many wives, who thinke themselves in every way as good as their husbands, and in no way inferiour to them.' This error was diagnosed as resulting from 'an ambitious and proud humour in women, who must needs rule, or else thinke themselves slaves.'[6] The Duchess of Newcastle believed that women wielded the actual power in society, but that their influence was concealed for prudential reasons, 'so as men perceive not how they are Led, Guided and Rul'd by the Feminine Sex'.[7]

As the three biographies recounted here have shown, there

were some grounds for this belief. In the arena of family politics, women's informal authority was far greater than we might infer from their official standing in society at large. Indeed the rites of adolescent courtship inverted the usual order of the sexes, albeit only temporarily.[8] During courtship, moreover, young women exploited the very conventions that were intended to circumscribe their activities. Margaret Lucas used her modesty (along with other traditional female weapons) as an aggressive lure, and Mary Boyle transformed her prerogative of a matrimonial veto into an instrument of active choice. Even after marriage, when a wife's legal and economic rights were reduced almost to nullity, there were many ways to manipulate not only her husband, but the entire nexus of kin and neighbourhood. The Duchess of Newcastle used her psychological ascendency over the duke to increase her jointure at the expense of her step-children; the Countess of Warwick dominated her household and local community through the sheer force of her moral stature. So long as women used the customary weapons of their sex and observed traditional rules of deportment, so long as their bids for power were confined to the private *milieu* of family and kin, their influence was tolerated in certain 'masculine' spheres. It was not so much feminine power *per se* as its public display that violated the canons of femininity.[9]

Nevertheless, even informal varieties of feminine presumption had their limits, and the boundaries were for the most part conceded and indeed enforced by women themselves. In the first place, English women evidently subscribed to the contemporary scientific worldview which affirmed their innate inferiority. Indeed, the more education women attained, the more solid grounding they received in the humoral theory and its postulates about gender differences. Thus the Duchess of Newcastle assumed she could never write 'so wisely or wittily as Men, being of the Effeminate Sex, whose brains Nature hath mix'd with the coldest and softest Elements...'.[10] The defective nature of the feminine intellect was taken to be an immutable fact, much like women's smaller physical stature, providing an automatic justification for their exclusion from all the more exalted spheres of the male domain—learning, politics, the professions. Until such doctrines began to decline in prestige towards the end of the seventeenth century, to be replaced by Lockean notions of a *tabula rasa*, educated women were presented with an almost insurmountable intellectual handicap.[11]

We do not know the extent to which the worldview of the elite penetrated the consciouness of the illiterate majority. 'Scientific' notions about gender differences may have had little or no effect on the day-to-day life of the lower ranks. According to a contemporary observer, among the country people subsisting on their daily labour 'the condition of the two sexes...is more level than amongst gentlemen' although 'not so equal as that of Brutes'.[12] In any case, the basic parameters which moulded female *mentalité* arose not from scholastic distinctions but from women's social and biological role in a pre-industrial demographic regime. As childbearers and childrearers, women were particularly vulnerable to the psychological stress of high mortality. While the religious doctrine of the time offered consolation for the horrors of material life, it did so at a price. Those who embraced a life of piety were thereby committed to a conservative social order whose keystone was the hierarchy of 'relative duties'. Popular beliefs about women's natural inferiority might be discounted whenever such prejudices seemed to contradict empirical experience. But it was impossible to pit common sense against Holy Writ, as the Countess of Bridgewater mused to herself: 'we are commanded, by those that are above our capacity of reason, by God himself'.[13] The same pattern which was delineated in the life of the Countess of Warwick appears unchanged in women of lower social stations. Mrs. Susanna Bell refused to accompany her husband to New England, but then the verse came to her mind, '*Wives submit yourselves unto your Husbands, as unto the Lord*'. Soon afterwards her infant died; she begged of God 'to know why he took away my child, and it was given in to me, that it was because I would not go to *New England*...then I told my husband I was willing to go with him'.[14] Protestantism may have promoted the ideology of sturdy individualism in male heads of households, but its long-term effect on their wives was to reinforce customary attitudes of dependence. Thus women, as the staunchest advocates of religious values at a time when elite male society was becoming more secularized, found themselves upholding the entire social framework which kept them in their 'place'.[15]

For the majority of women a traditional outlook on their role in life was almost inevitable. But seventeenth-century society was not a monolith. There were inconsistencies and ambiguities in the structure of the social order which occasionally blurred some of the sharp boundaries between the two sexes and cast doubt on the ubiquitous stereotype of the dependent wife. Widows were of course the most significant group of autonomous women. The career of the Countess of Warwick illustrates the great authority that could accrue to a woman of rank and wealth. But those of a lower social station, though less powerful, could be equally self-sufficient. Gervase Holles's charming portrait of his grandmother, and Sir John Bramston's description of the life of Mary Moundford are good examples of the type. Even Aphra Behn acted out the myth of the 'lusty widow', a role which made her behaviour more comprehensible, if not more commendable, to her contemporaries. Naturally the Stuart stereotype did not always conform to reality. Nevertheless, the autonomous status of widows was an important factor which modified the dependent role of the sex as a whole.[16]

Moreover it is clear that even ordinary women who were confined to the domestic setting could harbour interests and ambitions that transcended their limited domain. In order to reconcile such goals with a stereotyped female role, women found ways to encode their 'masculine' urges in a socially acceptable form. In conformity with the rule which assigned direct action in the material world to men, women arrogated to themselves the obverse of this masculine domain. They cultivated the mental or spiritual realm, leaving to men their monopoly of worldly power. Alternatively they made use of speech to compensate for their lack of physical prowess. From these perspectives, diverse types of Stuart womanhood can be seen as embodiments of a common urge to transcend feminine impotence and win control over a menacing environment. The female lay saint, exemplified by the Countess of Warwick, used prayer instrumentally to shower benevolent influence on her family, community and country. Sermons affirmed that 'good women are wonderfull helpefull to their husbands by their prayers...indeed the whole family fares the better for them'. There were innumerable examples of the type at every social level, like Baxter's step-mother,

whose holiness, mortification, contempt of the world and fervent prayer (in which she spent a great part of her life) have been so exceeding exemplary as made her a special blessing to our family...[17]

The witch harboured the same desire to alter her environment through non-physical means, but for malicious rather than benign ends. And the village scold cultivated the use of vituperative or scandalous speech as a specialized female weapon in default of physical weapons, which were reserved for men. Gossip, curses, defamation and other predominantly female social sanctions attained instrumental force in a community which believed in their power to do ill. All such feminine arts seemed to their practitioners to invert the normal order of things which placed women at the bottom of the hierarchy of power and prestige.[18]

These minor mutinies against the social order invoked familiar images of womankind. Over the course of the seventeenth century, however, political upheaval generated new modes of female behaviour based on different concepts of women's potentialities. The Civil War, whose abnormal atmosphere brought about turning points in the lives of the Duchess of Newcastle and the Countess of Warwick, wrenched women of every social class out of the domestic chrysalis. Royalist wives like the Duchess of Newcastle found themselves travelling and petitioning on behalf of their husbands, while Quaker women also left their families at home when setting off to deliver a 'testimony'. A new breed of female preachers, pamphleteers and politicians of all classes and political complexions created the 'effeminate' atmosphere which inspired the Duchess of Newcastle to print her first book, in 1653.

Perhaps the most enduring legacy of the Civil War was women's *entrée* into the male domain of publication. The huge flood of printed works by women of the Interregnum did not cease at the Restoration; instead there was a further incursion into masculine preserves as women like Aphra Behn turned to secular subjects.[19] This trend marks the beginning of a long process of evolution whereby literature lost its 'male' status as a professional discipline and became neutral intellectual territory, accessible to both sexes. So long as a woman avoided immodest subject matter and disguised her literary ambitions through anonymous or pseudonymous publication, she could write and even print her works without jeopardizing her personal reputation.

In social terms the cloistered housewife of Tudor times was gradually transformed into her urbane and ornamental counterpart of the late seventeenth century. The growth of London, along with a widespread process of economic and cultural differentiation, created a new class of leisured women who abandoned their manorial role as producers to become urban consumers. One symptom of this changing ideal was the mushroom growth of girls' schools, with their wide social and geographical range and their cultivation of those ornamental graces which now led to superior matrimonial prospects.[20]

Meanwhile developments in the intellectual realm supported these changes in fashion. By the end of the century it was increasingly argued that education rather than nature was responsible for perceived differences of intellect between the sexes. The trend was further reinforced by the flood of translations of Greek, Latin and continental works from the 1670s onward, for these made the 'great tradition' of the universities accessible to women. This expansion of secular literature helped put the female sex on equal footing with the male in the sphere of polite conversation, a talent for which women were just beginning to be commended. The Tudor ideal of silence had given way to what was to evolve into the 'salon' of the eighteenth century.[21]

But this apparent rise in the status of one sector of the female populace was attained only at a certain psychological cost. Their cloistered setting had had a protective function for women: shut up in their houses, occupied with their domestic tasks, they were thought to be safe from mischief. Young girls were guarded by the externals of deportment: the writers of conduct books thought a 'shamefast demeanour' or the 'veil of modesty' accomplished the same purpose as purdah.[22]

Now that some Restoration women had abandoned domesticity to mix freely with men, these external safeguards had crumbled. Aphra Behn, who in one sense heralded the new 'salon' type, also seemed to illustrate the pitfalls of a more public role for women in mixed society. The late seventeenth-century reaction to Restoration licence had a particular application to the female sex. As Halifax remarked, 'the unjustifiable Freedom of some of

your Sex have involved the rest in the penalty of being reduced'.
This did not mean a return to private domesticity, but rather the
adoption of a new behavioural code. Norbert Elias has suggested
that the greater social autonomy achieved by aristocratic women
at this period had as its corollary the necessity to enforce more
stringent *inner* controls. As Hume expressed it: 'A female has so
many opportunities of secretly indulging these appetites, that
nothing can give us security but her absolute modesty and
reserve'.[23]

While we can point to some changes in women's mental
universe by the end of the seventeenth century, the keynote is
one of underlying continuity. A tiny minority who had the means
and leisure might profit from a certain blurring of sexual
boundaries in the intellectual realm. But in the sphere of morality
and sexuality, gender distinctions were perhaps even more rigid
and comprehensive than before, as the Tudor code of shame and
honour evolved into the exaggerated prudery of the eighteenth
and nineteenth centuries.[24]

Abbreviations

Ashm.	Ashmole
BL (AM)	British Library, MS Additional.
BL (Birch)	British Library, MS Birch.
BL (Eg)	British Library, MS Egerton.
BL (Harl)	British Library, MS Harleian.
BL (Loan)	British Library, Portland Loan, Cavendish-Harley Papers.
Bodl.	Bodleian
Boyle MSS	Chatsworth, Devonshire Collection, Manuscripts of the Boyle family, 1604–43.
Clar.	Clarendon
Commons Journals	*Journals of the House of Commons.*
CSP (Col)	*Calendar of State Papers Colonial.*
CSPD	*Calendar of State Papers Domestic.*
DNB	*Dictionary of National Biography.*
Evelyn, *Diary*	*The Diary of John Evelyn*, ed. E. S. de Beer, 6 Vols. (Oxford, 1955).
HMC	*Historical Manuscripts Commission.*
Hutchinson, *Memoirs*	Lucy Hutchinson, *Memoirs of the Life of Colonel Hutchinson*, ed. J. Sutherland (Oxford, 1973).

193

Life (Firth)	Duchess of Newcastle, *Life of William Cavendish, Duke of Newcastle*, ed. C. H. Firth (2nd edn., n.d.).
Life (1667)	Duchess of Newcastle, *The Life of…William Cavendishe, Duke, Marquess and Earl of Newcastle…*(1667).
'Life' (1696)	'Memoirs on the Life of Mrs. Behn, Written by a Gentle-woman of her Acquaintance', in A. Behn, *The Histories and Novels* (1696).
'Life' (1698)	'The History of the Life and Memoirs of Mrs. Behn, Written by one of the Fair Sex', in A. Behn, *All the Histories and Novels* (1698).
Lismore I	*Lismore Papers*, ed. A. B. Grosart, 1st ser., 5 Vols. (1886).
Lismore II	*Lismore Papers*, ed. A. B. Grosart, 2nd ser., 5 Vols. (1889).
London Stage	*The London Stage 1660–1800*, Part I: 1660–1700, ed. W. Van Lennep (Carbondale, Ill., 1965).
Lords Journals	*Journals of the House of Lords.*
Love Letters	A. Behn, *Love Letters Between a Nobleman and his Sister…In three parts* (3rd edn., 1708).
Maddison, 'Philaretus'	'An Account of Philaretus during his Minority', by Robert Boyle, in R. E. W. Maddison, *The Life of the Honourable Robert Boyle, F.R.S.* (1969), pp. 2–45.

Nott. U., Cavendish MSS	University of Nottingham, Portland Collection, Cavendish Papers and Literary Manuscripts.
Pepys, *Diary*	*The Diary of Samuel Pepys*, ed. R. Latham and W. Matthews, 11 Vols. (1970–83).
POAS	*Poems on Affairs of State: Augustan Satirical Verse 1660–1714*, eds. G. de F. Lord, W. J. Cameron, G. M. Crump, F. H. Ellis, E. F. Mengel and H. H. Schless, 6 Vols. (New Haven, 1963–71).
PRO (SP)	Public Record Office, State Papers.
Ranger, 'Career of Richard Boyle'	T. Ranger, 'The Career of Richard Boyle, First Earl of Cork in Ireland, 1588–1643' (Oxford Univ. D. Phil. thesis, 1958).
Rawl.	Rawlinson
Works	*The Works of Aphra Behn*, ed. M. Summers, 6 Vols. (New York, 1915).

Notes

Note: Unless otherwise stated, the place of publication is London.

Introduction

1. K. Thomas, *Religion and the Decline of Magic* (Harmondsworth, Middlesex, 1973), p. 180; M. M. Dunn, 'Saints and Sisters: Congregational and Quaker Women in the Early Colonial Period', *American Quarterly*, xxx (1978), 600.
2. I. Illich *Gender* (1983) offers an idealized view of gender domains.
3. I. Maclean, *The Renaissance Notion of Woman* (Cambridge, 1980), pp. 6–81.
4. M. Roberts, 'Wages and Wage-earners in England: The Evidence of the Wage Assessments, 1563–1725' (Oxford Univ. D. Phil. thesis, 1981), pp. 184–5.
5. T. E., *The Lawes Resolutions of Womens Rights* (1632), p. 6.
6. A. Macfarlane, *Reconstructing Historical Communities* (Cambridge, 1977), p. 207.
7. For a comprehensive checklist and analysis see P. Crawford, 'Women's Published Writings 1600–1700', in M. Prior (ed.), *Women in English Society 1500–1800* (1985), Ch. 7.
8. See M. Ingram, 'Ecclesiastical Justice in Wiltshire 1600–1640' (Oxford Univ. D. Phil. thesis, 1976), pp. 1–14.
9. Servants of either sex tend to be hidden from historical view. A wife's occupation or social status often differed from that of her husband.
10. A. Clark, *Working Life of Women in the Seventeenth Century* (1919). A new edition (1983) contains an excellent introduction by M. Chaytor and J. Lewis.
11. E. Ardener, 'Belief and the Problem of Women', in J. LaFontaine (ed.), *The Interpretation of Ritual* (1972), pp. 135–58.
12. Contemporary proverbs assert women's propensity to talk excessively. M.

Tilley, *A Dictionary of the Proverbs in England in the Sixteenth and Seventeenth Centuries* (Ann Arbor, 1950), pp. 745-8.

13. J. Sharpe, *Defamation and Sexual Slander in Early Modern England*, Borthwick Papers no. 58 (York, 1980), pp. 19-20; M. Berg, *The Age of Manufactures: Industry, Innovation and Work 1700-1820* (1985), Ch. 7: 'Custom and Community'.

14. D. Cressy, *Literacy and the Social Order* (Cambridge, 1980), pp. 128-9, 144-7.

15. Crawford, 'Women's Published Writings', in Prior, *op.cit.*, pp. 221-3.

16. P. Clark, 'The Migrant in Kentish Towns 1580-1640', in P. Clark and P. Slack (eds.), *Crisis and Order in English Towns* (1976), pp. 142-4.

17. D. MacLaren, 'Fertility, Infant Mortality and Breast Feeding in the Seventeenth Century', *Medical History*, xxii (1978), 378-96.

18. BL(AM) 27351, 8 June, 29 July and 24 Dec. 1668.

19. J. Kinnaird, 'Mary Astell and the Conservative Contribution to English Feminism', *Journal of British Studies* (1979), pp. 53-75.

20. Maclean, *Renaissance Notion*, pp. 60-4; T. Hobbes, *Leviathan* (1651) Part II Ch. 20; R. Filmer, 'The Anarchy of a Limited or Mixed Monarchy', in P. Laslett (ed.), *Patriarcha and Other Political Works* (1949), p. 287, cited in K. Thomas, 'Women and the Civil War Sects', *Past and Present*, xiii (1958), 54.

21. P. Burke, *Popular Culture in Early Modern Europe* (1978), pp. 28, 49-50.

22. BL(AM) 27356.

23. A. Wilson, 'Childbirth in Seventeenth and Eighteenth-century England' (Sussex Univ. D. Phil. thesis, 1983), pp. 129-31.

24. A. F. Kendrick, *English Needlework* (2nd edn., 1967), pp. 59-142.

25. Thomas, *Religion*, pp. 16-17.

26. In C. Hill (ed.), *The Law of Freedom and Other Writings* (1973), p. 365.

27. Thomas, 'Women and the Civil War Sects', 44-5; M. Spufford, *Contrasting Communities* (Cambridge, 1974), pp. 302-3.

28. [R. Allestree], *The Ladies Calling* (1673), p. 144.

29. Sharpe, *Defamation and Sexual Slander*, p. 17; Ingram, 'Ecclesiastical Justice', Chs. 3, 5-7 and 9.

30. Blake, *Jerusalem*.

Chapter I: Margaret Cavendish, Duchess of Newcastle

1. P. Morant, *History and Antiquities of...Colchester* (1768), ii, 20-36. The best studies of Margaret are H.T.E. Perry, *The First Duchess of Newcastle and her Husband as Figures in Literary History* (Boston, 1918), and D. Grant, *Margaret the First* (1957).

2. CSPD 1625-49, Addendum, p. 468; *A True Relation...of the Gentry and Persons of Estate in...Essex that are Malignants...*(1643), p. 6.

3. *Natures Pictures drawn by Fancies Pencil to the Life* (1656), p. 370.

4. CSPD 1625-6, pp. 102, 111, 117 and 165.
5. *Natures Pictures*, pp. 369-370.
6. CSPD 1627-8, p. 497; 1633-4, pp. 50, 231, 249.
7. *Natures Pictures*, pp. 372-3.
8. *Ibid.*, p. 387.
9. *Ibid.*, p. 370.
10. *CCXI Sociable Letters* (1664), sig. b.
11. *Playes* (1662), p. 248.
12. *Sociable Letters*, p. 312; *Natures Pictures*, p. 387.
13. *Sociable Letters*, pp. 266-9; *Life* (1667), sig. a.
14. CSPD 1634-5, pp. 252-3; CSPD 1637, pp. 132-3; C. Holmes, *The Eastern Association in the English Civil War* (1974), p. 20.
15. PRO (SP) 16/449 ff. 46v-47 and PRO (SP) 16/451 ff. 49v-50; CSPD 1639-40, p. 594; *Lords Journals*, Vol. IV, pp. 272, 307, 313, and 322; B. Ryves, *Mercurius Rusticus* (1643), pp. 1-5; HMC 10 Rep. VI, pp. 146-7; W.L.F. Nuttall, 'Sir Thomas Barrington and the Puritan Revolution', *Trans. Essex Arch. Soc.*, 3rd ser., (1966) ii, 60-82; Holmes, *Eastern Association*, p. 36.
16. *Natures Pictures*, p. 373.
17. *Playes* (1662), p. 132.
18. *Plays Never Before Printed* (1668), 'The Presence', p. 49.
19. *Natures Pictures*, p. 374.
20. *Plays* (1668), 'Scenes', p. 96.
21. For his birthdate (incorrectly given as 1592 in the *DNB*) see Perry, *First Duchess of Newcastle*, p. 7. Charles was born in 1591. For a life of Newcastle see G. Trease, *Portrait of a Cavalier* (1979).
22. *Life* (Firth), pp. 2-5, 72, 104-6. Cavendish was created Viscount Mansfield to settle a pecuniary dispute with his relations (CSPD 1619-23, p. 190).
23. Hutchinson, *Memoirs*, p. 61; CSPD 1634-5, p. 149; Earl of Clarendon, *History of the Great Rebellion and Civil Wars in England*, ed. W. D. Macray (1888), Vol. I, pp. 104-5; *Life* (Firth), pp. 78, 181-7; BL (Loan) 29/235, ff. 113, 115-17, 128; BL (Harl) 6988, ff. 111-12.
24. HMC Portland I, p. 701; Sir P. Warwick, *Memoires* (1702), pp. 235-6, 274; Clarendon, *Rebellion*, Vol. III, pp. 383-5; BL (Harl) 6988, f. 104.
25. Clarendon, *Rebellion*, Vol. III, p. 384; Life (Firth), pp. 43-5.
26. W. Bray (ed.), *Diary and Correspondence of John Evelyn* (1857), Vol. IV, p. 8; Pepys, *Diary*, 27 April 1667.
27. 'The Phanseys of the Marquesse of Newcastle...', BL (AM) 32497, ff. 4, 12, 53 and 37.
28. *Natures Pictures*, pp. 374-5.
29. 'Poems Songs a Pastorall and a Play by...Lady Iane Cavendish and Lady Elizabeth Brackley', Bodl. MS Rawl. Poet. 16, ff. 5, 13.
30. BL (Loan) 29/235, ff. 176, 201; BL (AM) 32497, ff. 39v-40; *Playes* (1662), p. 269.
31. BL (Loan) 29/235, ff. 176, 178, 193; *Plays* (1668), 'Scenes', pp. 119-21.
32. For Margaret's identification with the character Lady Tranquillity in 'The Concealed Fansyes', a play written by two of Newcastle's daughters in

1645, see N.C. Starr, '"The Concealed Fansyes", A Play by Lady Jane Cavendish and Lady Elizabeth Brackley', *Publications of the Modern Language Association*, xlvi (1931), 837–8.

33. *Sociable Letters*, pp. 338, 394.
34. *Natures Pictures*, p. 375.
35. *Plays* (1668), 'Scenes', pp. 120–1; *Sociable Letters*, pp. 368–9.
36. *Natures Pictures*, sig. c2.
37. *Sociable Letters*, pp. 2, 27–8; *Playes* (1662), pp. 182–3.
38. *Sociable Letters*, pp. 27–8.
39. BL (Loan) 29/235, ff. 178, 184, 193, 208, 180, 182, 187, 201 and 212.
40. *Ibid.*, f. 212; Evelyn, *Diary*, 25 April 1667.
41. BL (AM) 32497, ff. 50, 54–54v.
42. BL (Loan) 29/235, f. 216, 20 Dec. 1645; *Calendar of the Proceedings of the Committee for Compounding*, p. 1439; Clarendon, *Life* (Oxford, 1857), Vol. I, pp. 195–6; Bodl. MS Ashm. 832, ff. 217–18.
43. *Life* (Firth), p. 64. For Newcastle's complicated finances at this time see *ibid.*, pp. 44, 47, 50–1, 57–9; Bodl. MS Clar. 46, f. 197; MS Clar. 48, f. 15; BL (AM) 23206, f. 24; BL (Loan) 29/236, f. 284, Nott. U., Cavendish MSS, Pw1. 406.
44. *Life* (Firth), p. 45.
45. *Sociable Letters*, pp. 183–4.
46. *Ibid.*, p. 186.
47. 'A Booke, Wherein is Contained Rare Minerall Receipts Collected at Paris', Nott. U., Cavendish MSS, PwV.90 (unfoliated). It contains letters from Sir Theodore Mayerne (c. 1648–9) and medical prescriptions for Margaret's infertility and related health problems. Mayerne mentioned Margaret's 'want of her courses'.
48. *Life* (Firth), pp. 48–9.
49. CSPD 1649–50, p. 39.
50. Her mother and a favourite sister had died just before the siege of Colchester, Sir Charles Lucas was executed after the siege, and her older brother Thomas was soon to die of a wound received about this time.
51. *The Worlds Olio* (1655), 'Epistle' between pp. 46–7; *Sociable Letters*, p. 22.
52. Bodl. MS Rawl. Poet. 16, written c. 1643–5.
53. *Calendar of Clarendon State Papers*, ii, nos. 283, 285, 548, 549, 556 and 557; Bodl. MS Clar. 40, f. 11; *Life* (Firth), pp. 205, 55.
54. See J. Jacquot, 'Sir Charles Cavendish and his Learned Friends', *Annals of Science* (1952), 13–27. For the Cavendish brothers' scientific concerns during the 1630s see BL (Loan) 29/235, ff. 89, 101, 127, 129–30; Bodl. MS Savile Q. 9. Sir Charles' letters to the mathematician John Pell are found in BL (Birch) 4278. His scientific MSS preserved in the British Library are BL (Harl) 6001–2, 6083 and 6796.
55. *Poems and Fancies* (1653), sig. A8.
56. *Sociable Letters*, pp. 29, 103, 120; *Worlds Olio*, pp. 1, 46, 117; *Philosophical and Physical Opinions* (1655), p. 29; *Poems and Fancies*, pp. 53, 58–9. Margaret's works display an inconsistent mixture of scepticism, deism, pantheism and occasional orthodoxy.
57. *Poems and Fancies*, sig. A8v; *Worlds Olio*, p. 1.

58. Other examples are Dorothy Leigh, *The Mothers Blessing* (1616); Elizabeth Clinton, *The Countess of Lincolnes Nurserie* (1622); Elizabeth Grymeston, *Miscelanea* (1604).

59. Thomas, 'Women and the Civil War Sects', 56.

60. *Poems and Fancies*, p. 162. For women's printed works during the Interregnum see Crawford, 'Women's Published Writings' p. 213.

61. *Poems and Fancies*, pp. 121–2.

62. Evelyn, *Diary*, ed. Bray (1857), Vol. IV, pp. 31–2.

63. *Poems and Fancies*, sig. A7; *ibid.*, 'Epistle Dedicatory to Fame', sig. A2.

64. *Ibid.*, sig. A7; *Sociable Letters*, sig. b; *Orations of Divers Sorts* (1662), sig. a; *Natures Pictures*, p. 120.

65. *Playes* (1662), p. 254.

66. *Ibid.*, p. 159.

67. *Ibid.*, p. 525.

68. *Ibid.*, pp. 28, 160. See also *Plays* (1668), 'Convent of Pleasure', pp. 24–9.

69. *Worlds Olio*, p. 85.

70. *Playes* (1662), pp. 121–80; *Natures Pictures*, pp. 287–356; *Playes* (1662), pp. 491–527.

71. For statistics see Crawford, 'Women's Published Writings', pp. 265–7.

72. G. Ballard, *Memoirs of Several Ladies of Great Britain…*(Oxford, 1752), pp. 285, 289; A. Walker, *Holy Life of Mrs. Elizabeth Walker* (1690), p. 5.

73. Maclean, *Renaissance Notion*, p. 62.

74. *Poems and Fancies*, sigs. A3–A3v.

75. *Sociable Letters*, p. 226.

76. See for example her essay on Shakespeare, *Sociable Letters*, pp. 244–7.

77. *Worlds Olio*, p. 93.

78. *Orations*, sig. a2.

79. BL (Loan) 29/235, f. 127.

80. *Worlds Olio*, sigs. E2–E3; *Phil. and Phys. Opin.*, p. 27; *Poems and Fancies*, sig. A6.

81. Bodl. MS Clar. 45, f. 409.

82. *Letters and Poems in honour of…Margaret, Duchess of Newcastle* (1676), p. 146.

83. 'An Epistle to Justify the Lady Newcastle…' [by the Marquis of Newcastle] prefixed to *Phil. and Phys. Opin.*; *Philosophicall Fancies* (1653), p. 85; *Worlds Olio*, sig. E2; *Phil. and Phys. Opin.*, sigs. A2–A3, B2.

84. See H.M. Cocking, 'Originality and Influence in the Work of Margaret Cavendish, First Duchess of Newcastle' (Reading Univ. M. Phil. thesis, 1972).

85. *Worlds Olio*, pp. 138, 140, 143, 177; *Sociable Letters*, sig. b, p. 262. For the influence of Montaigne on Margaret's sensibilities see K. Thomas, *Man and the Natural World* (1983), pp. 173–4.

86. BL (Loan) 29/236, f. 284. Henry married in 1653 and sent part of his portion to Newcastle. Jane did likewise the following year (she had already sold her jewels to send cash to her father). By 1654 Charles (Viscount Mansfield) was allowed to compound, and sent a regular income to Newcastle. See Nott. U., Cavendish MSS, Pw1. 644.

87. CSPD 1656–7, p. 279; Bodl. MS Smith 13, p. 45.

88. Newcastle to Nicholas, 15 Aug. 1654, printed in *Life* (Firth), pp. 205–6.
89. Bodl. MS Clar. 50, ff. 86, 111, and 119; *Life* (Firth), p. 63; CSPD 1657–8, pp. 296–7: Sir Edward Walker to Nicholas, 19 Feb./ 1 Mar. 1658; *ibid.*, pp. 300, 311: Thomas Ross to Nicholas, 24 Feb./6 Mar. and 1/11 Mar. 1658.
90. *Sociable Letters*, pp. 369–70. For Margaret's envy of 'State-Ladies' see *ibid.*, pp. 12–13. She may have been referring to women like Elizabeth Mordaunt, who played an active part in royalist plotting at this time.
91. *Ibid.*, p. 22.
92. *Natures Pictures*, sig. c.
93. *Life* (Firth), pp. 65, 68. Newcastle was sworn a gentleman of the bedchamber but this hardly answered his expectations.
94. The presentation copy is now Bodl. MS Clar. 109.
95. *Life* (Firth), p. 68.
96. *Ibid.*, p. 68, n.1. For Margaret's sour grapes see *Sociable Letters*, pp. 56–62 and 167–8.
97. BL (Loan) 29/236, ff. 282, 296; Nott. U., Cavendish MSS, Pw1. 630a; PRO (SP) 29/292, ff. 76–76v.
98. R. Goulding, *The Thrice Noble, Illustrious and Excellent Princess, Margaret Duchess of Newcastle* (1925), p. 20.
99. For Shadwell's composition of Newcastle's *The Triumphant Widow* see F. Needham (ed.), *Welbeck Miscellany no. 1* (1933), 'Introduction'. For Shirley's composition of *The Country Captain* (BL Harl. 7650, printed 1649) see A.H. Bullen (ed.), *A Collection of Old Plays* (1882), Vol. II, pp. 315–16. For Dryden's share in *Sir Martin Mar-all* see Pepys, *Diary*, 16 Aug. 1667.
100. *Phil. and Phys. Opin.*, p. 26.
101. *Ibid.*, pp. 26–7.
102. *Worlds Olio*, p. 6; *Playes* (1662), p. 279; *Worlds Olio*, p. 94; *Phil and Phys. Opin.*, sig. B2.
103. *Letters and Poems...*(1676), pp. 1–2, 98–105, 119–20, 123–7, 135–42; BL (AM) 28558, f. 65; Bodl. MS Smith 13.
104. *Life* (Firth), p.xxxvi. In 1664 Margaret purchased more than £39 worth of books; see Grant, *Margaret the First*, p. 200.
105. M. H. Nicolson (ed.), *Conway Letters* (New Haven, 1930), p. 237.
106. *Sociable Letters*, p. 298.
107. *Ibid.*, sig. b2.
108. *Phil. and Phys. Opin.*, sig. B2.
109. *Natures Pictures*, 'The Contract', pp. 183–204; *Playes* (1662), 'Youths Glory and Deaths Banquet'.
110. T. Birch, *History of the Royal Society* (1756), Vol. II, pp. 175–6; Pepys, *Diary*, 30 May 1667.
111. J. Evelyn, 'I'll tell the[e] Jo-', PRO (SP) 29/450, Item 102, f. 164; E. M. Thompson (ed.) *Hatton Correspondence* (Camden Soc., 1878), i, 47.
112. S. I. Mintz, 'The Duchess of Newcastle's Visit to the Royal Society', *Journal of English and Germanic Philology* (1952), 168–76.
113. *Sociable Letters*, p. 417.
114. *Letters and Poems...* (1676), p. 124.
115. Margaret mentioned having begun the project in the preface to her *Orations*.

116. *Sociable Letters*, p. 52. Margaret also imagined herself as general of an army: *Playes* (1662), pp. 212–13.

117. For a comparison of Margaret's military narrative with more objective accounts see *Life* (Firth), pp. ix–xiv; Perry, *First Duchess*, pp. 26–42.

118. For example *Life* (Firth), Discourse LXXXII, p. 140.

119. See Bodl. MS Clar. 45, f. 409, Hyde to Newcastle, 30 May 1653 (New Style).

120. Newcastle's association with Hobbes was close. See Hobbes' dedication of the MS 'Elements of Law' to Newcastle, BL (Eg) 2005, dated 9 May 1640. For Hobbesian or Machiavellian sentiments by Newcastle see BL (Harl) 6988, ff. 111–12; Bodl. MS Clar. 109, ff. 10–14, 54, 62, 79, 80–1; Nott. U., Cavendish MSS, PwV. 25: 'Meere Nature teacheth Mankinde both to Acknowledge a God and Religion'. For Clarendon's comments see *Rebellion*, Vol. III, p. 381.

121. *Life* (Firth), 'Notes of the Authoress', nos. XIV, XVII, pp. 146–7.

122. *Ibid.*, p. 79. At the Restoration Newcastle calculated the value of his total rentals at £8,999/10/7 per annum plus another £2,000 for iron works. See Nott. U., Cavendish MSS, Pw1. 331. Margaret used the figure £22,393/10/1 per annum for eighteen years at compound interest, then added other dubious 'losses'. Newcastle's list of rentals and those given by Margaret do not tally. See *Life* (Firth), pp. 75–6.

123. Pepys, *Diary*, 1 May 1667; CSPD 1667–8, p. 602.

124. *Poems and Fancies*, sig. A3; *Sociable Letters*, pp. 255–6.

125. *Sociable Letters*, p. 98.

126. *Letters and Poems...* (1676), p. 135; Evelyn, *Diary*, 18 April 1667; PRO (SP) 29/450, Item 102, ff. 164–165v.

127. *Worlds Olio*, p. 32.

128. *Sociable Letters*, pp. 14, 38, 42, 47–9, 113.

129. Evelyn, *Diary*, ed. Bray (1857), Vol. IV, pp. 8–9.

130. *Sociable Letters*, pp. 112–13; *Worlds Olio*, pp. 71, 213; *Playes* (1662), p. 155. Margaret gave the lower-class comic scenes of her plays to her husband to write, partly because of his superior gift for comedy and partly, it would seem, because of her own lack of interest in the lower orders.

131. *Worlds Olio*, 'The Preface to the Reader', affirms the humoral theory and its explanation of women's presumed inferiority.

132. 'Female Orations', in *Orations*, pp. 225–32.

133. *Natures Pictures*, sig. c.

134. Bodl. MS Smith 13, pp. 53–4.

135. *Worlds Olio*, p. 215.

136. Pepys, *Diary*, 11 April 1667. Some of Margaret's 'masculine' propensities should perhaps be attributed to Newcastle's influence. He was well known for his coarse bawdy humour and his habitual swearing.

137. BL (Loan) 29/236, ff. 313, 315, 19 March 1666.

138. Goulding, *Margaret, Duchess of Newcastle*, p. 20.

139. Nott. U., Cavendish MSS, Pw1. 90, 2 July 1668.

140. Nott. U., Cavendish MSS, Pw1. 315, three pages, unpaginated.

141. *Ibid.* Margaret knew all about the tricks practised by stewards and tenants; see her 'Tale of a Traveller' in *Natures Pictures*, pp. 279–80. No

doubt she had learned these matters, like the management of a grange, from her mother.

142. Goulding, *Margaret, Duchess of Newcastle*, p. 20.

143. Nott. U., Cavendish MSS, Pw1. 315.

144. Printed in S.A. Strong, *A Catalogue of the Letters and Other Documents Exhibited at Welbeck* (1903), p. 63.

145. PRO (SP) 29/292, f. 76, 12 Aug. 1671.

146. Among these were Sarah Jinner, in *A Prognostication for...1658* (1658), sig. B; [Bathsua Makin], *An Essay to revive the Antient Education of Gentlewomen...* (1673), p. 10; Mildmay Fane, Earl of Westmoreland, who wrote a laudatory poem on the fly-leaf of his copy of *Poems and Fancies* (cited in Grant, *Margaret the First*, p. 129).

147. Bodl. MS Ashm. 36, f. 186v.

148. D. Osborne, *Letters from Dorothy Osborne to Sir William Temple*, ed. E. A. Parry (1914), p. 100; *Poems on Affairs of State* (1699), p. 299.

149. For this topic see M. MacDonald, *Mystical Bedlam* (Cambridge, 1981).

150. Evelyn, *Diary*, ed. Bray (1857), Vol. IV, p. 9; Thomas Lawrence, 'An Elegy on ye Death of...Lady Jane eldest daughter of William Duke of Newcastle', 9 Oct. 1669, Nott. U., Literary MSS, PwV. 19, p. 3.

Chapter II: Mary Rich, Countess of Warwick

1. BL (AM) 19832, ff. 23–30; T. Ranger, 'The Career of Richard Boyle, First Earl of Cork in Ireland, 1588–1643' (Oxford Univ. D.Phil. thesis, 1958), p. 410.

2. A. Walker, *Eureka, or, the Virtuous Woman Found* (1678), p. 94.

3. See T. Ranger, 'Richard Boyle and the Making of an Irish Fortune, 1588–1614,' *Irish Historical Studies*, x (1957), 257–97.

4. *Lismore I*, Vol. I, entries for 19 Dec. 1627 and 8 March 1628.

5. BL (AM) 18023, f. 10v.

6. *Lismore I*, Vol. II, p. 111.

7. Mary thought she had been born on 8 November 1625, an impossibility in view of the indenture cited above, but perpetuated by the *DNB* and by two biographies of Mary printed in 1901, by C.F. Smith and M.E. Palgrave.

8. *Lismore I*, Vol. II, entry for 10 April 1628.

9. Maddison, 'Philaretus', p. 4.

10. BL (AM) 27357, f. 2v.

11. Boyle MSS., XVII, nos. 165, 166; XVII nos. 91, 101; see also Maddison, 'Philaretus', pp. 5–45.

12. Boyle 'Letter-Book', Boyle MSS, cited in Ranger, 'Career of Richard Boyle', p. 220. 'Civility' meant facility in conversation and social situations. For a discussion of the concept as applied to women see Robert Boyle's *Occasional Reflections* (1665), Sect. IV, pp. 130–3.

13. *Lismore I*, Vol. II, entry for 10 April 1628.

14. Boyle MSS, XVII, no. 124.

15. *Ibid.*, XIX, no. 75; Maddison, 'Philaretus', p. 17.

16. *Calendar of Patent Rolls Ireland*, James I, p. 76. Sir James Hamilton was raised to the Irish peerage as Viscount Clandeboye.
17. *Lismore I*, Vol. IV, entries for 4 March, 20 June, 10 Dec. and 23 Dec. 1635.
18. *Lismore I*, Vol. I, entries for 8 Aug. and 5 Dec. 1620; Vol. II, 29 July and 14 Sept. 1621, 26 July 1622; Vol. III, 9 May and 15 Aug. 1630, 6 Feb. 1632. Lettice was married at the late age of nineteen because two earlier matches fell through.
19. *Lismore I*, Vol. III, entry for 14 Oct. 1630, 15 June 1630; Boyle MSS., XVII, no. 152; *Memoirs of the Verney Family* ed. F. P. Verney (1892), Vol. II, pp. 204, 206; Lismore I, Vol. IV, entries for 1 April 1635, 24 Aug. 1634.
20. *Lismore II*, Vol. IV, Viscount Clandeboye to Cork, 2 Aug. 1639, pp. 80–1.
21. BL (AM) 27357, f. 3v.
22. See for example W. Gouge, *Of Domesticall Duties* (1622), pp. 449–50 and 564.
23. Boyle MSS, XX, no. 145.
24. For the provisions of the treaty with Margaret see *Lismore I*, Vol. III, entry for 9 May 1630.
25. BL (AM) 27375, f. 4v.
26. *Lismore I*, Vol. V, entries for 6 Aug., 6 Sept., 24 Oct., 1 Nov., 7 Dec. and 26 Dec. 1639 and 28 June 1640; Boyle MSS, XIX, no. 129, XX, nos. 1, 102, 106 and 109, XXI, no. 83.
27. CSPD 1639–40, pp. 297 (2 Jan. 1641), 341 (16 Jan. 1641) and 365 (23 Jan. 1641).
28. BL (AM) 27357, ff. 22v–23.
29. BL (Eg) 1290, f. 2. The motto is dated '1634. 10 Apr. Gen[eva]'.
30. BL (AM) 27357, ff. 8v–9.
31. *Ibid.*, f. 8.
32. *Ibid.*, ff. 12–14.
33. For contemporary examples see D. G. Green (ed.), *The Meditations of Lady Elizabeth Delaval* (Surtees Soc., 1978), 90, and J. Loftis (ed.), *The Memoirs of Anne Lady Halket and Ann Lady Fanshawe* (Oxford, 1979), p. 19.
34. Osborne, *Letters*, p. 191.
35. For an analysis of Cork's motives at this time see Ranger, 'Career of Richard Boyle', pp. 371–6.
36. Mary was to haggle over the same issue when conducting negotiations for her niece Essex Rich. See HMC Finch MSS, ii, p. 16.
37. BL (AM) 27357, f. 15v.
38. George Fox would not attend a wedding but instead would visit the couple the next day. For feminine revulsion at a public wedding see Osborne, *Letters*, p. 250. See also the Duchess of Newcastle, 'The Bridals', in *Plays Never Before Printed*, pp. 11–12 and 18–20.
39. [Allestree], *Ladies Calling*, pp. 159–60, Marquis of Halifax, *The Lady's New Years Gift* (1688), p. 25; S. Bufford, *An Essay Against Unequal Marriages* (1692), pp. 57–9.
40. *Lismore II*, Vol. IV, p. 210; *Lismore I*, Vol. V, entry for 9 March 1643.

41. *Commons Journals*, Vol. V, p. 42.
42. BL (AM) 27357, f. 17v.
43. *Ibid.*, ff. 33v–34.
44. *Ibid.*, f. 18v.
45. Diary of Arthur Wilson printed in F. Peck, *Desiderata Curiosa*, Vol. II, Book XII, Part 6, p. 23.
46. Clarendon, *Rebellion*, Vol. II, p. 544.
47. E. Calamy, *A Patterne for All* (1658), pp. 34–6.
48. Walker, *Eureka*, p. 52.
49. BL (AM) 27357, f. 23.
50. *Ibid.*, f. 19v.
51. J.R. Jacob, *Robert Boyle and the English Revolution* (New York, 1977), pp. 120–1; BL (AM) 27357, f. 23v.
52. For examples see Green, *Meditations of Lady…Delaval*, pp. 186–7; Loftis, *Memoirs of Lady Halkett and Lady Fanshawe*, p. 20.
53. Walker, *Eureka*, p. 54.
54. BL (AM) 27357, f. 19v.
55. *Ibid.*
56. Bodl. MS Add. A. 119.
57. For duties of daughters-in-law see Halifax, *Lady's New Years Gift*, p. 62.
58. BL (AM) 27357, ff. 20–20v.
59. Peck, *Desiderata*, Vol. II, Book XII, Part 6, p. 31.
60. 'Preface' to Robert Boyle, *Some Motives and Incentives to the Love of God* (1659).
61. BL (AM) 27357, ff. 24–5.
62. Bodl. MS Clar. 62, f. 104.
63. BL (AM) 27357, ff. 24–5.
64. *Hatton Correspondence*, Vol. I, p. 40; BL (AM) 27357, f. 33v.
65. BL (AM) 27357, f. 29v.
66. Printed in George, Earl of Berkeley, *Historical Applications and Occasional Meditations* (1670), pp. 131–57.
67. BL (AM) 27351, April 1667.
68. G. Burnet, *A Sermon Preached at the Funeral of…Robert Boyle* (1692), p. 33. For her intellectual influence see C. Webster, *The Great Instauration* (1975), pp. 40, 62–3, 86, 308, 419, 433 and 501.
69. For Mary's Court visits see BL (AM) 27351, 16 Feb., 19 March, 23 April, and 22 Oct. 1667; 31 Jan. 1668.
70. *Ibid.*, 23 April 1667.
71. *Ibid.*, 31 Jan. 1668; Walker, *Eureka*, p. 54.
72. *Nicholas Papers*, ed. Sir G. Warner (Camden Soc., 1920), iv, 265; Bodl. MS Clar. 61, ff. 204–5.
73. *Ibid.*, f. 342; *Lords Journals*, Vol. XI, p. 12; *Calendar of Treasury Books 1660–67*, pp. 371, 376, 560, and 566.
74. BL (AM) 27357, f. 31v.
75. Walker, *Eureka*, p. 91; BL (AM) 27357, f. 31v.
76. Duchess of Newcastle, *Natures Pictures*, p. 378; Calamy, *A Patterne for All*, p. 38; A. Hayes, *A Legacy or Widows Mite* (1723), p. 14.
77. A. Walker, *The Holy Life of Mrs Elizabeth Walker* (1690), p. 116.

78. See Thomas, *Religion and the Decline of Magic*, pp. 95–6.
79. A. Walker, *Planctus Unigeniti* (1664), p. 13.
80. Walker, *Holy Life*, pp. 61–4, 99, 116.
81. Walker, *Planctus Unigeniti*, p. 45.
82. *Ibid.*, sig. A3.
83. Bodl. MS Add. B. 58, f. 118v.
84. Walker, *Eureka*, p. 49.
85. *Hatton Correspondence*, i, 40.
86. BL (AM) 27357, f. 34v.
87. BL (AM) 27351–5. Dates given in the text refer to diary entries.
88. The most impressive example of Mary's self-discipline with regard to the diary is the period following Warwick's death. Although unable to sleep, eat, read or pray, Mary still filled in daily entries.
89. Peck, *Desiderata*, Vol. II, Book XII, Part 6, p. 21.
90. In 1666 Beadle still lived in the neighbourhood, where Mary periodically visited him for 'holy conference'.
91. Robert Burton remarked that there were 'so many commentators, treatises, pamphlets, expositions, sermons, that whole teams of oxen cannot draw them' (*Anatomy of Melancholy*, 1621, 'Preface'). Bestselling guides like Lewis Bayly's *Practise of Pietie* (3rd edn, 1613) ran into scores of editions, but minor clerics were so prolific that Mary could form an entire devotional library written by local divines. For examples of female devotional practice see BL (Eg) 607; Bodl. MS Rawl. Q.e. 26; S. Savage, *The Life of Mrs. Savage* ed. J.B. Williams (1848).
92. Some female devotional guides are Susanna Hopton, *Daily Devotions* (1673) and Elizabeth Burnet, *A Method of Devotion* (2nd edn., 1709).
93. N. Ranew, *Solitude Improved by Divine Meditation* (1670), p. 91.
94. See for example Bodl. MS Rawl. Q.e. 26, ff. 5v, 6, 8; E. Mordaunt, *The Private Diarie of Elizabeth, Viscountess Mordaunt* (Duncairn, 1856), pp. 226–31; Bodl. MS Add. B. 58, ff. 14v, 18v.
95. J. Beadle, *The Journal or Diary of a Thankful Christian* (1656), pp. 66, 70.
96. BL (AM) 27354, 27 April 1676.
97. See for example Walker, *Holy Life*, p. 28.
98. John Bunyan is a well-known example.
99. BL (AM) 27356, f. 269v.
100. BL (AM) 27351, 13 June 1667.
101. *Ibid.*, 5 Aug. 1666.
102. Thomas, *Religion and the Decline of Magic*, Chs. 4–5.
103. For the career of Lucy Hay, Countess of Carlisle see DNB.
104. Bodl. MS Add. B. 58, ff. 2–4v, 36–52; Mordaunt, *Private Diarie*, pp. 33–4; S. Bury, *An Account of the Life and Death of Elizabeth Bury* (1721), p. 37.
105. See particularly A. MacFarlane (ed.), *The Diary of Ralph Josselin 1616–1683* (1976).
106. For other examples of women's terror of childbirth see BL (Eg) 607, ff. 22v, 26v, 32v; Bodl. MS Add. B. 58, ff. 28–34.
107. A. Walker, *Leez Lachrymans Sive Comitis Warwici Justa* (1673), p. 3.
108. BL (AM) 27356, f. 139.
109. BL (AM) 27357, f. 33.

110. For example BL (AM) 27351, 6 Jan., 20 Jan., 27 Jan., and 3 Feb. 1667, 28 Jan. 1670; BL (AM) 27352, 19 July 1671.

111. BL (AM) 27356, f. 245.

112. BL (AM) 27357, f. 16v.

113. BL (AM) 27356, f. 82.

114. BL (AM) 27351, 7 Jan. and 16 Dec. 1668.

115. See for example *The Life and Death of Mr. Vavasor Powell* (1671) p. 4.

116. BL (AM) 27356, f. 156v.

117. Walker, *Leez Lachrymans*, p. 4.

118. BL (AM) 27351, 3 March and 10 March 1667; BL (AM) 27353, 22 Sept. 1672 and 7 June 1673.

119. BL (AM) 27353, 10 Nov. 1672. Charles 'cursed' Mary for 'deasireing my Lord should doe what was charetable and fitt to a poore orphan'.

120. Earl of Berkeley, *Historical Applications*, p. 140; BL (AM) 27356, f. 114; BL (AM) 27351, 1 Feb. 1667; BL (AM) 27356, f. 195.

121. BL (AM) 27356, f. 92.

122. BL (AM) 27351, 25 Dec. 1668.

123. Ranew, *Solitude Improved*, p. 110.

124. M. Penington, *Some Account of the Circumstances of the Life of Mary Penington* (1821), p. 24; A. Beaumont, *The Singular Experiences...of Mrs. Agnes Beaumont* (1822), p. 12.

125. For these passages see BL (AM) 27351, 18 Dec. 1668, 11 March 1669; BL (AM) 27352, 24 Dec. 1669, 22 Aug. 1670, 17 Oct. 1670.

126. Mary laid particular stress on 'relationes duties' in her catalogues of sin, i.e., her duties as wife, mother, mistress of the household.

127. For attacks of spleen, melancholy or 'the Mother' (hysteria) see 18 July 1667, 4 Jan. 1668, 20 Feb. 1668, 25 Jan. 1670, 19 Sept. 1672, 10 Oct. 1672, 14 April 1673 (on this occasion Mary crossed out 'malencolly' and wrote 'the spleene'), 18 April 1673, 9 July 1673, 30 July 1673, 18 Aug. 1673. Warwick died on 24 August. Mary recorded only one fit of spleen for the period 1673–8.

128. BL (AM) 27352, 8–9 Feb. 1672.

129. BL (AM) 27353, 2 Feb. 1673. 'Divel' is in the margin.

130. BL (AM) 27357, f. 34v; BL (AM) 27353, 24 Aug. to 26 Sept. 1673.

131. BL (AM) 27357, f. 36; BL (AM) 27353, 24 and 27 Oct. 1673.

132. BL (AM) 27357, f. 36.

133. BL (AM) 27353, 20 Aug. 1673.

134. For disputes about the will and about religion between Mary and Lord Manchester, see BL (AM) 27354, 11 May and 21 Sept. 1675 and 8 May 1676.

135. Charitable donations are mentioned on nearly every page of the diary. For Mary's scholars at Little Lees see 10 May 1672, 5 February 1674.

136. Walker, *Eureka*, p. 107. The same work lists Mary's main charities, pp. 96–101.

137. See BL (AM) 27355, 1 March, 30 May, 8 and 23 June, 12 July, 20 and 21 Aug. 1677.

138. Macfarlane (ed.), *Diary of Ralph Josselin*, 2 July 1674.

Chapter III: Aphra Behn

1. Although R. A. Day concludes his analysis of the earliest contemporary
    biography of Aphra with the suggestion that she was the 'author' of this
    posthumous account, there is no evidence that she wrote the sections
    about her family origins. See R. A. Day, 'Aphra Behn's First Biographer',
    Studies in Bibliography, xxii (1969), pp. 227–40.
2. The only modern work based on scholarly methods is W. J. Cameron,
    New Light on Aphra Behn (Auckland, 1961). All other accounts suffer
    from the failure to distinguish between fact and speculation. The best of
    these, although marred by this same defect, is G. Woodcock, *The
    Incomparable Aphra* (1948); almost wholly untrustworthy are Edmund
    Gosse's article in the *DNB*; V. Sackville-West, *Aphra Behn* (1927); M.
    Summers' introductory 'Memoir of Mrs. Behn' in *Works*, Vol. I, pp.
    xv–lxi. The most recent accounts are M. Duffy, *The Passionate
    Shepherdess, Aphra Behn 1640-89* (1977) and A. Goreau, *Reconstructing
    Aphra* (New York, 1980). For more extensive discussion and
    documentation of controversial points see my doctoral thesis, 'Women in
    Seventeenth-century England: Three Studies' (Oxford Univ. D.Phil.
    thesis, 1982), pp. 214–337.
3. T. Colepeper, 'Adversaria', BL (Harl) 7588, f. 453v; see also f. 426v.
4. The colonel spent his childhood at Hakington near Canterbury, a locality
    where the name 'Aphra' was localized during the seventeenth and
    eighteenth centuries. See P. D. Mundy, 'Aphra Behn, Novelist and
    Dramatist, 1640?–1689', *Notes and Queries*, cxcix (1954), 199–201. The name
    'Johnson' is also a common Kentish surname.
5. The evidence is consistent with the assumption that Aphra was about
    fourteen in 1663, and seventeen or eighteen in 1666-7 and hence was born
    about 1649.
6. Folger MS N.b. 3, p. 43.
7. Day, 'Aphra Behn's First Biographer', pp. 227–40. For comparison see G.
    Langbaine, *An Account of the English Dramatick Poets* (1691), pp. 17–24;
    G. Jacob, *The Poetical Register* (1723), Vol. I, pp. 14–17.
8. *Works*, Vol. V, p. 265.
9. G. Duchovnay, 'Aphra Behn's Religion', *Notes and Queries*, ccxxi
    (May–June 1976), 235–7.
10. Many examples could be cited. An interpolation Aphra introduced into
    an otherwise faithful plagiarism of a Middleton play reads: 'I was not
    above seven years old when my mother carried me beyond Sea...with a
    design to put me into a nunnery...'. Compare *The Counterfeit
    Bridegroom* (1677), p. 36, and T. Middleton, *No Wit, No Help Like a
    Woman's*, Act IV, sc. i, lines 175–87. In Aphra's story 'The Lucky
    Mistake', the younger sister Charlot is eight years old when placed for her
    'probationer year' in a nunnery where her father's kinswoman is abbess. In
    'The Fair Vowbreaker', Isabella is educated in an Augustinian nunnery
    where her father's sister is abbess. Calista, of *Love Letters*, had spent her
    childhood from the age of six in an Augustinian convent where her aunt

was abbess. Hellena of *The Rover* (1677) is a younger sister 'design'd for a nun' who has been in an Augustinian convent. Cornelia of *The Feign'd Curtizans* (1679) is a younger sister 'bred in a monastery'. In *The Younger Brother* (1696) the audience is irrelevantly informed that Mirtilla has come from England to Ghent to see her younger sister initiated in the English monastery there.

11. All the English nunneries took in female scholars to supplement their income. See the account of Abbé Mann in *Archeologia*, xiii, 251-73, and xxxvi, 74-7. For an Augustinian English nunnery see *The Troubles of Our Catholic Forefathers* (1872), Vol. I, pp. 251-316. The practice of putting on plays, mentioned in the latter work, was referred to by Aphra in her story 'The Fair Vow-Breaker' (*Works*, Vol. V, p. 276).

12. *Oroonoko* (1688), p. 148; 'Life' (1696), sig. a.

13. CSP (Col) 1661-8, nos. 451, 477 and 489; *Acts of the Privy Council Col. 1613-80*, p. 355.

14. Ernest Bernbaum's claim that Aphra Behn had never been to Surinam has been refuted by modern scholarship. See E. Bernbaum, 'Mrs Behn's "Oroonoko"', *George Lyman Kittredge Papers* (1913), pp. 419-33; Cameron, *New Light*, pp. 5-13. As to whether Oroonoko itself is fiction or fact, my own view is that the 'eyewitness' sections have been corroborated by independent evidence but other sections (e.g. Oroonoko's previous history in Coromantien) are probably fiction. See BL (Loan) 29/180, f. 196, 176-176v, and 183 for indirect evidence of Aphra's visit and its duration.

15. *Oroonoko*, p. 142.

16. See J. A. Ramsaran, '"Oroonoko": A Study of the Factual Elements', *Notes and Queries* ccv (1960), 144; B. Dhuicq, 'Further Evidence on Aphra Behn's Stay in Surinam', *Notes and Queries*, (new ser.), xxvi no. 6 (Dec. 1979), 524-6.

17. *Oroonoko*, pp. 103-4.

18. P. M. Seward, 'Calderon and Aphra Behn's Spanish Borrowings in *The Young King*', *Bulletin of Hispanic Studies* xlix (1972), 149-64.

19. BL (Loan) 29/180, f. 131, c. March 1664.

20. See Cameron, *New Light*, p. 20.

21. I.e., Henry Marten the regicide.

22. Nott. U., Portland MSS, Letter from Byam to Harley, cited in Duffy, *Passionate Shepherdess*, pp. 44-5; BL (Loan) 29/180, f. 131. See also CSPD 1660-1, p. 594.

23. *Works*, Vol. V, p. 265.

24. *Love Letters*, p. 120. See also Aphra's 'On the Marriage of the Right Honourable the Earle of Dorset...' appended to *Lycidus* (1688).

25. This is clear from Aphra's letter to Killigrew, PRO (SP) 29/172 no. 14, 7 Sept. 1666.

26. *Miscellany...by Several Hands* (1685), p. 295.

27. CSPD 1664-5, pp. 426-7, cited in Cameron, *New Light*, p. 21; PRO (SP) 29/167, no. 160.

28. PRO (SP) 29/172 no. 14. The clerk who briefed Aphra for her mission always referred to her as 'Mistress Aphora', a mode of address reserved for

adolescent young ladies sufficiently genteel to require the prefix 'mistress' but still too young to drop the given name for the surname.

29. PRO (SP) 29/170, no. 75, and Cameron, *New Light*, p. 56, n. 1; PRO (SP) 29/167 no. 160.
30. 'Life' (1698), p. 6. The close correspondence between this passage and Aphra's letter, PRO (SP) 29/167 no. 160, suggests that this part of the 1698 'Life' (as well as the short novella and the 'Letters' which follow) were composed by Aphra.
31. PRO (SP) 29/167 no. 160. Scot's repeated attempts to persuade Aphra to come to the Hague, as dangerous a place for her as Antwerp was for him, betray a suspicious lack of gallantry. See PRO (SP) 29/169, no. 118.
32. PRO (SP) 29/169 no. 117 and no. 118; PRO (SP) 29/171 no. 120.
33. PRO (SP) 29/177 no. 42; PRO (SP) 29/172 nos. 14, 81.
34. PRO (SP) 29/172 no. 14I.
35. PRO (SP) 29/169 no. 118; PRO (SP) 29/170 no. 75; PRO (SP) 29/168 no. 118.
36. PRO (SP) 29/172 no. 14.
37. PRO (SP) 29/171 no. 65.
38. 'Life' (1698), pp. 8–10. Rumours of Arlington's treasonable connexions with the Dutch (because of his marriage) were widespread at the time. See *POAS 1660–78* p. 81, n. 300.
39. PRO (SP) 29/177, no. 42.
40. PRO (SP) 29/182, no. 143; 'Life' (1698), p. 32.
41. For conclusive arguments for Aphra's editorship see G. Thorn-Drury (ed.), *Covent Garden Drolery* (1928), pp. xvii–xviii.
42. At least three amateur Court theatricals can be identified from prologues included by Aphra: *The Indian Emperor* (13 Jan. 1668), *Horace* (4 Feb. 1668) and *The Faithful Shepherdess* (6 April 1670).
43. See H. A. Hargreaves, 'New Evidence of the Realism of Mrs. Behn's "Oroonoko"', *Bulletin of the New York Public Library*, 74, 437–44.
44. PRO (SP) 29/251, nos. 90, 91, 91I (in Aphra's autograph).
45. PRO (SP) 29/251 no. 92.
46. For a payment to 'Mr Behn' [*sic*] in February 1668 see 'Extracts from an account book of Mr. Baptist May...', Bodl. MS Malone 44, f. 106v.
47. Evelyn, *Diary*, 2 Feb. 1668.
48. For an idealized portrait of Katharine Philips see P. W. Souers, *The Matchless Orinda* (Cambridge, Mass., 1931).
49. A. Clifford (ed.), *Tixall Letters* (1815), Vol. II, p. 60. As Duffy has pointed out, the letter is dated mid-January 1669. See Duffy, *Passionate Shepherdess*, pp. 93–4.
50. A. Clifford (ed.), *Tixall Poetry* (1813), pp. 228–9.
51. See E. Polwhele, *The Frolicks (1671)*, ed. J. Milhous and R. Hume (Ithaca, 1977), pp. 18–49, and Bodl. MS Rawl. Poet. 195, ff. 49–78.
52. J. Downes, *Roscius Anglicanus* (1708), p. 34. The play was revived within a few months.
53. *Poems Upon Several Occasions* (1684), p. 59.
54. *POAS 1660–78*, pp. 338–41; John Dennis's account in *London Stage* p. 253.

55. Many MS copies exist including Bodleian copies Don.b.8 and Rawl. Poet. 173. J. H. Wilson's arguments for Rochester's authorship in *Review of English Studies*, xxii (1946), 109–16 are persuasive. For Aphra's charms see Wycherly's poem 'To the Sappho of the Age', in *Miscellany Poems* (1704), p. 191.

56. *Poems* (1684), pp. 33–44.

57. G. J. Gray, 'The Diary of Jeffrey Boys of Gray's Inn, 1671', *Notes and Queries*, clix (1930), 452–6.

58. The poem as reprinted from the 'MS' copy by *The Muses Mercury* (July, 1707), p. 161, is entitled 'To Mrs. Harsnet…'. A later version is printed in *Poems* (1684) as 'To My Lady Morland'.

59. D. Vieth (ed.), *The Complete Poems of John Wilmot, Earl of Rochester* (New Haven, 1968), p. 42; J. Wright, *Humours and Conversations of the Town* (1693), p. 87.

60. Gray, 'Diary of Jeffrey Boys', p. 455.

61. *Poems* (1684), p. 32.

62. Alexander Radcliffe in 'News from Hell' mentions the rumour that a 'Gray's Inn Lawyer'—presumably Hoyle—had written Aphra's works instead of 'presenting scarf and hood' (i.e. marrying her). See Radcliffe's *Poems* (1682), p. 7. Matthew Prior's 'Session of the Poets' (c. 1688) represents Aphra swearing 'she'd prove, that she and Jack Hoyle taught the whole Age to Love'. *Works of Prior*, ed. Wright and Spears, Vol. I, p. 65.

63. *Bibliotheca Hoyleana* (1692); Earl of Dorset, 'A Faithful Catalogue of Our Most Eminent Ninnies', in *POAS 1685–88*, pp. 213–14 and notes 451, 455, and 459; Whitelocke Bulstrode, MS Commonplace Book, cited in *Works*, Vol. I, p. xxxvi.

64. *Lycidus*, pp. 161–3.

65. *Poems* (1684), pp. 32, 62–3, 106–9; *Lycidus*, p. 162.

66. *The Histories and Novels* (1696), pp. 44–60.

67. For example, the phrase 'my soul is form'd of no other material than love' was repeated half a dozen times throughout her works.

68. *The amours of Philander and Silvia* (1687), pp. 289–90. Other passages in this section, for example the character analyses on p. 4 and p. 59, and the 'gamester' image on p. 115 (which appears in Letter IV in similar form), are strongly reminiscent of 'Love-Letters to a Gentleman'.

69. *The Young King* (1683), *The Forc'd Marriage* (1671), *The Amorous Prince* (1671) and *The Dutch Lover* (1673) had all been finished by 1672, and *The Woman turn'd Bully* (1675) was at least half finished. Aphra produced a total of twenty-two works for the stage including anonymous adaptations and two posthumous plays.

70. See Dryden's 'Essay of Dramatick Poesie', in *The Works of John Dryden*, eds. E. N. Hooker and H. T. Swedenberg, jr., Vol. XVII (1971), pp. 17–20.

71. *Poems* (1684), p. 116.

72. Its composition can be dated, thanks to a Dryden line which Aphra misquotes on p. 38: 'A sudden thought is sprung within my breast (as the New Play has it)'. This line (the correct word is 'mind' not 'breast') can be

found in *The Assignation, or, Love in a Nunnery*, premièred sometime between July and November 1672. The play betrays Aphra's authorship through numerous details of characterization and style, including lines which Aphra re-used elsewhere. For example, 'You are a good Catholick lover, and have a strong implicit faith' (p. 39) became 'By this Hand, child, I have an implicit Faith' in *The Rover* in exactly the same dramatic context. Aphra often re-used material in this way. She disguised her sex in both *The Woman Turn'd Bully* and *The Rover* by using the pronoun 'he' for the author in prologue and epilogue.

73. Aphra was clearly influenced by scenes of female duellists such as Viola in *Twelfth Night*. The main difference is that Aphra's female duellists win.

74. See J. Milhous, 'The Duke's Company's Profits, 1675-77', *Theatre Notebook*, xxxii (1978), no. 2, 76–88, particularly p. 80.

75. See 'A Session of the Poets' (1676), in *POAS 1660-78*, p. 354.

76. *Familiar Letters of Love and Gallantry*, ed. T. Brown (1718), Vol. I, pp. 31-2. Although almost all the letters attributed to Aphra in this collection are spurious, this one may be taken as genuine.

77. Langbaine devoted an entire book to the subject, his *Momus Triumphans: or, The Plagiaries of the English Stage* (1687).

78. Divorce was not always granted even on grounds of non-consummation. For a non-consummated marriage which the House of Lords refused to dissolve, see *Cases of Divorce* (1715), pp. 31-9.

79. *The Town-Fopp* (1677), p. 47.

80. *The Rover*, p. 34, p. 30.

81. *Ibid.*, p. 13.

82. H. Baker, 'Mrs. Behn Forgets', *Studies in English* (Univ. of Texas, 1942), no. 4226, 121-3.

83. 'Epistle Dedicatory', *The Souldiers Fortune* (1681).

84. *Love Letters*.

85. *The Roundheads* (1682), sig. A2v.

86. *Miscellany*, pp. 74–5.

87. See *The Second Part of the Rover*, 'Prologue'.

88. 'A Pastoral to Mr. Stafford...' (the Earl of Stafford's son), in *Miscellany*, pp. 294-6; dedication to *The City-Heiress* (1682).

89. *Juvenalis Redivivus* (1683), p. 1; 'The Epistle Dedicatory' to *Love Letters from a Nobleman to his Sister, The Second Part* (1693).

90. A posthumous play, *The Younger Brother* (1696), was filled with 'the old bustle of Whig and Tory' according to its editor, Charles Gildon; he removed all the politics.

91. Printed in HMC, 2 Rep., p. 70.

92. 'Tom Brown's Last Letter to his Witty Friends and Companions', quoted in P. Pinkus, *Grub Street Stripped Bare* (1968), pp. 119-20.

93. *Miscellany*, p. 74; W. Oldys' MS note to Langbaine, BL (AM) 22592, f. 37v. A verse recipe 'for making a Sack Posset' is in Aphra's MS 'Book for Songs and Satyrs', Bodl. MS Firth c. 16, pp. 138-9.

94. T. Wilkes, *A General View of the Stage* (1759), p. 246; Folger MS c.c.1 (4).

95. *Familiar Letters*, Vol. I, pp. 31-2.

96. *Poems* (1684), pp. 80-1; *Sir Patient Fancy* (1678), sig. A.

97. HMC, 2 Rep., p. 70; *Miscellany*, p. 75; 'Returns of Lodgers and Inmates', St. Bride's Parish, New Street, in Corp. of Lond. Records Office. The rate books list Dryden as living on Fleet Street (at Fetter Lane), and Shadwell at Salisbury Court next to the Duke's Theatre.

98. M. Prior, 'A Satyr on the Modern Translators' (1685).

99. 'To the Unknown Daphnis on his Excellent Translation of Lucretius', in T. Creech, *Titus Lucretius Carus*, 3rd edn. (Oxford, 1683), sig. cv.

100. *The Woman Turn'd Bully* quotes the motto 'Hanc venium petimus Damusq' on its title page. There is a good deal of peculiar Latin sprinkled throughout the play itself, presumably to mock the legal profession. The postscript to *The Rover* has a 'translated' tag: 'I will only say in English what the famous Virgil does in Latin: I make Verses and others have the fame'.

101. See for example two couplets in Aphra's 'translation' of *Aesop's Fables* (1687), p. 20.

102. Actually Sandys did not translate the *Heröides*.

103. For Aphra's theory of translation, see the preface to her translation of Fontenelle's *A Discovery of New Worlds* (1688), sig. A4.

104. C. Cotton, *Poems on Several Occasions* (1689), p. 154.

105. *Poems* (1684), p. 127.

106. Printed in *Amusements Serious and Comical and Other Works by Tom Brown*, ed. A. L. Hayward (1927), p. 439.

107. Many satires mention Aphra's propensity to talk at great length. See for example 'A Journal from Parnassus', Bodl. MS Don. e. 18, f. 13.

108. Cited in Woodcock, *The Incomparable Aphra*, p. 83.

109. Preface to *The Younger Brother*.

110. Printed in the miscellany of poems following *The History of Adolphus* (1691), p. 54. As W. J. Cameron pointed out, this volume contains some of the 'Remaines' of Aphra Behn. W. J. Cameron, 'George Granville and the "Remaines" of Aphra Behn', *Notes and Queries*, ccix (1959), 88–92.

111. 'Ephelia', *Female Poems on Several Occasions* (1679), p. 72; *Lycidus*, p. 116.

112. *The Temple of Death* (1695), p. 242.

113. Quoted in *Signet Classic Poets of the Seventeenth Century*, ed. J. Broadbent (N.Y., 1974), Vol. II, p. 442.

114. 'Life of Mrs. Anne Wharton', in P. Bayle *et al.*, *A General Dictionary* (1741), Vol. X, pp. 126, 129.

115. *The Temple of Death*, p. 242.

116. *Poems* (1684), p. 59.

117. *A General Dictionary*, Vol. X, pp. 126–7.

118. R. Gould, *Poems* (1689), p. 303; E. H. Sloane, *Robert Gould, Seventeenth Century Satirist* (Phila., 1940), pp. 26, 34.

119. BL (Harl) 7319, ff. 165v–167; B. Harris, 'Aphra Behn's "Bajazet to Gloriana"', *Times Literary Supplement* (9 Feb. 1933), p. 92. Aphra also wrote a prose satire on Mulgrave, 'The Court of the King of Bantam', composed in 1683 but printed posthumously. See *Works*, Vol. V, pp. 13–34.

120. Gould, *Poems* (1709), Vol. II, p. 16.

121. BL (Harl) 6913, f. 126, dated 'temp Charles II'; the mention of the Countess of Stamford dates it between 1675 and 1687. The awkward stopped end-rhymes, the prevalence of certain rhymes and resemblance of several lines to those found in Gould's published poems identify it as his.
122. BL (Harl) 7319, f. 165v.
123. Torquato Tasso's *Aminta Englisht—The Henry Reynolds Translation*, ed. C. Davidson (Fennimore, Wisc., 1972), p. 67, note 26 to First Chorus.
124. *Dutch Lover*, sig. A2.
125. *Miscellany*, p. 49.
126. *Ibid.*, p. 75.
127. *The Young King*, p. 5; 'To Henry Higden, Esq., on his Translation of the Tenth Satyr of Juvenal', in [H. Higden], *A Modern Essay on the Tenth Satyr of Juvenal* (1687), sig. a.
128. *Poems* (1684), p. 118; Creech, *Lucretius*, sig. C; *Amours of Philander and Silvia*, p. 29.
129. *Amours of Philander and Silvia*, p. 246.
130. *Miscellany*, p. 197.
131. *Works*, Vol. V, p. 281; *Lycidus*, p. 115.
132. *Lycidus*, pp. 145–51.
133. *Love Letters*, p. 65.
134. R. Gould, 'Love Given O're', in *Satires on Women* (Augustan Reprint, Los Angeles, 1976), p. 5.
135. *Love Letters*, pp. 65–7; 'Lysander' is erratically substituted for the name of the hero, Philander, in the first two editions.
136. *Poems* (1684), p. 101.
137. *Ibid.*, p. 110.
138. *Love Letters*, p. 69; *Poems* (1684), sig. A8 and pp. 8–10.
139. *Poems of Rochester*, ed. Vieth, p. 14.
140. *Ibid.*, p. 10.
141. *Works*, Vol. V, p. 404.
142. *Love Letters*, p. 69.
143. 'A poem against fruition on the reading in Mountains Essay: By Alexis'; it immediately precedes Aphra's reply in *Lycidus*, p. 129. Neither poem mentions which essay, but it could only be 'Of Friendship'. See *Essays of Montaigne Translated by Charles Cotton*, ed. W. C. Hazlitt (1877), Vol. I, p. 266.
144. *Works*, Vol. V, p. 263.
145. *Lycidus*, p. 40.
146. An exception is the genre of poems counselling rape. For examples see three poems printed in the Duke of Buckingham's posthumous *Works* (1705): Radcliffe's 'A satire against love and women' (Vol. II, p. 106), Sedley's 'Advice to Lovers' (Vol. I, pp. 116–17), and the Earl of Dorset's 'The Advice' (Vol. II, Part 2, p. 57).
147. *Amours of Philander and Silvia*, p. 152.
148. [Higden], *Tenth Satyr of Juvenal*, sig. a; *Miscellany*, p. 293.
149. *Poems* (1684), p. 8; *Ibid.*, p. 4.
150. The two other poems are her paraphrase 'The Disappointment' in *Poems*

(1684), p. 75 and 'To the Fair Clarinda, who made love to me, imagin'd more than Woman', in *Lycidus*, p. 164.

151. It seems unlikely that Aphra would have been younger than sixteen when sent to Antwerp in 1666.

152. *Amours of Philander and Silvia*, pp. 385–7; Prior, 'A Satyr on the Modern Translators', *Works of Prior*, ed. Wright and Spears, Vol. I, p. 21; *Love Letters from a Nobleman to his Sister. The Second Part* (1693), p. 139.

153. J. H. Wilson, *Nell Gwyn* (New York, 1952), p. 278; 'An Elegy Upon the Death of Mrs. Behn', in *A Little Ark*, ed. G. Thorn-Drury (1921), p. 56.

154. The book is Bodl. MS Firth c. 16. Satires copied either wholly or partly in Aphra's autograph are found on pp. 101, 102, 103, 104 (two), 111 (two), 115 (part), 122, 129, 130 (part), 134, 135 (two), 139, 143, 145, 147 (part), 165, 199 (part), 217, 241 (part), 243, 245, 263 (part), 269, 276, 283 (part). Clearly her friends contributed the other satires and sometimes shared the burden of copying. Contemporaries pronounced her surname 'bean'.

155. It is a rough working copy covering pages 217–26, with corrections in her own and another hand. It is signed 'A Behn', and the signature crossed out. Aphra's autograph has been identified by comparison with her note to Tonson for a loan, now Folger MS c.c.1 (4). The satire 'Tunbridg Lampoone 1686' on pp. 111–15 in Aphra's autograph may be her own composition as it is very much in her style.

156. Bodl. MS Firth c. 16, p. 103, entitled 'Another on Mr. Bays'; other satires on Dryden are found on pp. 101–11.

157. *Ibid.*, pp. 104–111.

158. R. Hume, 'The Dorset Garden Theatre', *Theatre Notebook*, xxxiii (1979), 12–13.

159. HMC, 2 Rep., p. 70; Folger MS c.c.1 (4).

160. References to the Duke of Norfolk occur throughout the decade. In 1682 Aphra dedicated *The City-Heiress* to him; in 1685 she called him 'Maecenas of my Muse' in her Coronation poem; his name and Paris address (probably for 1688) are scrawled on the title page of her 'Book for Songs and Satyrs'.

161. 'Life' (1696).

162. *Poems* (1684), sig. A5v; 'A Journal from Parnassus', Bodl. MS Don. e. 18, ff. 13v–14.

163. P. B. Anderson, 'Buckingham's Chemist', *Times Literary Supplement* (1935), p. 612.

164. 'To Julian', BL (Harl) 7317, f. 58.

165. *Works*, Vol. I, pp. l–li; *Ibid.*, pp. vi, 405.

166. 'To the Memory of the Most Illustrious Prince George Duke of Buckingham', in Buckingham's *Works* (1705), Vol. II, p. 206.

167. *Aesop's Fables*, p. 203.

168. *A Discovery of New Worlds*, sig. a–a2.

169. In 1688 Aphra printed 'A Poem to Sir Roger L'Estrange', thanking him for having solved the mystery of Sir Edmund Bury Godfrey's death with his suicide theory, published in the third part of his *A Brief History of the Times* (1687–8). Her poem summarizes her view of the Popish Plot. Aphra's dedication to Lord Jeffreys praises him for his public services,

repeating views she had expressed in *Aesop's Fables* (1687) in favour of death sentences for all those implicated in Monmouth's Rebellion. See *Aesop's Fables*, pp. 29, 31, 45, 49, 61, 87, 101, 113, 143, 145, 161, 197.

170. See G. Duchovnay, 'Aphra Behn's Religion', *Notes and Queries*, (new ser.), ccxxi (1976), 235–7.

171. Bodl. MS Firth c. 16, pp. 259, 261, 295, 300; *Ibid.*, pp. 264, 276, 283, etc.

172. Cowley, *The Second and Third Parts of the Works...The Third Containing his Six Books of Plants* (1689), Book VI, 'Of Trees', p. 143. The editor's note reads: 'The Translatress in her own Person Speaks'.

173. Bodl. MS Firth c. 16, p. 303. The next few pages were left blank. On pp. 307–8 are six short poems dating from 1736–8.

174. 'A Pindaric Poem to the Reverend Doctor Burnet...' (1689), pp. 5–6.

175. C. Gildon, 'Preface' to *The Younger Brother*.

176. Printed in broadside, 22 April 1689. It has been persuasively argued that the author was Delarivière Manley. See R. Foxton, 'Astrea's Vacant Throne', *Notes and Queries*, (new ser.) xxxiii no. 1 (March 1986), 41–2.

177. Pepys, *Diary*, 3 Nov. 1662.

178. T. Brown, 'To a Lady, whom he refus'd to Marry because he Lov'd her', in Duke of Buckingham, *Works* (1705), Vol. II, p. 107.

179. Folger MS N.b.3, p. 69.

180. A MS poem to Anne Wharton in the Bodleian copy of Edward Young's *The Idea of Christian Love* (1688), pp. vii–viii. A note ascribes it to 'Will Atwood'.

Epilogue

1. *The Luckey Chance* (1687), 'Preface'.

2. *Orations* (1662), p. 229.

3. *Playes* (1662), p. 254.

4. Proverbs listed by Tilley include 'All women are ambitious naturally' (W697) and 'Women think place [plaice] a sweet fish' (W719). M. Tilley, *A Dictionary of the Proverbs in England in the Sixteenth and Seventeenth Centuries* (Ann Arbor, 1950), pp. 747, 748. For Samuel Butler's satire on the 'proud lady', see *Characters from the Notebooks*, ed. A. R. Waller (1908), p. 250. Concern for status was not confined to the aristocracy, as we can infer from numerous disputes over church seating by women of the artisan and labouring classes throughout this period. The same preoccupation is shown in the growing practice of recording family histories and genealogies.

5. The usual response to feminine incursions into the male domain was ribald mockery, as in the popular Civil War genre which depicted imaginary 'female Parliaments' whose aims were grossly sexual. English attitudes were not simply an expression of the 'spirit of the times'; contemporary France saw a well-developed feminist movement. See I. Maclean, *Woman Triumphant: Feminism in French Literature 1610–1652* (Oxford, 1977).

6. W. Gouge, *Of Domesticall Duties* (1662), pp. 271, 286. Gouge also speculated that wives assumed they were equal to their husbands because of the small degree of difference in the matrimonial relationship, compared with other familial and household relations.

7. *Sociable Letters*, pp. 27–8. Class mobility was also concealed in a society with a static, hierarchical and intensely conservative frame of mind, through the buying of titles, the manufacture of genealogies, etc.

8. For more evidence of courtship practices among various classes see S. Mendelson, 'The Weightiest Business: Marriage in an Upper-Gentry Family in Seventeenth-Century England', *Past and Present*, lxxxv (1979), pp. 126–35, and M. Ingram, 'The Reform of Popular Culture? Sex and Marriage in Early Modern England', in *Popular Culture in Early Modern England*, ed. B. Reay (Beckenham, Kent, 1985), pp. 129–65.

9. A good contemporary example is the career of Lady Ranelagh. See above, p. 86.

10. *Worlds Olio*, 'The Preface to the Reader'.

11. Unlike their counterparts in contemporary France, Englishwomen did not produce a countervailing philosophy which might have challenged the cultural implications of the humoral theory. In her *Prognostication for...1658* Sarah Jinner questioned some of the implications of the humoral theory but not its main postulates. For the decline of the humoral theory see below, note 21.

12. *An Essay in Defence of the Female Sex* (2nd edn., 1696), sigs. B8–B8v. Contemporary ecclesiastical court records give a similar impression of women's greater equality and autonomy among the lower ranks.

13. BL (Eg) 607, f. 78v.

14. *The Legacy of a Dying Mother...Being the Experiences of Mrs. Susanna Bell* (1673), pp. 45–6.

15. For the conservative effect of religious doctrine on women's familial role early in the eighteenth century, see for example Mary Astell, *Some Reflections upon Marriage* (1706), pp. 83–9.

16. *Memorialls of the Holles Family* (Camden Soc., 1937) 3rd ser., lv, 226; *Autobiography of Sir John Bramston* (Camden Soc., 1845), xxxii, 13–16; C. Carlton, 'The Widow's Tale: Male Myths and Female Reality in Sixteenth and Seventeenth Century England', *Albion*, x (1978), 118–29; B. Todd, 'The Remarrying Widow: a Stereotype Reconsidered', in *Women in English Society 1500–1800*, ed. M. Prior (1985), pp. 54–92. Childless women of whatever matrimonial status shared some of the same characteristics, and it is not a coincidence that most of the female authors who forged a literary career during this period were single, widowed or barren.

17. S. Geree, *Ornament of a Woman* (1639), p. 28; R. Baxter, *Autobiography*, ed. J. M. Lloyd Thomas (Everyman, 1931), p. 15.

18. A. Macfarlane, *Witchcraft in Tudor and Stuart England* (1970), pp. 147–98; Thomas, *Religion and the Decline of Magic*, pp. 517–680; Butler, *Characters*, ed. Waller, p. 255; *A Pepysian Garland*, ed. H. E. Rollins (Cambridge, 1922), pp. 72–7; S. Amussen, 'Gender, Family and the Social Order, 1560–1725', in *Order and Disorder in Early Modern England*, ed.

A. Fletcher and J. Stevenson (Cambridge, 1985), pp. 196–217; D. Underdown, 'The Taming of the Scold', in Fletcher and Stevenson, *ibid.*, pp. 116–36.

19.   P. Crawford, 'Women's Published Writings 1600–1700', in *Women in English Society 1500–1800*, ed. M. Prior (1985), p. 213.

20.   F. J. Fisher, 'The Development of London as a Centre of Conspicuous Consumption in the Sixteenth and Seventeenth Centuries', *Transactions of the Royal Historical Society* (1948); A. Clark, *Working Life of Women in the Seventeenth Century* (1919), p. 38; E. Chamberlayne, *An Academy or College...* (1671), pp. 1–2; D. Gardiner, *English Girlhood at School* (1929), pp. 274–5.

21.   S.W. Jackson, 'Melancholia and the Waning of the Humoral Theory', *Journal of the History of Medicine and Allied Sciences* xxxiii (1978), 367–76; W. Walsh, *A Dialogue Concerning Women* (1691); N. Tate, *A Present for the Ladies* (1692); [P. Motteux], *The Ladies Journal* (1693); N. H., *The Ladies Dictionary* (1694), pp. 18–21; *An Essay in Defense of the Female Sex* (1694), p. 36.

22.   [R. Allestree], *The Ladies Calling* (1673), p. 147.

23.   Marquis of Halifax, *The Lady's New Years Gift* (1688), p. 96; N. Elias, *The Civilizing Process* (New York, 1978), pp. 184–6; D. Hume, *An Enquiry Concerning the Principles of Morals* (La Salle, 1953), p. 74. See also *Examen Miscellaneum* (1702), p. 115.

24.   For the importance of gender distinctions in eighteenth-century manners and morals see F. Childs, 'Prescriptions for Manners in English Courtesy Literature, 1690–1760, and Their Social Implications' (Oxford Univ. D.Phil. thesis, 1984).

Select Bibliography

A. Manuscript Sources

I. BODLEIAN LIBRARY
Additional MSS
  A.119 Letters of the Fairfax family.
  B.58 Prayers of Lady Pakington.
Ashmole 36, f. 186v. Epitaph on the Duchess of Newcastle.
Clarendon MSS
  29–72 Clarendon State Papers.
  109 Marquis of Newcastle's 'Advice' to Charles II.
Don. e. 18 'A Journal from Parnassus'.
Eng. Misc. d. 133 Diary of Lady Anne Clifford.
Eng. Misc. d. 436–7 Cookery and Medicinal Receipts.
Firth c. 16 Aphra Behn's 'Book for Songs and Satyrs'.
Malone 44 Extracts from Baptist May's Privy Purse Accounts for Charles
  II.
Rawlinson MSS
  D.421 'Mulieres non Homines, ou la Femme Deshumanisée'.
  Poet. 16 'Poems Songs a Pastorall and a Play by . . . Lady Iane Cavendish
    and Lady Elizabeth Brackley'.
  Q.e.26–27 Stuart female spiritual diary.
Smith 13 Walter Charleton's commonplace book.

II. BRITISH LIBRARY
Additional MSS
  18023, ff. 7–9 Indenture of Sir Richard Boyle.
  19831–2 Autobiography and other MSS of Sir Richard Boyle.
  22592 W. Oldys' MS notes on Langbaine.
  23206 Bond of Marquis of Newcastle.
  27351–5 Diary of Mary Rich, Countess of Warwick.

27356 'Occasional Meditations' of the Countess of Warwick.

27357 'Some Specialities in the Life of M. Warwicke'.

28558, f. 65. Letter from the Marchioness of Newcastle to Christiaan Huygens.

28693 'Lover Martyr' by Anne Wharton.

32497 'The Phanseys of the Marquesse of Newcastle'.

Birch 4278 Letters of Sir Charles Cavendish to John Pell.

Egerton MSS

80 Correspondence of the Earl of Cork.

607 Religious Meditations of the Countess of Bridgewater.

1290, f. 2 Motto of 'Charles Riche', 1634.

2005 Hobbes' presentation copy of 'Elements of Law' to the Earl of Newcastle, 1640.

2551 Bill for restoring the Marquis of Newcastle's estates.

2648, f. 46 Letter of recruitment by Charles Rich.

Harleian MSS

379 D'Ewes correspondence.

6001–2 Scientific MSS of Sir Charles Cavendish.

6083 Scientific MSS of Sir Charles Cavendish.

6796 Scientific MSS of Sir Charles Cavendish.

6913, f. 126 'The Description of a Poetress'.

6988, ff. 111–12 Earl of Newcastle's advice to Prince Charles.

7317, f. 58 'To Julian'.

7319, ff. 165v–167 'The Female Laureate'.

7367 'The Humorous Lovers' [by the Duke of Newcastle].

7588 T. Colepeper, 'Adversaria'.

7650 'The Country Captain' [by the Duke of Newcastle].

Portland Loan

29/180 Harley Papers.

29/235 Cavendish Papers, 1604–60.

29/236 Cavendish Papers, 1661–95.

Sloane 4454 Diary of Katharine Austen.

III. CHATSWORTH, DERBYSHIRE

Calendar of the Lismore Manuscripts of the Boyle family (typescript).

Lismore Manuscripts of the Boyle family, 1604–43.

IV. FOLGER SHAKESPEARE LIBRARY

c.c.1 (4) Autograph note by Aphra Behn.

N.b.3 Poems of the Countess of Winchelsea.

V.a.312 'A Discourse against Plays and Romances'.

V. PUBLIC RECORD OFFICE
State Papers

Dispatches of Aphra Behn to Major Halsall, Thomas Killigrew and Lord Arlington: 29/167 no. 160; 29/168 no. 118; 29/169 no. 117 and no. 118; 29/170 no. 75; 29/171 no. 65 and no. 120; 29/172 nos. 14, 14I and 81; 29/177 no. 42; 29/182 no. 143.

Petitions of Aphra Behn to Thomas Killigrew and Charles II: 29/251 nos. 90, 91, 91I, and 92.

29/450, Item 102 ff. 164–v Ballad by John Evelyn.

Wills

Thomas Lucas, 23 Sept. 1625.

Charles Rich, fourth Earl of Warwick, 14 April 1673.

Mary Rich, fourth Countess of Warwick, 12 March 1678.

VI. UNIVERSITY OF NOTTINGHAM
Portland Collection

Pw1. Cavendish Manuscripts.

PwV. Literary Manuscripts.

VII. THESES

Cioni, M., 'Women and Law in Elizabethan England', Cambridge Univ. Ph.D. Thesis, 1976.

Cocking, H. M., 'Originality and Influence in the Work of Margaret Cavendish, First Duchess of Newcastle', Reading Univ. M. Phil. Thesis, 1972.

Ingram, M. J., 'Ecclesiastical Justice in Wiltshire, 1600–1640', Oxford Univ. D. Phil. Thesis, 1976.

Ranger, T., 'The Career of Richard Boyle, First Earl of Cork in Ireland, 1588–1643', Oxford Univ. D. Phil. thesis, 1958.

B. Printed Sources

I. PRIMARY SOURCES

[Allestree, R.], *The Ladies Calling* (1673).

Beadle, J., *The Journal or Diary of a Thankful Christian* (1656).

Behn, Aphra,

—— *Abdelazar* (1677).

—— *Aesop's Fables* (1687).

—— *All the Histories and Novels* (3rd edn., 1698).

—— *The Amorous Prince* (1671).

—— *The amours of Philander and Silvia* (1687).

—— *The City-Heiress* (1682).

—— *A Congratulatory Poem...on the Happy Birth of the Prince of Wales* (1688).

—— *A Congratulatory Poem to her...Majesty...*(1688).

—— *A Congratulatory Poem to...Queen Mary...* (1689).

—— *The Counterfeit Bridegroom* (1677).

—— *Covent Garden Drolery* (1672).

—— *The Debauchee* (1677).

—— *A Discovery of New Worlds*, trans. from B. de Fontenelle (1688).

—— *The Dutch Lover* (1673).

—— *The Emperor of the Moon* (1687).

—— *The False Count* (1682).

—— *The Feign'd Curtizans* (1679).

—— *The Forc'd Marriage* (1671).

—— *The Histories and Novels* (1696).

—— *The History of Oracles...*, trans. from B. de Fontenelle (1688).

—— *Love Letters between a Nobleman and his Sister* (1684).

—— *Love Letters from a Nobleman...the Second Part* (1693).

—— *Love Letters between a Nobleman and his Sister...In three parts.* (3rd edn., 1708).

—— *The Luckey Chance* (1687).

—— *Lycidus* (1688).

—— *Miscellany...by several hands* (1685).

—— *La Montre*, trans. from B. de Bonnecourse (1686).

—— *Oroonoko* (1688).

—— *A Pindaric Poem to...Doctor Burnet* (1689).

—— *A Pindarick on the Death of our late Sovereign* (1685).

—— *A Pindarick Poem on the Happy Coronation* (1685).

—— *A Poem Humbly Dedicated to the Great Patern of Piety...Catharine* (1685).

—— *A Poem to Sir Roger L'Estrange* (1688).

—— *Poems upon Several Occasions* (1684).

—— *The Roundheads* (1682).

—— *The Rover* (1677).

—— *The second part of the Rover* (1681).

—— *Sir Patient Fancy* (1678).

—— *To poet Bavius* (1688).

—— *To the Most Illustrious Prince Christopher* (1687).

—— *The Town-Fopp* (1677).

—— *The Widdow Ranter* (1690).

—— *The Woman Turn'd Bully* (1675).

—— *Works*, ed. M. Summers, 6 Vols. (New York, 1915).

—— *The Young King* (1683).
—— *The Younger Brother* (1696).
Berkeley, George, Earl of, *Historical Applications and Occasional Meditations* (1670), pp. 131–57.
Boyle, R., *The Works of the Honourable Robert Boyle*, ed. T. Birch, 5 Vols. (1744).
Braithwait, R., *The English Gentlewoman* (1631).
Brown, T. (ed.), *Familiar Letters of Love and Gallantry*, 2 Vols. (1718).
Calamy, E., *A Patterne for All* (1658).
Calendar of the Clarendon State Papers, 4 Vols. (Oxford, 1869–1932).
Calendar of Patent Rolls Ireland.
Calendar of State Papers Domestic.
Calendar of State Papers Colonial.
Calendar of the Proceedings of the Committee for Compounding.
Calendar of Treasury Books.
Clarendon, Edward Hyde, Earl of, *The History of the Great Rebellion and Civil Wars in England*, ed. W. D. Macray, 6 Vols. (Oxford, 1888).
Conway Letters, ed. M. H. Nicolson (New Haven, 1930).
Cowley, A.,...*Six Books of Plants...Now made English...* (1689).
Dryden, J., *The Works of John Dryden*, eds. E. N. Hooker and H. T. Swedenberg, jr., 19 Vols. (Berkeley, Calif., 1956–79).
Downes, J., *Roscius Anglicanus* (1708).
E., T., *The Lawes Resolutions of Womens Rights* (1632).
'Ephelia', *Female Poems on Several Occasions* (1679).
Evelyn, J. *Diary and Correspondence*, ed. W. Bray, 4 Vols. (1857).
Evelyn, J. *Diary*, ed. E. S. de Beer, 6 Vols. (Oxford, 1955).
Gouge, W., *Of Domesticall Duties* (1622).
Gould, R., *Satires on Women* (Augustan Reprint, Los Angeles, 1976).
Halifax, George Savile, Marquis of, *The Lady's New Years Gift* (1688).
Historical Manuscripts Commission Reports.
Hoyle, J., *Bibliotheca Hoyleana* (1692).
Hutchinson, L., *Memoirs of the Life of Colonel Hutchinson*, ed. J. Sutherland (Oxford, 1973).
Jinner, S., *A Prognostication for...1658* (1658).
Journals of the House of Commons.
Journals of the House of Lords.
Langbaine, G., *An Account of the English Dramatick Poets* (1691).
Letters and Poems in Honour of...Margaret, Duchess of Newcastle (1676).
Lismore Papers, ed. A. B. Grosart, 1st and 2nd ser., 10 Vols. (1886–9).
[Makin, B.], *An Essay to Revive the Antient Education of Gentlewomen...* (1673).

[Manley, D.], *An Elegy Upon the Death of Mrs. A. Behn* (1689).

Markham, G., *The English Housewife* (1618).

Newcastle, Margaret Cavendish, Duchess of, *CCXI Sociable Letters* (1664).

—— *The Description of a New World, called the Blazing-World* (1668).

—— *Grounds of Natural Philosophy* (1668).

——The Life of William Cavendish, Duke of Newcastle, ed. C. Firth (2nd edn., n.d.).

——*The Life of...William Cavendishe, Duke, Marquess, and Earl of Newcastle...*, (1667; Latin edn; 1668).

—— *Natures Pictures drawn by Fancies Pencil to the Life* (1656).

——*Observations upon Experimental Philosophy* (1666).

—— *Orations of Divers Sorts* (1662).

——*Philosophical and Physical Opinions* (1655).

——*Philosophicall Fancies* (1653).

——*Philosophical Letters* (1664).

—— *Playes* (1662).

—— *Plays Never Before Printed* (1668).

—— *Poems and Fancies* (1653).

—— *The Worlds Olio* (1655).

Newcastle, William Cavendish, Duke of, *La Methode Nouvelle et Invention Extraordinaire de dresser les Chevaux* (Antwerp, 1658).

—— *The Phanseys of William Cavendish Marquis of Newcastle, ed.* D. Grant (1956).

Peck, F., *Desiderata Curiosa*, 2 Vols. (1732–5).

Pepys, S., *Diary*, ed. R. B. Latham and W. Matthews, 11 Vols. (1970–83).

Poems on Affairs of State, eds. G. de F. Lord, W. J. Cameron, G. M. Crump, F. H. Ellis, E. F. Mengel, H. H. Schless, 6 Vols. (New Haven, 1963–71).

Polwhele, E., *The Frolicks [1671]*, ed. J. Milhous and R. Hume (Ithaca, 1977).

Prior, M., *The Literary Works of Matthew Prior*, eds. H. B. Wright and M. K. Spears, 2 Vols. (Oxford, 1959).

Ryves, B., *Mercurius Rusticus* (1643), pp. 1–5.

Strong, S.A., *A Catalogue of the Letters and Other Documents Exhibited at Welbeck* (1903).

Walker, A., *Eureka, or, the Virtuous Woman Found* (1678).

—— *The Holy Life of Mrs Elizabeth Walker* (1690).

—— *Leez Lachrymans Sive Comitis Warwici Justa* (1673).

—— *Planctus Unigeniti* (1664).

Warwick, Mary Rich, Countess of, *Autobiography*, ed. T. C. Croker (Percy Society, 1848), xxii.

II. SECONDARY SOURCES

Amussen, S., 'Gender, Family and the Social Order, 1560–1725', in *Order and Disorder in Early Modern England*, ed. A. Fletcher and J. Stevenson (Cambridge, 1985), pp. 196–217.

Ballard, G., *Memoirs of Several Ladies of Great Britain...* (Oxford, 1752).

Birch, T., *History of the Royal Society*, 4 Vols. (1756–7).

Bowerbank, S., 'The Spider's Delight: Margaret Cavendish and the "Female" Imagination', *English Literary Renaissance* (1984), 392–408.

Bredvold, L. I., *The Intellectual Milieu of John Dryden* (Ann Arbor, 1934).

Camden, C., *The Elizabethan Woman* (New York, 1952).

Cameron, W. J., 'George Granville and the "Remaines" of Aphra Behn', *Notes and Queries*, ccix (1959), 88–92.

—— *New Light on Aphra Behn* (Auckland, 1961).

Clark, A., *Working Life of Women in the Seventeenth Century* (1919).

Crawford, P., 'Women's Published Writings 1600–1700', in *Women in English Society 1500–1800*, ed. M. Prior (1985), pp. 211–82.

Davids, T. W., *Annals of Evangelical Nonconformity in the County of Essex...* (1863).

Day, R. A., 'Aphra Behn's First Biographer', *Studies in Bibliography*, xxii (1969) 227–40.

Delany, P., *British Autobiography in the Seventeenth Century* (1969).

Dhuicq, B., 'Further Evidence on Aphra Behn's Stay in Surinam', *Notes and Queries*, new ser., xxvi no. 6, (Dec. 1979) 524–6.

Duchovnay, G., 'Aphra Behn's Religion', *Notes and Queries*, ccxxi (May-June 1976) 235–7.

Duffy, M., *The Passionate Shepherdess, Aphra Behn 1640–89* (1977).

Fraser, A., *The Weaker Vessel* (1984).

Gagen, J. E., *The New Woman: her Emergence in English Drama* (1954).

Gardiner, D., *English Girlhood at School* (1929).

Goreau, A., *Reconstructing Aphra* (New York, 1980).

Goulding, R., *The Thrice Noble, Illustrious and Excellent Princess, Margaret Duchess of Newcastle* (1925).

Grant, D., *Margaret the First* (1957).

Gray, G. J., 'The Diary of Jeffrey Boys of Gray's Inn, 1671', *Notes and Queries* clix (1930) 452–6.

Hargreaves, H. A., 'New Evidence of the Realism of Mrs. Behn's "Oroonoko",' *Bulletin of the New York Public Library*, 74, 437–44.

Harris, B., 'Aphra Behn's "Bajazet to Gloriana",' *Times Literary Supplement* (9 Feb. 1933), p. 92.

Hume, R., 'The Dorset Garden Theatre', *Theatre Notebook*, xxxiii (1979) 12–13.

Jacquot, J., 'Sir Charles Cavendish and his Learned Friends', *Annals of Science* (1952) 13–27.

MacCarthy, B. G., *Women Writers: their Contribution to the English Novel, 1621–1744* (Oxford, 1944).

Maclean, I., *The Renaissance Notion of Woman* (Cambridge, 1980).

Mendelson, S., 'Stuart Women's Diaries and Occasional Memoirs', in *Women in English Society 1500–1800*, ed. M. Prior (1985), pp. 181–210.

Milhous, J., 'The Duke's Company's Profits, 1675–77', *Theatre Notebook*, xxxii (1978), no. 2, 76–88.

Mintz, S. I., 'The Duchess of Newcastle's Visit to the Royal Society', *Journal of English and Germanic Philology* (1952) 168–76.

Morant, P., *History and Antiquities of...Colchester*, 2 Vols. (1768). *History and Antiquities of...Essex*, 2 Vols. (1768).

Mundy, P. D., 'Aphra Behn, Novelist and Dramatist, 1640?–89', *Notes and Queries*, cxcix (1954), 199–200.

Nicoll, A., *A History of Restoration Drama, 1660–1700* (Cambridge, 2nd ed., 1952).

Paloma, D., 'Margaret Cavendish: Defining the Female Self', *Women's Studies*, vii (1980) 55–66.

Perry, H. T. E., *The First Duchess of Newcastle and her Husband as Figures in Literary History* (Boston, 1918).

Ramsaran, J. A., '"Oroonoko": A Study of the Factual Elements', *Notes and Queries*, ccv (1960) 144.

Ranger, T., 'Richard Boyle and the Making of an Irish Fortune, 1588–1614', *Irish Historical Studies*, x (1957) 257–97.

Reynolds, M., *The Learned Lady in England, 1650–1760* (Boston, 1920).

Seward, P. M., 'Calderon and Aphra Behn's Spanish Borrowings in *The Young King*', *Bulletin of Hispanic Studies*, xlix (1972) 149–64.

Smith, C. F., *Mary Rich, Countess of Warwick* (1901).

Smith, H., *Ecclesiastical History of Essex...* (Colchester, 1932).

Smith, H., *Reason's Disciples* (Urbana, 1982).

Souers, P. W., *The Matchless Orinda* (Cambridge, Mass., 1931).

Starr, N. C., '"The Concealed Fansyes", a Play by Lady Jane Cavendish and Lady Elizabeth Brackley', *Publications of the Modern Language Association*, xlvi (1931) 837–8.

Stone, L., *The Family, Sex and Marriage in England, 1500–1800* (1977).

Thomas, K. V., 'The Double Standard', *Journal of the History of Ideas*, xx (1959) 195–216.

—— *Religion and the Decline of Magic* (Harmondsworth, Middlesex, 1973).

—— 'Women and the Civil War Sects', *Past and Present*, xiii (1958) 42–62.

Thorn-Drury, G.(ed.), *Covent Garden Drolery* (1928), 'Introduction'.

Townshend, D., *The Life and Letters of the Great Earl of Cork* (1904).

Trease, G., *Portrait of a Cavalier* (1979).

Underwood, D., *Etherege and the Seventeenth Century Comedy of Manners* (New Haven, 1957).

Wallas, A., *Before the Bluestockings* (1929).

Warnicke, R., *Women of the English Renaissance and Reformation* (Westport, Conn., 1983).

Watkins, O., *The Puritan Experience* (1972).

Wilson, J. H., *All the King's Ladies* (Chicago, 1958).

—— *The Court Wits of the Restoration* (Princeton, 1948).

Woodcock, G., *The Incomparable Aphra* (1948).

Van Lennep, W. (ed.), *The London Stage 1660–1700*, Part I (Carbondale, Ill., 1965).

Wrightson, K., *English Society 1580–1680* (1982).

Index